Leadership and Management in Education

Cultures, Change and Context

Leadership and Management in Education

Cultures, Change and Context

Marianne Coleman and Peter Earley

OXFORD

UNIVERSITY PRESS

OXFORD
UNIVERSITY PRESS

Great Clarendon Street, Oxford OX2 6DP

Oxford University Press is a department of the University of Oxford.
It furthers the University's objective of excellence in research, scholarship,
and education by publishing worldwide in

Oxford New York

Auckland Bangkok Buenos Aires Calcutta Cape Town Chennai
Dar es Salaam Delhi Hong Kong Istanbul Karachi Kolkata
Kuala Lumpur Madrid Melbourne Mexico City Mumbai Nairobi
São Paulo Shanghai Taipei Tokyo Toronto

Oxford is a registered trade mark of Oxford University Press
in the UK and in certain other countries

Published in the United States
by Oxford University Press Inc., New York

British Library Cataloguing in Publication Data

Data available

ISBN-0-19-926857-6

10 9 8 7 6 5 4 3 2 1

Typeset by Newgen Imaging Systems (P) Ltd, Chennai, India
Printed in Great Britain on acid-free paper by
Antony Rowe Limited, Chippenham

Foreword

This book arose from work undertaken for a distance learning course in applied educational leadership and management, developed by my colleagues at the Institute of Education for a University of London external master's degree. It soon became evident that the materials produced for the course would be of interest to a much wider audience. This includes those studying on face-to-face master's and doctoral courses in educational leadership and management, as well as many others involved in the practical tasks of leading and managing educational institutions—or preparing to do so.

The book is written by some of the leading experts in this field working at the Institute of Education and elsewhere. Although most of the authors are based in the UK, they also have substantial international experience. The issues they are writing about are relevant to leaders and managers in many parts of the world, as the local contexts in which leadership is exercised are increasingly intersected by global trends. In particular, educators in many countries are experiencing that paradoxical blend of devolution and centralisation associated with what Guy Neave terms the rise of the 'evaluative state'. This entails state schools and other educational institutions being given more autonomy to manage their own affairs while, at the same time, often being subjected to greater government regulation and surveillance. The modality of state control, however, shifts from the detailed prescription of how schools should operate to the setting and monitoring of performance targets that they have to meet. While this often gives greater scope for imaginative approaches to management, the consequences of failure are also heightened. In some cases, school leaders find themselves adopting similar approaches to the management of their own institutions.

A particular value of this book is that, even while identifying some common themes, it maintains a strong awareness of context. Unlike some other texts, it does not position leaders and managers as simply either 'agents' or 'victims' of contemporary fashions in educational management. Rather, it addresses how both the possibilities and the limitations of current developments need to be worked with by leaders and managers as they pursue agendas of institutional improvement in their own schools and colleges. What is especially refreshing about the approach is the recognition that the task is not just one of managing and changing institutions but centrally about the leadership of learning and learning communities.

For these reasons, I am confident that you will find this volume both intellectually stimulating and helpful to your own work as today's and tomorrow's leaders in education.

Professor Geoff Whitty
Director
Institute of Education
University of London

Neave, G. (1989) 'On the cultivation of quality, efficiency and enterprise: an overview of recent trends in higher education in Western Europe', 1968–1988, *European Journal of Education*, 23(1/2), 7–23.

Neave, G. (1998) 'The Evaluative State Reconsidered', *European Journal of Education*, 33(3), 265–284.

Preface

This book is about the leadership and management of schools and colleges in a range of international settings. We hope that it will be of interest and benefit to everybody who is concerned with the provision of education. The inclusion of examples from many countries will make the book relevant to international practitioners and students and will encourage readers in the UK to take a fresh perspective on issues of importance in leading and managing educational institutions.

The book is designed to be used as a core text by post-graduate students of courses in educational leadership, management, administration and policy, working at both masters and doctoral level and for professional qualifications such as the National Professional Qualification for Headship (NPQH) in England and the Scottish Qualification for Headship (SQH). However, the topics that are covered will be of interest to all professionals in educational organisations and to those responsible for the oversight of schools and colleges at regional and national level.

Many of the chapters in this book are drawn from the distance learning materials that have been written specifically for the MA in Applied Educational Leadership and Management, a degree of the University of London's External Progamme, offered through the Institute of Education. This degree is offered as an online course and students are provided with specially written materials. This book which is largely derived from the distance learning materials, reflects the work of teachers of post-graduate courses who are experienced in both research and writing and who have knowledge and experience of working with both UK and a wide range of international practitioners. The authors are drawn from the Institute of Education, University of London and from those who have contributed to the writing of the distance learning materials.

Marianne Coleman and Peter Earley, March 2004

Acknowledgements

Chapters by Marianne Coleman, Peter Earley, Pamela Sammons, Eileen Carnell, Caroline Lodge, Phil Woods, David Oldroyd, Lesley Anderson and Marian Shaw have been adapted and developed from material originally produced for the MA in Applied Educational Leadership and Management by distance learning offered by the University of London External Programme (www.londonexternal.ac.uk).

The Situational Leadership® Model is used with permission of the Center for Leadership Studies, Escondido, California.

The photograph in Chapter 12 is from the private collection of Eileen Carnell.

Contents

Notes on Contributors

Lesley Anderson Lesley is Director, Postgraduate Professional Development and Senior Lecturer in Educational Leadership and Management at the Open University. Her main research interests are policy and practice relating to the organisation of schools, and finance and resource management including human resource management.

Tim Brighouse Tim is presently Commissioner for London Schools and visiting Professor at the Institute of Education at London University. He has written extensively especially on school improvement and has a number of books and articles to his name. He has also broadcast on radio and television and has spoken at many national and international conferences. Tim has received honorary doctorates from the Open University, University of Central England, Oxford Brookes University, Exeter University, Warwick University, Birmingham University, University of the West of England and Sheffield University.

Eileen Carnell Eileen is a Senior Lecturer in Education at the Insitute of Education. Her particular expertise is in effective learning, action research, professional development, consultation, group work, team and institutional development. She has contributed to a range of publications including research reports, journal articles, professional development materials and authored books.

Marianne Coleman Marianne is the Course Director and Reader in Education Leadership and Management at the Institute of Education. She has written extensively in the field of leadership and management in education and has taken part in research projects in China and South Africa. Her main interest is in leadership, particularly women in leadership and management and also in practitioner research. Her research has also focused on school-based management and mentoring, particularly the mentoring of new head teachers.

Peter Earley Peter is Reader in Education Management and Head of the Management and Leadership Development Section at the Institute of Education. He is also a member of the International School Effectiveness and Improvement Centre at the Institute. A central research interest is leadership and he has recently completed studies of school leaders for the government, independent schools sector, and the National College for School Leadership. As well as school leadership and management, his research interests include school governing bodies, school inspection and self-evaluation, and professional development. He is also an external adviser to governing bodies, an area he is currently researching.

Derek Glover Derek was Course Director, MBA (Education) at Keele University and continues to act as consultant to the course and Honorary Professor within the education department. He is currently involved in a major investigation of the pedagogic requirements of teaching with new technologies. He is a research associate at the Institute of Education for development of distance learning for international audiences. He has written extensively in the areas of educational leadership and management.

Anil Khamis Anil was previously Assistant Professor, The Aga Khan University Institute for Educational Development. He is presently a lecturer and course leader on the MA in Education and International Development at the Institute of Education. His specialist interests include school improvement, education and development with special reference to Muslim societies, teacher education and education in emergencies.

Rosalind Levačić Rosalind is Professor of Economics and Finance of Education at the Institute of Education. Her main research interests are school funding systems, financial and resource management of schools, and the relationships between school resourcing and student outcomes. Specific topics include school-based management, education production functions, school quasi-markets, specialist schools and cost effectiveness analysis applied to educational provision. Her work with the Centre for the Economics of Education is concerned with the relationship between school resources and student outcomes. She has worked as a consultant on school finance for internationally funded projects in Poland, Bosnia and Herzegovina, and China.

Caroline Lodge Caroline was formerly a secondary headteacher and now works as Senior Lecturer in School Effectiveness and School Improvement at the Institute of Education. She researches into and has written for a range of publications on learning in schools, teacher enquiry into learning in schools and discourses of learning in schools.

David Oldroyd Formerly a Senior Lecturer at the University of Bristol and the National Development Centre for Educational Management and Policy, David is now a Polish-based educational development consultant. He specialises in leadership and teacher development in transition countries in Europe, Asia and Africa mainly on EU, DfID and Asian Development Bank projects. He has published extensively in the area of educational management and staff development and has recently been visiting fellow at Dalarna University in Sweden. He is a founding member of the European Network for Improving Research and Development in Educational Management (ENIRDEM) and editor of their Newsletter.

Kathryn Riley Kathryn is Visiting Professor at the Institute of Education University of London and has been in education for many years, beginning as a volunteer teacher in Eritrea and then teaching in inner city schools in London before holding senior academic positions at Birmingham University and University of Surrey, Roehampton. She was an elected member of the Inner London Education Authority from 1986 until its abolition and in 1999–2001 headed the World Bank's *Effective Schools and Teachers Group*. She is interested in how educational change takes place, particularly in urban contexts, and the ways in which parents, communities, teachers and pupils can be brought into the change process.

Pamela Sammons Pam has recently taken up a Chair at the University of Nottingham. Previously she was Professor of Education, Co-ordinating Director and Research Project Director at the International School Effectiveness and Improvement Centre, Institute of Education. Her main areas of research are in the two related fields of school effectiveness and improvement. During the last 20 years she has been involved in school effectiveness and improvement research at both the primary and secondary level. Consultancy work has been conducted for the National Education Agency in Sweden (Skolverket), the Scottish Executive Education Department (SEED), the Department of Education Northern Ireland and a number of UK LEAs.

Marian Shaw Marian is a consultant in educational management, mainly working in international contexts. Her main area of interest (practical, writing and research) is in the transference of management theories and models across cultures. She recently developed and led the Policy, Planning and Management track on the MA for International Schools at Oxford Brookes University.

Philip Woods Philip is Professor of Applied Research in Education at the University of the West of England, Bristol. He has written extensively on educational policy, leadership and governance. Current research includes investigation of diversity and collaboration amongst schools (including the challenges and potential of Steiner schools entering the state sector), democratic leadership, and the impact of private principles meeting public values in the drive to modernise leadership. He has also explored issues of creative social action and governance in sociological theory.

Leading and Managing in Education: National and International Trends and Contexts

INTRODUCTION

Marianne Coleman and Peter Earley

This book is concerned with leadership and management in education, focusing particularly on the relationship of leading and managing to maximising learning and improvement within individual educational institutions. Schools and colleges are not seen in isolation, but are contextualised in relation to their external environment at local, regional, national and global levels. Although the book is derived from a course at the Institute of Education in London, it draws on international examples to illustrate current theory and practice in the context of two major trends in education.

One of the underlying trends is the impact of the move to site-based management for educational institutions, a change that is both linked with improvement and seen as a move towards a managerialist agenda, a context of greater accountability and a culture of performativity. Decentralization and the devolution of power and responsibility are, experienced differentially throughout the world, but these trends are an influence on the development of educational institutions globally and on their management and leadership. The delegation of resources to local level, often linked with a greater centralized control and strengthened 'high stakes' accountability systems, has highlighted the importance of leadership and management, especially at institutional level and has led to a debate on the role of the state and the nature of teacher professionalism. This debate provides the context for the discussion of leadership and management within institutions.

Since the central purpose of education is learning, the other key theme of the book is the importance of learning for all: students, teachers, and educational leaders and managers. The book investigates the ways in which leadership and management can contribute towards the development and enhancement of student learning, staff development and institutional growth. It is based on two beliefs:

- that high performing educational organisations institutionalise, share and maximize learning;

> **Your own learning**
>
> In order to promote your own learning, in each of the chapters you will be asked on a number of occasions to 'reflect' on what you have just read and to relate it to your own experience. In addition, each author has outlined what they see as the learning objectives for each chapter. We would like you to pause at the beginning of each chapter to consider the extent to which the listed objectives relate to your particular needs. A further learning objective for the whole book is that you develop your skills of critical reflection and critical reading. In particular, you may wish to question the extent to which the theories and empirical research reported in the book fit your understanding of what is occurring in your own society and environment. At the end of each chapter you will be given some suggestions for further reading that will give you the opportunity to extend your understanding and provide you with a range of views on the specific areas or issues that have been covered.

- that educational organisations that give high priority to learning, and which maintain a culture to support it at all levels, are the ones most able to react imaginatively to and meet the challenges of an uncertain world.

The book is intended to serve as an introductory text, as we are starting from a point where knowledge of theory is not taken for granted. In particular, the first three chapters introduce you to some of the underpinning concepts and theories that will be helpful to you in reading the rest of the book. The editors have sought coherence in the book through its underlying themes, but each chapter has a particular locus and does to some extent represent the voice of its author.

The first chapter, written by Marianne Coleman, aims to provide an introduction to the key theoretical issues of educational leadership, examining the differences between leadership and management and outlining the development of leadership theory to include some of the more recent contributions such as emotional intelligence and distributed leadership. The relationship between gender and leadership and current trends in leadership development and training are also briefly introduced. In the second chapter, Marian Shaw provides the international contexualisation for leadership theory, and the other theories introduced in the book by pointing out that most of the research which informs theory has generally been carried out in the 'West' (i.e. richer countries, regardless of geography). This chapter considers the larger issues of culture, as outlined by Hofstede, that underpin the cross-cultural transference debate, ensuring that every reader, from whichever part of the world, has the means to situate and interrogate the concepts of leadership and management within the context of their own culture and society. Shaw shows us how cross-cultural analysis can help us understand the causes of behaviour, and provide insights into professional development and learning.

The third chapter introduces further key theories and concepts, first considering general organisational theory and then moving on to consider how organisations can be seen through the frames of power, structure or institutional culture. In this chapter, the way that power is used within the organisation is a central theme, but power is also considered in terms of the wider society and is related to issues of equity and social justice. Therefore this chapter also considers factors associated with access to power and the ways that access is differentiated.

In Chapter 4, Lesley Anderson extends the analysis of power through her careful consideration of the current moves towards decentralisation and site-based management. She shows that although similar trends towards devolution of power and responsibility can be discerned internationally, the reality of institutional management is experienced differently according to national context. In the UK, and in other English speaking countries such as New Zealand, Australia, parts of Canada and the USA, there has been at least some devolution of finance and management functions to the level of the institution. In other countries there has been some experimentation with devolution or more minor changes. In addition, the move towards devolution has often been accompanied by a move towards a market in education, an increase in central power, accountability and an emphasis on performance indicators and the achievement of targets and standards. One of the major implications of increased site-based management is the additional power and responsibility given to principals and other educational leaders. They have experienced an increase in responsibility for the relationship of the school or college with its external environment and claims have been made about links between institutional autonomy and improvement as well as tensions arising from an increased emphasis on performance, standards and targets. In this chapter the relationship between the national and regional levels of government and the institution are considered mainly in terms of the distribution of power, whilst in Chapter 5 Phil Woods considers the place of education in its wider economic, political and social context, critically examining the purposes of education in society, as well as models of governance and types of accountability. Focusing more narrowly on the role of the community in relation to the educational institution, the key role of parents is also analysed and the importance of parental involvement in the process of schooling is considered.

The voice of the 'remote' leader, in this case that of a Chief Education Officer at the regional level, is heard in Chapter 6, where Tim Brighouse reflects on a time of change in the large conurbation of Birmingham, England. The role of the 'remote' leader is seen to be that of a moderator of political and economic factors as they impinge on the individual institutions in the area. The chapter is a kind of case study of change and improvement of systems and institutions in an urban environment, and draws on examples from individual schools within the area showing how school leaders can effect cultural change.

The theme of change and improvement is developed further in Chapter 7 where Kathryn Riley and Anil Khamis provide three contrasting and illuminative examples of how education reforms can lead to improvements in the learning opportunities of children and young people. The chapter begins by introducing a framework which enables both policy-makers and practitioners to identify the problems they face in an education system; to map the choices and the decisions which they have already made; and to consider future possible courses of action. Although the chapter mainly considers reform and improvement at a system level, the final conclusions focus on the school improvement lessons to be learned from these explorations.

If improvement takes place, measurement of that improvement is part of the process and Chapter 8 focuses on school effectiveness research which at its best sensitively harnesses statistical techniques to inform leadership for learning. This chapter by

Pam Sammons and colleagues reviews what is meant by effectiveness and 'value added' approaches whilst also addressing equity issues, the concept of differential effectiveness and the size of school effects. Full coverage is given to the debate critiquing school effectiveness and school improvement research and readers are encouraged to establish the extent to which different types of criticism may be justified and to identify the main strengths and limitations of the studies outlined in the chapter.

Effectiveness research is one way of evaluating the extent of improvement and in Chapter 9, Marianne Coleman focuses on the concept of evaluation in education, first by defining what is meant by evaluation and then looking briefly at research methods appropriate to evaluation. The chapter is mainly concerned with the differences in the way that evaluation can be used. On the one hand it can be used internally in relation to the self-defined agenda of the school or college and is then linked with collaborative learning, professional development and improvement. Alternatively, it can be imposed externally to measure the extent to which an institution has reached a certain level or accomplished a specified outcome. This aspect of evaluation tends to be associated with a managerialist agenda. In the field of evaluation, the tensions between accountability and improvement are exemplified well in England where the purpose of regular school inspection, via the Office for Standards in Education (Ofsted), is officially seen as that of improvement but the experience of the inspected teachers tends to focus on the more punitive and controlling aspects of the process.

In Chapter 10 the focus is on the importance of financial and material resources for learning. In this chapter Ros Levačić and Derek Glover specifically develop one of the major themes of the book, the devolution of aspects of power and of leadership and management of resources from the centre to the institution. The advent of different levels of site-based management has meant that senior managers in educational institutions have taken on a range of responsibilities for the management of both finance and material resources. Leaders and managers therefore need to be aware of the responsibilities and possibilities that are available to them as managers of their own resources whether this is control of their budget within a decentralised system, or topping up centrally distributed revenue through 'entrepreneurial' activity. This chapter reviews decision-making on resource and financial management within the context of the options that may be available to schools and colleges and reviews them in the light of the key concepts of effectiveness, efficiency and equity.

The key resource of any educational institution is the people that work within it. Spending on human resources takes the major part of all educational expenditure, the effective deployment of human resources is therefore vital if education is to operate to the benefit of students and the community at large, nurturing learning and educational improvement. In Chapter 11, David Oldroyd considers and contrasts the 'hard' aspects of human resource management (HRM) related to new public management and managerialism, with the 'soft' aspects of HRM, the dimension that he sees as relating to the empowering and motivation of staff. Through the use of case examples drawn from Poland, Oldroyd maps key processes, but the stress is on the differences between the two models. He sees hard HRM as focusing on the needs of the organisation, whilst soft HRM centres on the individuals as people as well as employees of the organisation.

Therefore key elements of HRM are likely to include the importance of employee commitment. Leaders need to motivate and inspire all who work within the school or college if improvement is to occur and this chapter considers theories of motivation and offers examples of motivational leadership.

Throughout the book the authors are aware of the central significance of learning, and Chapter 12 draws our attention to what we mean by learning. This chapter by Carnell and Lodge draws attention to recent developments in research into learning, recognising that the impact of this research does vary across cultures. Different conceptions or theories of learning are examined—transmission, construction and co-construction— whilst implications for practice, at classroom, teacher and whole school/institution level, are also considered. The authors argue that effective learning relates to context, and to national, international and local influences. They point to increasing international recognition that learners need to co-construct knowledge rather than absorb knowledge and that effective learning involves activity, collaboration, learner responsibility and especially learning about learning. Carnell and Lodge point out that principles involved in managing for effective learning are the same as those for effective learning: the principles of engagement; responsibility; collaboration/dialogue and meta-learning. Different levels of management of learning are explored: managing learning in classrooms, supporting professional development of teachers and managing the whole school learning community.

These themes are taken forward in Chapter 13 where Peter Earley continues with the idea that learning is at the heart of any educational institution. This chapter considers the professional and personal development of all adults as a key part of a learning organisation or learning community. An important part of the chapter focuses on leading and managing continuing professional development (CPD) to help bring about a learning community for all who work or study within it, examining the role of the CPD coordinator and the training and development cycle. The chapter finishes with a consideration of how an organisation's priorities can be combined with individuals' needs. It also examines the characteristics of effective CPD and adult learning.

The book ends with an endnote relating to the key themes of the book—leading for learning within a semi autonomous or autonomous self-improving institution with shared vision and values. Also it points to some of the issues and debates as we move towards leadership being conceived primarily in terms of being 'learning centred'. Clearly, leadership in education that fails to consider the learning needs of all can hardly be described as such. It is hoped that this edited collection, drawing on a range of international examples will help to provide you with insights into the nature of effective leadership and management and by so doing ensure that 'learning' is at the heart of all your practice; a key consideration in all you do.

1

Theories and Practice of Leadership: An introduction

Marianne Coleman

INTRODUCTION AND LEARNING OUTCOMES

In this chapter you will be introduced to some of the major theories about leadership in educational institutions. The examples are drawn from a number of different countries and cultures and this will help you to reflect on leadership as an abstract concept, and also on how culture affects leadership practice. The chapter ends with a short review of aspects of leadership development and training.

By the end of this chapter you should be able to:

- distinguish the concepts of leadership and management;
- identify and summarise major strands of leadership theory and current thinking on leadership and management in education;
- formulate your reflections on how current models of leadership apply to you and your institution;
- reflect on training and preparation for leadership.

LEADERSHIP, MANAGEMENT, ADMINISTRATION AND POLICY—DEFINITIONS

The three concepts of leadership, management and administration overlap and, as we shall see, their usage varies at different times, in different countries and in different professional cultures. Thus, like many concepts in this field of study, they are best regarded as contested. In the UK at the present time, 'leadership' tends to be seen as the most important of these concepts, 'management' tends to relate to more operational matters and 'administration' to relate to tasks which are routine. However, until fairly recently, management was seen as the broader concept and leadership as a subset of it.

In North America, the term 'administration' relates to the most prestigious level and may even be synonymous with 'leadership'. 'Educational administration' in the USA therefore means more or less the same as 'educational leadership' in the UK. It is important to be aware of this difference in the use of words when reading literature that was written in the USA or Canada as opposed to the UK.

There is also the issue of separating out what happens within the institution (a school or college) with what happens outside it in the educational system at regional or national level. This brings us to consider the concept of 'policy'. Policies that impact on the institution are often made outside the school or college. For example, in many countries central governments have policies that control aspects of the curriculum delivered in the schools. In the UK, where there is a national curriculum, the government instituted tightly defined literacy and numeracy hours in primary schools. In Israel, the Ministry of Education annually puts forward a curricular theme to be followed in all schools e.g. the history of Jerusalem, or Israel's 50th anniversary (Gibton et al, 2002). In Hong Kong, many government reforms impact on schools, for example the introduction of site-based management to all aided schools and the compulsory benchmark testing of the English language capability of all teachers.

At the local level, policies can also be made inside the institution, for example the development of a behaviour policy or an equal opportunities policy for a single school or college. Such policies may be influenced by national legislation, but tailored to the needs of the individual institution.

Despite the different interpretations that can be put on them, the words leadership and management are often used interchangeably in everyday speech, particularly in the UK. The blurring together of these two concepts is not entirely surprising as in practice it is often the same people who are both leading and managing, for example the principal of a college or a head of department or a school. When observing such a person in action, it may be very difficult to decide which of their functions and actions could be labelled 'leadership' and which 'management'. However, in general:

> Leadership is frequently seen as an aspect of management, with 'real leaders' often characterised as charismatic individuals with visionary flair and the ability to motivate and enthuse others—even if they lack the managerial or administrative skills to plan, organise effectively or control resources. On this basis it is often argued that managers simply need to be good at everything that leaders are not! (Law and Glover, 2000, p.13)

In his book *The Making of Educational Leaders* Gronn (1999) states that in his view: 'Leadership, . . . is a qualitatively different function from both management and administration' (pp.4–5). He sees leadership as a quality that does not automatically come with status. Generally, leadership is viewed as something special. In the Law and Glover quotation, the word 'charismatic' is used, in Gronn's definition, the quality of leadership is thought to be something that does not automatically arrive with the job. However, the more technical skills of management and the more esoteric skills of determining values and reflecting on practice are both important. Leadership may be identified with one person, for example a headteacher or principal, but it is exercised by others at different levels of the organisation. The concept of 'distributed' leadership is one that will be considered further in this chapter. A different view of 'remote' leadership—that of a local education authority leader is considered in Chapter 6.

What is expected of a headteacher as leader has been quite tightly defined in the training offered in England and Wales for the National Professional Qualification for Headteachers (NPQH) which is compulsory for all candidates for headship to possess. It includes consideration of:

- strategic direction and development of the school;
- teaching and learning;
- leading and managing staff;
- efficient and effective deployment of staff and resources;
- accountability.

You could argue that it is in the first of these, covering issues of vision and values that the key areas of leadership can be found and that in the other areas leadership and management merge and overlap.

Reflection 1

How would you define leadership as distinct from management? What are the most important qualities in your view?

After a comparison of 100 leaders in business and 100 successful headteachers, the Hay Group (2000) identified five characteristics of effectiveness in leaders, how does their list of characteristics coincide with the qualities that you thought of? Their list included:

1. Teamwork and developing others;
2. Drive and confidence;
3. Vision and accountability;
4. Influencing tactics and politics; and
5. Thinking styles (i.e. the big picture)

(cited in *Fullan*, 2002, p.4).

THEORISING LEADERSHIP

The main thing that is notable about current writing on leadership is the sheer quantity of commentary and analysis, what Day et al (2000, p.7) refer to as the 'swamp of literature on leadership'. There is an enormous amount of material written about leadership in general and leadership in education in particular.

Some of the ways in which leadership has been theorised include:

1. Focusing on the qualities of the individuals who have leadership status, seeing a leader as a 'great man' or as having special traits or qualities that make them different.

2. Seeing leadership as contextual, in other words that leadership is a two-way process dependent on followers as well as leaders working in a particular context. This would mean that one leader might fit one set of circumstances but not another.

3. More recently there has been a move away from seeing leadership as identified with one person and a growing interest in the idea of leadership being 'distributed' throughout the organisation and shared amongst its members.

4. Leadership and management theories are often based on underlying dimensions such as the extent to which a leader focuses on people or task achievement, or the way in which decisions are made.

5. Sometimes styles are identified with gender and there seems to be a generally unexamined belief that men and women lead and manage in different ways.

6. Finally an aspect of leadership that is now recognised is the importance to leadership of the emotions and of emotional intelligence, this emphasises the importance of a particular range of skills that leaders may need if they are to be truly effective and stresses the affective rather than the rational aspect of leadership.

These ideas are now going to be explored a little further, before going on to look at a number of styles of leadership in more detail illustrated by case examples indicating how the styles might operate in practice in different contexts.

1. QUALITIES OF INDIVIDUALS

The great man theory

Early discussions of leadership tended to identify leadership with the quality or qualities of the individual. The most basic illustration of this is the 'great man' theory. The implication is that leaders are not made but born. This could be rather a depressing thought as it implies a sort of predestination and that there could be no such thing as effective leadership training. It is however, a persuasive idea and hard to avoid in everyday life. However, it tends to be linked with stereotypes of leaders in the heroic mould, who are usually of the male gender: thus it is known as the great *man* theory.

Trait theories

A similar idea is that there are a range of traits that are common to leaders (Stogdill, 1969). However, it has proved impossible to empirically identify a *particular* set of traits that are clearly present in a range of leaders and transferable across cultures and both the great man and trait theories are not considered adequate for the identification of leadership qualities and skills.

However, current interest in competencies could be seen as something of a return to the idea that leaders should possess certain traits. The expected skills and attributes for headteachers are set out in a list in the National Standards for Headteachers in England (*DfES*, 2000) and see www.dfes.gov.uk. The difference between competencies and traits is that it is expected that leaders could be coached to gain competencies, whereas traits were seen as something that people either have or do not have.

The great man and trait theories of leadership have limited impact on theorising of leadership today, but the idea of contextual leadership underpins much of our thinking about leadership.

2. CONTEXTUAL, SITUATIONAL AND CONTINGENCY THEORIES

A further set of theories are those that relate the leader to the situation in which they find themselves. These theories allow for the fact that the leader does not operate in isolation but will be affected by his or her circumstances. Churchill is often identified as a 'great man' but he was much more successful as a leader in war than in peace.

The best known of these contextual theories is that of Hersey and Blanchard (1988) (see also Chapter 2 in this volume) who considered the relationship of the leader to the led on the basis of two variables, one was the experience of the person being led and the other their level of commitment. On this basis leaders might vary their behaviour with different people, for example *delegating* a lot with experienced and committed staff, *directing* the inexperienced staff and *coaching* or *supporting* the experienced but less committed staff. Again this theory appeals to our intuition but it does depend on the leader being able to switch his or her attitudes to accord to the needs of a particular individual.

Another classic contingency leadership theory is that of Fiedler (1967) who considered the leader's style might be more or less successful in the context of favourable and unfavourable situations for leaders. He showed for example that a leader who is more directive and focused on achieving targets might be a better leader in an unfavourable situation. We might be able to see aspects of this in our own work life. For example in England, when schools have been identified as failing, a more directive leadership style seems to work well initially. This style can then be modified as the situation improves.

3. DISTRIBUTED LEADERSHIP

In most models of leadership there is an underlying assumption that there is one main leader in each school or institution. In fact the leadership of schools is often presumed to be in the hands of the principal or headteacher. However, there is a growing belief that leadership should and can be shared throughout an organisation. The idea of a common vision is important to this. Harris (2002) identifies distributed leadership with the collective leadership of teachers working together to improve classroom practice and therefore pupil outcomes. This ideal of distributed leadership is often normatively preferred, that is it may be stated that it is better for leadership to be shared rather than to be vested in one person. This could happen in practice in different ways. Gronn (2003, p.35) refers to leadership practice being 'stretched' over the school, for example:

> when sets of two or three individuals with differing skill and abilities, perhaps from across different organisational levels, pool their expertise and regularise their conduct to solve a problem, after which they may disband.

In practice, distributed leadership could happen in different ways. Another example of distributed leadership suggested by Gronn (2003) includes quite formal arrangements, for example where a school or college is on two campuses, so that leadership has to be shared between the sites. A more informal, and rarely recognised manifestation of distributed leadership is the role of a secretary who ensures that the intentions of the leader are coordinated and implemented.

Gronn also talks about the division of labour as distributed leadership and quotes examples including this one from a college in Australia:

> We're trying to develop a way that we take some college responsibility as well as campus responsibility. So, for example, one of the new campus principals, who'll take over next year, is very good in IT [information technology] so she'll look after the IT side of things and guide the rest of us along. Another one is very good and has a lot of experience with integration [of students with special needs] so she will probably run the college integration program as one of her responsibilities. And I'll probably assist [the college principal] with staffing or finance or something like that. So we're looking at doing that (*ibid*, p.49).

One of the most important types of distributed leadership is that exercised by middle managers, for example heads of academic departments in schools or colleges, or subject leaders in primary schools.

4. UNDERLYING DIMENSIONS OF LEADERSHIP THEORIES

Two of the basic leadership (and management) styles focus on:

1. decision-making (Tannnenbaum and Schmidt, 1973); and
2. the centrality of people or production/task (Blake and Mouton, 1978).

In the first of these, the style of leadership varies along a spectrum from autocratic at one end, where the leader tells people what to do, to democratic at the other where the leader gives authority over decision-making to the group (see Figure 1.1).

In the second major theory, Blake and Mouton (1978) developed a grid with two axes, one showing concern for production/task, the other concern for people. Nine points were identified on each axis. It was then possible to identify where an individual

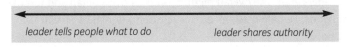

leader tells people what to do   *leader shares authority*

Figure 1.1 Tannenbaum and Schmidt continuum (1973)

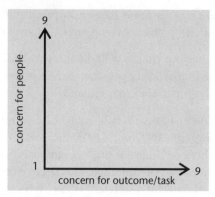

Figure 1.2 Blake and Mouton (1978)
Concern for People v. Task

leader/manager might be placed on this grid. Originally this theory was intended to identify training needs for managers and leaders, as the ideal position on the grid was the 9/9 manager who manages to place equal and high emphasis on both concern for people and concern for achieving tasks (see Figure 1.2).

The idea of leadership being more or less democratic or autocratic and the idea of leaders and managers being more or less task or people focused are both important ones and underpin a number of other styles which will be considered a little later in the chapter.

5. GENDER AND LEADERSHIP

When it comes to gender in the context of leadership style, a binary distinction is often made in terms of masculine and feminine styles of leadership. There are stereotypes about how men and women in management and leadership operate. Women are thought to be caring, tolerant, emotional, intuitive, gentle and predisposed towards collaboration, empowerment and teamwork. Men are supposed to be aggressive, assertive, analytical, decisive and more inclined to act independently. There are also firmly held cultural expectations that managers and leaders are male. These expectations are pervasive, and are held by most men, to a lesser extent by women and by both younger and older age groups in a range of international settings (Schein, 1994). A good example of this can be seen in some responses from a research project in China that included questions about gender and leadership:

Sometimes male leaders have strong abilities and are brave and act quickly and are wise. Female leaders are reluctant and hesitant (male year head of secondary school).

Women are careful and cautious and too kind which is not appropriate [for a leader] (male year head, secondary school).

Male leaders grasp the overall picture. Females stress detail and teacher relationships and affections. Female teachers are more careful (female assistant principal of professional school).

Women are careful and men are strategic (female dean of student affairs, professional school). (Coleman et al, 1998, p.151.)

As you can see from these quotations stereotypes are held by women as well as men.

However, these divisions are simplistic and essentialise women and men. Research with all the male and female secondary headteachers in England and Wales showed that they did not see themselves as operating in different ways. The majority of both men and women saw themselves as managing in a way that was actually more stereotypically feminine than masculine, i.e. nurturing, caring and collaborative (see Coleman, 2002, Chapter 7).

The tendency to essentialise the ways in which women and men lead helps to perpetuate the stereotypes that identify men with leadership in the public sphere and women in the nurturing role which is identified with the less valued private sphere of the home. (Equity issues relating gender to accessing power will be considered in Chapter 3.)

6. EMOTIONAL INTELLIGENCE

There is increasing interest in the concept of emotional intelligence (Goleman, 1998) and how this impinges on leadership. The five domains of emotional intelligence are identified as:

- self-awareness—the ability to recognise one's own emotions, and strengths and weaknesses, this is related to the sense of self-worth and confidence;
- self-regulation—the ability to control one's own emotions rather than allowing them to control;
- motivation—the strength of will needed to meet goals, the drive to improve;
- empathy; and
- social skills.

All of these are seen to be important to leadership, the last two particularly relating to the management and leadership of others. The importance of emotional intelligence will be considered in more detail in Chapter 11. However, it is worth noting in the context of theories of leadership, that the new interest in the emotions of leaders and the emotional relationship between leaders and followers is a real contrast to the traditional view of a formal leader where rationality rather than emotion was expected to prevail.

Making use of empathy and social skills is one aspect of emotional leadership, but there is a growing body of research into the emotional aspect of being a headteacher which has identified how leaders may experience a range of negative emotions associated with the role:

- anger caused by carrying (that is, taking into themselves) the weight of other peoples' emotions, behaviour, demands and expectations;
- distress created by their own and others' expectations added to an overdeveloped sense of personal responsibility;
- anxiety associated with enacting their role, and the consequent tendency to avoid anxiety by accentuating the positive;

- anger about the isolation that they experience, and the pressure they feel (created by themselves as well as others) to be 'perfect' managers.

(James and Vince, 2001, p.313)

Such negativity may be fuelled by current demands to meet targets and continually to improve.

You have now been introduced to some of the basic ways of theorising leadership which underpin current theories about styles of leadership; some of these styles will be considered in the next section.

At the start of this discussion on theorising leadership it was pointed out that there were considerable difficulties in finding a way through the huge range of relevant literature on leadership, what Day et al (2000) referred to as a 'swamp'. To simplify the 'swamp', we are going to make use of a framework developed by Leithwood et al (1999, pp.7–17) which is derived from a review of articles from 1988 to 1999 concerned with leadership in four English-language journals that focus on educational management and leadership. The four journals do not represent views from the whole world, but are representative of thinking in the Western world and will be illustrated by case examples from a range of international settings.

You may be interested to know that the journals used for the Leithwood et al selection were:

Educational Administration Quarterly (EAQ)—North America
Journal of School Leadership (JSL)—North America
Journal of Educational Administration (JEA)—Australia, New Zealand and North America
Educational Management and Administration (EMA)—mainly UK, but includes articles from a range of countries and cultures.

STYLES OF LEADERSHIP

The framework that is derived from the review by Leithwood and colleagues is divided into six broad categories or styles, which represent models of leadership in education today. Each of these categories has a different focus. The leadership styles are defined in terms of influence: who is exerting it; what is it exerted for; and what are its outcomes. The categories defined are:

1. *Instructional leadership* which assumes that the key focus for leaders in education is the learning of their students, so the influence of leaders would tend to be based in their expert knowledge and intended to improve the effectiveness of teachers in the classroom.

2. *Transformational leadership* (often contrasted with transactional leadership) which relates strongly to building the capacity of members of the organisation. Leadership of this type might be exercised by people other than the formal leader, and the outcomes would be greater capacity and continuing improvement.

3. *Moral leadership* which stresses the importance of values in leadership and aims for morally justified actions and democratic schools.

4. *Participative leadership* which focuses on the sharing of decision-making within the educational institution, thus leadership is distributed amongst the group and the organisation becomes more democratic.

5. *Managerial leadership* which may also be called transactional, technical or organisational leadership. Leadership is formal, the aim is for efficient achievement of goals.

6. *Contingent leadership* which stresses the variation in response of leaders to different leadership situations with the aim of increasing capacity of the organisation to respond productively to demands for change.

Although these six categories are useful as a framework for considering leadership, there are obviously many ways in which leadership can be classified. The Leadership Programme for Serving Heads (LPSH) and training for the National Professional Qualification for Headteachers (NPQH) offered in England and Wales identifies six styles, different to those offered below, all of which might be used by an effective leader. You might like to look at these styles identified by the HayGroup at the following web-site: www.nscl.org.uk.

We now return to the first five of the Leithwood categorisations illustrated with some case study examples. The last of the six categories is that of contingent leadership and this has already been briefly discussed (see p.10 above).

1. INSTRUCTIONAL LEADERSHIP

In this type of leadership, the stress is on the centrality of learning. A more appropriate term may therefore be 'learning-centred leadership', focusing on good teaching, effective learning and achievement.

Instructional leaders will focus on the core activity of the school or college; the learning and teaching of the students. This type of leadership is also likely to be linked to the concept of the learning community, or learning organisation. Other terms which might be used in place of 'instructional leadership' are 'pedagogic leadership', 'educative leadership' or 'educational leadership'. Key concerns of instructional leaders are likely to be the curriculum, teaching and learning, monitoring of learning.

Although it might be thought that the focus of any leadership in education should be on learning, in practice this is not always the case. In practice there can often be tension between instructional leadership and administrative or other tasks. A review of the work of primary headteachers in England, Scotland and Denmark found that:

> Danish headteachers in our study spent much more of their working day with teachers than Scottish or English heads. Scottish headteachers spent considerably more time with pupils than did their Danish and English counterparts, while English heads were more likely to spend their time with outside agencies or individuals, managing external politics. (Riley and MacBeath, 2003, p.182.)

A potential tension for English headteachers showed itself in a recent review of school leadership in England (Earley et al, 2002, p.3) which had amongst its conclusions:

The majority of headteachers still spend some of their working week in the classroom, either teaching, observing or coaching; and

Leaders in schools are de-motivated by the bureaucracy and excessive paperwork which they associate with the role and also by constant change in the education system.

In Papua New Guinea, Boe Lahui-Ako (2001) carried out research related to the instructional leadership capacity of high school principals, their management of the curriculum and promotion of a positive learning climate. The main conclusions were that the principals generally did not carry out the instructional leadership tasks and that they were being encouraged by inspectors to prioritise administrative procedures over their instructional leadership role.

2. TRANSFORMATIONAL LEADERSHIP

Transformational leadership should be seen in terms of its relationship with transactional leadership. Transactional leadership is identified as a contract between the leader and the led. A simple relationship which implies that the leader will look after the interests of the led as long as they carry out their contractual duties. Transformational leadership is very different and is seen as the one most likely to:

offer a comprehensive approach to leadership that will help those in, and served by, current and future schools respond productively to the significant challenges facing them. (Leithwood et al, 1999, p.21.)

It is therefore the style that is normatively favoured in Western thinking about leading in education. What is meant by transformational leadership? Probably the best-known version of transformational leadership is that identified by Bass and Avolio (1994), although Burns (1977) is credited with the origins of the idea.

Transformational leaders do more than transactional leaders in a number of ways that have been identified as the 'Four Is'. These are:

1. *Idealized influence.* Transformational leaders are role models and their followers emulate them. The leader considers the needs of others rather than his or her personal needs. The leader demonstrates high standards of ethical and moral conduct and avoids using power for personal gain.

2. *Inspirational motivation.* The leaders inspire followers by providing meaning to the work of others through the development of a vision for the future. Team spirit and enthusiasm are encouraged as the vision for the future is communicated.

3. *Intellectual stimulation.* Leaders encourage innovation and creativity and question the existing state. However, there is a positive and supportive environment where

new ideas and approaches are not criticised because they are different from those of the leader.

4. *Individualised consideration*. The needs of each individual are considered and coaching and mentoring are the norm.

There is a stress on development including new learning opportunities within a supportive climate; individual differences in needs are recognised; a two-way communication is encouraged; interaction with followers is personalised, e.g. the leader remembers previous conversations; the leader listens effectively; tasks are delegated, but supportive monitoring offered (based on Bass and Avolio, 1994, pp.3–4).

It may be that transformational leadership is a rather Western concept. For example, in a study in Hong Kong it was noted that 'Chinese managers favoured indirect tactics, such as offering gifts, or involving another person, whereas American managers favoured direct tactics such as rational persuasion' (Huen et al, 2002, p.368). This study of transformational leadership in Hong Kong elementary schools asked:

- To what extent do the teachers perceive their principals to be exercising transformational leadership?

- What is the nature and extent of teachers' commitment to change?

- To what extent do teachers' perceptions of principals' transformational leadership explain variation in teachers' professional commitments?

The results were that the teachers moderately agreed that their principals were providing some elements of transformational leadership. The conclusions of the authors were that:

> the nature of transformational leadership's influence on teachers' commitment to change is very similar across studies, and perhaps across cultural contexts, but the magnitude of its effects may be quite different (*ibid*, p.383).

The authors also consider that many of the qualities historically valued in Chinese leaders are quite typical of those that might be attributed to transformational leaders . . . 'qualities such as kindness, benevolence and trustworthiness (*ibid*, p.384).

3. MORAL LEADERSHIP

Moral leadership places values at the heart of leadership.

An argument can be made that moral leadership is particularly important in the area of education, since professionals in education are charged with the care and development of young people. An example of a type of moral leadership is outlined by Bhindi and Duignan (1999, p.120) who make a plea for 'authenticity in leadership' which 'is centrally concerned with ethics and morality and with deciding what is significant, what is right and what is worthwhile'. It may be that moral leadership is a concept that can be applied internationally.

Although it forms a strand of Western thinking about leadership it can be applied in many contexts. Bhindi and Duignan are mainly writing about Western contexts but draw on a range of sources and relate their work in particular to South East Asia. The idea of moral leadership could easily be applied to Chinese societies where leadership may be seen as 'a process of influencing relationships and modelling what are deemed to be "desirable" behaviour.' (Dimmock and Walker, 2000, p.305).

A particular aspect of moral leadership relates to areas of the world where adverse political factors including repression linked with economic deprivation have been the context for education. In such situations, Harber and Davies (1997) argue for the development of democratic attitudes and values in schools as a means of promoting a more stable society. They also argue for the universality of certain educational values, including 'for example, inclusion, participation and transparency' (*ibid*, p.152).

> To develop education for democracy we must develop democratic education . . . Our learners must study how democratic societies operate and the obligations and rights of their citizens. Our learners must understand that democracy means more than voting . . . [and] . . . that they cannot simply receive democracy from those who rule the society. Instead, they must build, nurture and protect it. And they must learn that they can never take it for granted. . . . Nor will learners today be deceived by an education system that talks about democracy and says it is for someone else at some other time. To teach about democracy our teachers and our education system as a whole must practise democracy. (Namibian Ministry of Education and Culture, 1993, p.41, quoted in Harber and Davies, 1997, p.154.)

Democratic values will translate into the classroom through a change in the power relationships of teachers and students. In a more democratic learning environment, students take charge of their own learning with teachers acting as facilitators. Democratic schools will encourage the participation of pupils in the running of the school. In South Africa, in an attempt to move towards a more democratic society, the governing bodies of schools include representatives of the community including parents and learners from age 14 upwards.

Another implication for moving towards a more democratic style in educational institutions is the acceptance of a more equal relationship between teachers and learners which may be more problematic in societies with a greater degree of deference to authority (Hofstede, 1991; Dimmock and Walker, 2000).

4. PARTICIPATIVE LEADERSHIP

This style of leadership focuses on the sharing of decision-making. It is exemplified by the right side of the spectrum in the Tannenbaum-Schmidt continuum. There are overlaps with the democratic leadership that we have identified as part of moral leadership. Participative leadership also has a relationship to the collegial style of management that is discussed in Chapter 3 (p.53). As with transformational leadership, it may be that this style of leadership fits better with Western modes of thinking.

In Thailand the educational system has been highly centralized and 'participants assume that orders from above are orders for all concerned. This has resulted in . . . a compliance culture' (Hallinger and Kantamara, 2000, p.191). The Ministry of Education has tried to bring about 'empowering' reforms which include school-based management and parental involvement. The authors claim that cultural norms within Thai society will need to be taken into account if the reforms are to succeed. Some of these norms are respect for authority and a high value on social relationship and harmony in social groups. Interviews in three schools that had successfully implemented the reforms over a seven-year period indicated that:

1. The predominant leadership style was surprisingly participatory, with principals making every effort to get views not only from teachers but also from students;

2. All three principals led by example;

3. All three encouraged teamwork and peer coaching;

4. The three had avoided forcing teachers to join in new initiatives, and had built on the initial voluntary participation, thus reducing stress and minimising the disruption of harmony;

5. A range of techniques was adopted with resistant teachers. One met a resistant teacher informally for a *jap-kao-kui-gun* or 'touch the knee' talk, an informal open discussion;

6. Over time the public recognition of the schools' success became in itself a source of pressure to keep up the change.

Superficial change could have been enforced because of respect for authority in Thai culture, but in these schools the principals had encouraged the gradual introduction of change over time towards a genuine participatory style of leadership.

5. MANAGERIAL LEADERSHIP

The technical and functional aspects of leadership are emphasised in this style, the origins of which can be traced back to scientific management and the work of Taylor (1911). In a managerially led school or other educational institution, structures and procedures tend to be important. This style of leadership is often equated with bureaucratic and hierarchical organisations with one key leader at the apex of the hierarchy who is exercising strong leadership. The institution is run according to rules and targets. (For further discussion of bureaucracy and hierarchy see Chapter 3 on power, structure and culture.) In the Leithwood et al (1999) framework, managerial leadership is simply taken to be a style which draws heavily on classical management theories. However, the term 'managerial' has taken on overtones which imply a 'cold' approach to leadership which stresses efficiency at the cost of more humanistic values. It implies a stress on working to targets with little consideration of people (remember the Blake and Mouton grid—Figure 1.2). Many commentators consider that managerial leadership is encouraged by government initiatives which stress accountability and performativity. Wright (2001) draws a contrast between moral and managerial leadership:

> It is in many ways the moral dimensions of schools, for their teacher, and more importantly their pupils, which provide the most challenging issues and demands for school leaders. The values schools pass on to their pupils could have the most profound effects on the next generation. How should pupils view their fellow human beings? Fundamentally as cogs in the managerial, economic machine or as other humans with real feelings, concerns, worries? What has happened to empathy? . . . What of the moral dimensions of working and leading other teachers? What messages do pupils pick up from our schools about the real worth of their teachers as adult role models if the school management sees teachers primarily as a 'cost' on the school budget? What model of learning do pupils receive from our schools when their work is so directly couched in terms of targets and tests? (2001, pp.277–278).

Managerialism has become identified with the New Right agenda in the UK and therefore carries political overtones which link this target-driven style of leading with the agenda of, first the Thatcher and Major Conservative governments and then the aims of the Blair Labour administration. This agenda is seen as trying to make schools more business-like in what is termed a 'post-welfarist' environment (Gerwitz, 2002). However, in the Leithwood et al (1999) framework the managerial style of leading is not necessarily linked to a political stance.

In Western literature the critical stance on management in education sees the focus on the institution as too narrow, distracting us from the wider problems of society, that simply cannot be remedied by educational institutions. It is also felt that the managerial practices advocated by governments reduce the professionalism of teachers and affect the educational values that schools and colleges transmit. Leadership has generally been seen as a concept that was separate enough from management to be free of these criticisms. However, this is contested:

> The leadership literature is generally so unquestioning of problem solving and managerialist assumptions that attempting to extract leadership as a conceptual category of higher calling is a lost cause (Thrupp and Wilmott, 2003, p.142).

Some of these criticisms of leadership are particularly linked to narrow or superficial conceptualisations of leadership training (see end section).

Within the current theories, there are similarities and links between instructional leadership, transformational leadership, moral leadership and participatory leadership. Of the types of leadership that we are reviewing only managerial leadership stands alone and relatively unrelated to the other types. However, there are alternative typologies of leadership and there are styles of leadership that are not encompassed within any of the definitions reviewed.

The following case example is drawn from research undertaken by an Israeli teacher, Orit Cohen, investigating the role of headteachers in the implementation of change. The particular focus of change was the introduction of Bagrut 2000, a new matriculation exam which affects the style of assessment and therefore the style of teaching of students in their final school years. More autonomy has been given to the schools to carry out their own assessment and there are implications for the relationships between teachers and students as the teachers have the potential to take on a new role as a facilitator of learning. The reform has been piloted in 22 schools and these extracts from two interviews show very different approaches to school leadership and the management of change.

Case Example 1 Contrasting styles of leadership in Israel

Headteacher No. 8:

'. . . The good points of Bagrut 2000 are that first of all it advanced the whole teaching staff . . . One of the great things was developing the teachers' expertise. It created endless possibilities for learning. The teachers were given the opportunity to ask essential questions about the goals and values, to re-evaluate their role as teachers, not only choose between one textbook or another . . . people, people, people. It's all about people; the extent to which you can connect to people, connect them to your ideas and be attentive to their input. That's the key to everything . . . . The ability to connect people to a change without intimidating them, but through giving them the feeling it would give their lives much more meaning. No change would succeed if it is not connected to the self-fulfilment of the people in the organization. Today I feel that the people in my school go around with the feeling that their lives have been made much more significant following 'Bagrut 2000' . . . '.

The issue of opposition to the change also indicates the style of leadership of this headteacher:

'. . . We never forced anybody to do anything. We gave people time they needed. The same for Mr. "K"—I didn't confront him or say "how could you not see what I saw?" If he didn't share my enthusiasm from the beginning, that's OK, he'll come around in time . . . '

Whilst headteacher No. 7 represents a contrasting leadership style:

'. . . I change things every year. If somebody isn't up to making the effort, I replace him. I also replace my vice headteacher once in a while . . . I don't keep anybody on a permanent basis . . . I decide alone. You have to understand that the Arab authority and government system is based on centralism . . . . We are a people without traditions of institutions or democracy. School headteachers also operates that way. There is a school board, but in reality, the headteacher makes all the decisions by himself. I don't know if it is good or bad, but that's the way it is . . . . If somebody tries to bring in political or national issues, I show him the way out. Because here, only I am in charge. Not the council, nor the Ministry of Education. Everybody knows that I am capable of dismissing teachers. I don't usually resort to this, but I would do it if I had to . . . '

(from Cohen, 2003).

Reflection 2

What styles of leadership do these extracts represent? How would you label them in terms of the theories that have been outlined? Which fits best with your experience of leadership? In the case of headteacher no. 7, the style might be termed autocratic (compare with the Tannenbaum-Schmidt continuum). However, the headteacher is certainly operating according to his values and not the influence of the state. In the case of headteacher no. 8 would you consider the style to be mainly instructional?

From these two examples of leadership style in Israel you can see that different educational leaders can interpret state initiatives differently. In these examples the differences reflect both the agency of the individual principal, but also the differing cultural norms of communities within the state. You are now going to consider a different case example showing how school leaders in England may also be able to operate individualistically, exemplifying their values as leaders rather than being driven by the demands of government initiatives.

Case Example 2   Values-driven leadership

This case example is derived from Gold et al (2003, pp.131–132) and is based on visits to ten schools, four primary, four secondary and two special, in each of which leadership and management had been highly rated by Ofsted.

The school leaders in our case-study schools were clearly . . . mediating government policy through their own values systems. We were constantly reminded by those to whom we spoke of the schools' strong value systems and the extent to which vision and values were shared and articulated by all who were involved in them . . . . In almost all the schools, staff commented on the importance of teamwork as a way of developing and sharing vision and values and as a means of making sure that they shared the same values and adopted the same approach to the young people and to learning and teaching the school. The whole idea of sharing and teamwork within staff groups could be difficult to foster at a time when external forces (e.g. pay differentials and performance management) could so easily encourage internal competition.

We were keen to explore the ways in which school leaders managed to promote and encourage such shared values. It seems to us that almost all of them retained, articulated and communicated their values by:

- working with, managing and even searching out change;
- paying careful attention to information management within the school—thus keeping staff constantly informed;
- working very closely and sometimes seamlessly with their leadership groups;
- developing leadership capacity and responsibility throughout their schools.

These schools were notable for the way in which they were driven by shared values and moral leadership which was distributed through the schools by good information and teamwork. The close working between senior management and the rest of the staff, and the development of leadership capacity illustrate transformational leadership. The clear message from the observations of these leaders was of moral (or values driven) leadership, with no evidence of them succumbing to a managerialist style simply because of external demands.

Reflection 3

How much can you relate the discussion of leadership styles to your experience of your present institution, and which style is most likely to be regarded as ideal in your society? It is unlikely that you will ever find a 'pure' example of any style of leadership in any one person or institution, but you may find that one style is dominant.

TRAINING AND DEVELOPMENT FOR LEADERSHIP

Leadership is difficult and complex drawing on a range of understanding and skills and development for leadership can take place at a number of levels. Until relatively recently, training and development courses for principals were only formalised in a small number of countries including the USA, but internationally it is becoming more common for training and development to occur before or immediately after appointment to headship. In England and Wales there is now in place a range of programmes, organised through the National College for School Leadership. The programmes are targeted at different levels and stages and include formalised training for middle and senior managers. Five stages of leadership, each with their own training programme are identified:

Emergent: When a teacher begins to take on leadership responsibilities.
Established: For those who are experienced leaders but do not intend to pursue headship.
Entry to headship: Including a teacher's preparation for and induction into a senior post in a school.
Advanced: The stage at which leaders look to widen their experience, refresh themselves and update skills.
Consultant: When an able and experienced leader is ready to take on training, mentoring or coaching (NCSL, 2003).

Opportunities for formal professional development are to be welcomed but the insistence on leadership training and development run to a government agenda can be seen as narrow and as an attempt to embed government policy (Thrupp and Wilmott, 2003). The NPQH training, which is now mandatory has been criticised as narrow and summative (for example, Bush, 1999).

In a wide-ranging international review of training for leadership in Australia, New Zealand, Canada, USA, Hong Kong, Singapore and Sweden, Bush and Jackson (2002) identified differences in the types of training which highlight the difficulties of transferring programmes from one country to another, but they did identify certain trends that were common to all programmes:

- the acknowledgement that leadership is not confined to the principal of a school;
- the development of more integration of leadership programmes across careers;

- the use of many types of learning including virtual learning environments;
- development programmes for teams;
- using experienced principals as trainers;
- recognising that schools are learning organisations;
- the need for leadership centres.

The quality of leadership in education is consistently seen as a vital element in the success of a school or college. This chapter has aimed to present some of the basic ideas about leadership to increase your own understanding of this important concept.

SUMMARY

This chapter has introduced you to aspects of theory and how they can relate to the practice of leadership. The aspects reviewed include:

- defining the concepts of leadership, management and administration and the extent to which you consider them to be different, the same or over-lapping;
- ways of theorising leadership including a focus on the individual or on the situation, some of the underlying dynamics of leadership (Tannenbaum and Schmidt, and Blake and Mouton), distributed leadership, gender and leadership and emotional intelligence and leadership;
- the Leithwood et al analysis of styles of leadership based on the exercise of influence:
  — instructional leadership or learning-centred leadership;
  — transformational leadership (often contrasted with transactional leadership);
  — moral leadership;
  — participative leadership, focusing on the sharing of decision-making;
  — managerial leadership which may also be called transactional, technical or organisational leadership and which is linked to targets and performativity;
  — contingent leadership which stresses the variation in response of leaders to different leadership situations;
- a brief review of leadership training and development issues.

At the end of this chapter stop now and reflect on your understanding of the concepts that have been covered and how they relate to your experience.

RECOMMENDED FURTHER READING

You will be able to take some of the ideas in this chapter further by reading the following:

Law, S. and Glover, D. (2000) *Educational Leadership and Learning: Practice, Policy and Research*, Buckingham: Open University Press. Chapter 2, 'Developing leadership and management effectiveness', will give you an overview and more detail in relation to some of the areas covered in this chapter.

Foskett, N. and Lumby, J. (2003) *Leading and Managing Education: International Dimensions*, London: Paul Chapman Publishing. Chapter 14, 'Leadership', discusses leadership in an international context.

Other useful edited volumes include:

Brundrett, M., Burton, N. and Smith, R. (eds.) (2003) *Leadership in Education*, London: Paul Chapman Publishing. Particularly Chapter 1, Dimmock, C., 'Leadership in learning-centred schools: cultural context, functions and qualities, Chapter 3, Coleman M., 'Gender in educational leadership'; and Chapter 9, Harber, C. and Davies, L., 'Effective leadership for war and peace'.

Bennett, M., Crawford, M. and Cartwright, M. (eds.) (2003) *Effective Educational Leadership*, London: Paul Chapman Publishing.

Begley, P.T. and Johansson, J. (eds.) (2003) *The Ethical Dimensions of School Leadership*, Dordrecht: Kluwer Educational Publishers, provides a comprehensive and stimulating overview of theories relating to ethics and educational leadership.

Gunter, H. (2001) *Leaders and Leadership in Education*, London, Paul Chapman Publishing, outlines the more critical and theoretical view of leadership whilst, Gronn, P. (2003) *The New Work of Educational Leaders*, London: Paul Chapman Publishing, analyses distributed leadership.

For more information and analysis of leadership training, see Bush, T. and Jackson, D. (2002) 'A Preparation for School Leadership: International Perspectives', *Educational Management and Administration*, 30(4), 417–429.

In addition, a review of the literature on school leadership by Tony Bush and Derek Glover (Spring, 2003) is available from www.ncsl.org.uk/literature reviews. Other literature reviews can also be downloaded from this website, including a review of distributed leadership by Nigel Bennett, Christine Wise and Philip Woods.

Another useful website is www.dfes.gov.uk for the latest on UK government thinking.

2

The Cultural Context of Educational Leadership

Marian Shaw

INTRODUCTION AND LEARNING OUTCOMES

By opening up the topic of culture, and examining how culture affects the way educational organisations operate, this chapter aims to establish a principle that underpins the rest of the book by contextualizing its various concepts. After an introduction, the second section examines some of the theory that has grown around cross-cultural research, and touches on its relationship to organisational culture. The third section then explores what this means practically to educational leaders and managers by reference to two case studies. The fourth section is the nub of the chapter. First, it demonstrates through one example how a theory, proven to be useful in its own context, can fail leaders if used out of its relevant cultural context, and then it goes on to propose a means of adapting theories across cultures by introducing a "theory-interrogation" model. This can subsequently be used as a tool with which to interpret dominant theories of leadership and management in different cultural contexts. The overall contention of the chapter is that, by using a sensitive combination of this tool and cross-cultural theory, schools, regions, ministries—or, indeed, individual teams within these systems—can forge the most appropriate *organisational* culture to guide, support and inform all members of the educational community.

By the end of this chapter you should be able to :

- understand the key elements of cross-cultural theory;
- recognise and analyse some of the challenges presented by cross-cultural interactions in educational organisations;
- analyse your own situation through the theory;
- interpret dominant theories of leadership and management in different cultural contexts.

CULTURAL CONTEXT

Education is widely recognised as the crucible where the next generation's attitudes and values are forged. Through it, citizens are shaped, and leaders emerge. Much effort goes into developing appropriate curricula, but how much into defining the way people interact in their educational systems? The 'hidden curriculum' is very powerful: people tend to learn through what they experience from their leaders rather than through what they are told, as Harber found in his research into education for democracy (Harber, 1995; 1998). For the educational manager this can present a real challenge. This is especially so where a mix of cultures is represented, whether this is through association by borrowing theories from different cultures, or by personal influence from overseas consultants. In either case, the potential for dissonance is huge.

Some readers, such as those working in countries in receipt of donor-aided educational projects, will already recognise the nature of this challenge. But even if we are working and living in a single country, it is likely that most of us have greater contact with people of different cultures than we may have had in the past. In opening up discussion about inter-cultural interaction, therefore, the issues raised in this chapter are relevant to virtually everyone working in the education service, including students studying in overseas schools and universities, teachers leading such courses, expatriates working in different cultural environments, leaders in schools with mixed-culture teams of staff, consultants supporting aid-funded projects, and their counterparts in-country. It is so easy to assume that the principles of educational leadership and management are universally applicable, but this is not so.

Our knowledge of leadership and management has developed by observations and hypotheses, followed by research to test these out. But this costs money, and so such research has largely been carried out in the richer, more developed countries which can afford it. The research is then written up and published as journal articles, which are eventually turned into text books on theories of leadership and management. With globalised marketing, such books are then sold around the world as 'how to' books, or 'the way to do it'.

There has frequently been an implicit assumption—in practical, operational terms—that the materials in these books are equally relevant to all situations, but such models and theories nevertheless cannot apply universally across the world (e.g. Little, 1996; Rodwell, 1998). Educational leadership and management is a social science; it concerns the human interactions between people. In achieving the goals of an organisation, whether this is at the level of a team, a school, a college, an education authority or a ministry, leaders and managers need to know how to treat *all* the people with whom they work in such a way that the organisation becomes more effective, as the school improvement research shows (see Chapter 7). To do this, they must understand what is appropriate (and inappropriate!) behaviour to use with everyone.

Successful leaders rely heavily on human relationships. They need to understand how X will react, what motivates Y, or why Z did that when confronted by W. Employee expectations vary from one country to another: in more developed countries, employees assume that they will be treated with individual respect, but leaders also know that an approach that works for some people does not work for others. As others in this book testify, a huge amount of research demonstrates the complexity of effective leadership, even where team members from a single culture share an implicit set of assumptions about the way they work together. But where there are differing cultural expectations, and a shared set of assumptions is missing, the challenges are even greater.

In order to illustrate how cross-cultural encounters can lead to puzzling mis-understandings, and to introduce the theme of the chapter, case example 1 provides an example of an incident facing an educational leader with a mixed-culture team of staff. Try to examine the situation from all perspectives, regardless of your own cultural background and experience.

Case Example 1

Noriko is a 13-year-old Japanese student attending an international school in Tokyo, her home town. The staff consists of some local teachers, and some teachers from overseas. The students are drawn from local and international communities.

Noriko asks her teacher a question concerning the lesson topic. John, an experienced Australian teacher in his first year overseas, acknowledges the importance of the question. Then, pointing her towards the relevant resources, suggests that Noriko finds out the answer herself, and then tells the rest of the class the following day.

The next day, however, there is no answer. Instead, Noriko's parents complain to the Principal that her teachers are not properly qualified, as they don't seem to be able to answer questions in class.

John is invited to discuss the issue with the Principal. As a successful teacher at home, he is shocked and upset about what has happened—not least that the parents went directly to the Principal rather than to him.

In this case, the consequences are significant: a successful teacher has lost confidence in his teaching abilities, a sound student has been confused by her teacher, a parent-client is in danger of losing confidence in the school of their choice, and the Principal now has to build bridges across cultures and move things forward. The *specific* issues raised in case example 1 will be discussed later in the chapter, but in order to establish a theoretical basis for such a discussion, the next section now introduces some cross-cultural theory.

THEORETICAL PERSPECTIVES

Over the last 30 years, an increasing body of research has focused on the effect that culture has on the way we perceive situations and the way we react. Here we focus briefly on two related, but distinct, areas: (a) cross-cultural theory, and (b) organisational culture, bringing these together in a brief examination of their relationship with each other. In a mixed-culture workforce, managers may want to know whether organisational culture has more—or less—effect on the way people work than national or ethnic culture. Discussing culture is fraught with difficulty—there are too many meanings of the word; so, to avoid confusion, where the word 'culture' appears alone, it represents the values and assumptions of groups of people bound by their ethnicity, as described below in case example 2. Where it refers to the climate or atmosphere of an organisation, the word 'culture' is preceded by, for example, a descriptor such as organisational, school, team or ministry.

Cross-cultural theory

This is a rapidly expanding field, and this section does no more than highlight some of the concepts that can help to improve cross-cultural understanding and communication. Research has sought to help people understand better what is going on between cultures, enabling them to communicate more effectively, thus eventually improving organisational performance at all levels. There is a key difficulty in carrying out research of this nature, however: it is impossible to do a scientific piece of experimental research, as there are so many human variables. Nevertheless, Hofstede's well-known and seminal research, carried out between 1967 and 1973, involved so many different cultures, and such huge numbers of people, that broad generalisations were able to be made with confidence (Hofstede, 1980; 1991). This work led to his international recognition for ground-breaking work on cultures and organisations, and, while it invited many challenges, it did at least set the scene for many further investigations.

Hofstede uses an onion metaphor: as one peels away the outer layers of an onion, more of what is hidden inside is revealed. The outer, more visible layers of the 'culture onion' are concerned with *symbols* and *practices*, while the concealed innermost layer consists of *values*. Unlike the outer layers, which are relatively easy to observe and to understand, the core values are usually hidden; these are the *assumptions* inherent in the culture. They define the norms by which people of the same group live, and because they *are* assumptions they are not discussed. It is widely assumed that this inner core of cultural values is 'transmitted from generation to generation, with the responsibility given to parents, teachers, religious leaders, and other respected elders in the community' (Brislin, 1993, p.6). Hofstede adds that 'developmental psychologists believe that by the age of ten most children have their basic value system firmly in place, and after that age, changes are difficult to make' (1991, p.8).

Values—and therefore culture—may be derived from various sources, such as national or ethnic group, generation, work organisation, gender, class and religion—and these are not necessarily all consonant with each other (Hofstede, 1991, p.10). In addition, though not discussed by Hofstede, any group of people working together is likely to have a series of sub-cultures operating within them—quite often influenced by recent history. Mbiti, writing about religions in general, and Africa in particular, posited in 1969: 'religion is the strongest element in traditional background, and exerts probably the greatest influence upon the thinking and living of the people concerned' (Mbiti, 1969, p.1).

Hofstede defines culture as: 'the collective programming of the mind which distinguishes the members of one group or category of people from another. Culture is learned, not inherited. It derives from one's social environment, not from one's genes' (1991, p.5). Brislin, who trains people in managing their own cross-cultural encounters more successfully, defines some characteristics of culture:

- Culture consists of ideals, values, and assumptions about life that guide specific behaviours.

- Culture consists of those aspects of the environment that people make.

- Culture is transmitted from generation to generation, with the responsibility given to parents, teachers, religious leaders, and other respected elders in the community.

(Brislin, 1993, Ch.1)

Values, the 'broad tendencies to prefer certain states of affairs over others' (Hofstede, 1991, p.8), are central to the examination of culture, as they are 'the weights with which people evaluate or judge their world' and they 'give rise to certain presuppositions from which they act with little or no conscious awareness' (Brislin et al, 1986, p.299). That is to say, people make judgements about what to do in any given set of circumstances according to the way their value system has been programmed. However, cultural difference—even conflict—may arise where 'individuals and societies order these values in differing hierarchies' (Brislin et al, 1986, p.299).

The researchers argue that cultural values are attached to groups of people, and that such groups are often defined by nationality. Nationality alone, however, may be problematic. A nation state may itself consist of many different cultures, for example, or groups of people may have migrated to another land through war or famine, taking their cultures with them. Whatever the cause of cultural affiliation, the researchers have sought to find a reliable way of categorising cultures into various dimensions, and nationality is one such way.

By way of a reminder, and as the case studies later depend on using these terms, Box 2.1 summarises the practical outcomes of Hofstede's seminal work; his cultural dimensions.

One of the reasons that Hofstede's work was so widely taken up was that Hofstede attached index values to these dimensions for individual countries, and, by making these evidence-based generalisations about the way people from specific national cultures tended to react under various circumstances, he was able to compare the cultural attitudes and expectations of people *stereotypically* across the world. His results have been used by researchers 'to put their theories and explanations into a clarifying perspective' (Søndergaard, 1994, p.453), and many researchers have sought to replicate, prove or disprove his theory, though few have produced comparable large-scale studies of values, Schwartz (1992) being an exception.

Stereotyping carries health warnings, however. No-one is culture-free, and people readily feel 'labelled' if such research is presented badly, or used insensitively. Carried to extremes, this sentiment carries the further danger of labelling *individuals*—believing that everyone of a certain nationality thinks and behaves in the same way, and the researchers themselves are keen to highlight this danger (Hofstede, 1991, p.253;

Box 2.1 Hofstede's Five Dimensions (Hofstede, 1991)

Individualism-Collectivism: The degree to which people see themselves or their collective group as more important. Individualistic societies tend to emphasise the 'I' above the 'we', while collectivist societies respect the goals of their own group more than individual achievement.

Power Distance (PD): The amount of emotional distance between employers and employees. In high power distance cultures, employees tend to prefer their managers to lead visibly, and paternal-autocratic leadership styles are seen as caring. In low power distance cultures, the opposite is true; employees express a preference for consultative management styles.

Uncertainty Avoidance (UA): The degree to which people feel threatened by uncertain or unknown situations. People with a high uncertainty avoidance index tend to prefer to know where they are, with rules of precision to guide them, while the opposite is the case with those with a low UA index, where more risks may be taken.

Masculinity-Femininity: This is concerned with the degree of achievement-orientation built into the culture, taking its name (perhaps unhelpfully) from stereotypical gender expectations. High masculinity cultures value status, challenge and achievement, while high femininity cultures value good working relationships and cooperation.

Confucian Dynamism (long-term vs. short-term orientation): This dimension emerged after the others following studies of entrepreneurial development in East Asia, which did not fit into the previous dimensions. It represents an emergence of the long-term orientation of 'virtue' (persistence, thrift, ordering relationships by, and observing, status, and having a sense of commitment to others) out of the more traditional short-term orientation of 'truth' (personal stability, protecting 'face', respect for tradition). The interaction between the two makes up this cultural value.

Brislin, 1993, p.174). Another danger lies in using national cultural stereotypes as an excuse, and failing to examine the real processes under the surface (Kanter and Corn, 1994; Goffee and Jones, 1995; Tayeb, 1994).

Nevertheless, in spite of the problems around their misuse, stereotypes can be useful: they help people to categorise, and they provide a point of reference, because 'people have so many decisions about their behaviour during a given day that they need guidance, hints, helpful rules, and so forth. Stereotypes serve this purpose' (Brislin, 1993, p.173).

Some of the other relevant cross-cultural phenomena emerge from research include:

- *Disconfirmed expectancies:* if people have a strong expectation about something, then any deviation from it is perceived as greater than it really is (Helson, 1964). Brislin remarks (1993, p.44) that 'disconfirmed expectancies are certain in intercultural encounters'.

- *Fundamental attribution error,* the mistake of making judgements about the characters of others without taking situational factors into account (Ross, 1977). Actions of other people are judged through the value system of the perceiver, who may then form incorrect conclusions about the motive for the action—often thinking the worse of them.

- *Symbolism:* sometimes others do not understand the value and importance of the way people relate to the symbols inside their own culture, which can be the cause of misunderstanding, sometimes disenfranchising others.

- *Universalism vs. particularism,* i.e. the degree to which universal rules can be applied within the culture to everyone equally. Particularist cultures may give preference to those closer to them (e.g. family, village, tribe), which universalists might perceive, through their own particular cultural lens, as unfair nepotism. Trompenaars (1993) gives several examples of this dimension.

Cross-cultural research, being immensely complex, is not without problems, particularly when applied to educational issues, which can be notoriously labyrinthine. For example, it is largely Western-centric (Trompenaars, 1993); it is mainly industry-based, and can be easily misused when attempt at transference is made to other areas (Jameson, 1994); and it has tended to attach stereotypes to nation states (Hofstede, 1980; Trompenaars, 1993). Crossley and Vulliamy (1997) also highlight the dangers of carrying out research in developing countries, where 'cultural imperialism continues to take many forms' (p.11). In addition, the research tools are not appropriate in all cultures (different concepts, inappropriate language to express concepts), which means suspect validity (Riordan and Vandenburg, 1994).

Organisational culture: its relationship to cross-cultural theory

The concept of organisational culture has been the focus of much educational research, brought into prominence partly by Ball's seminal study of micro-politics in schools (1987), and lent impetus in more recent times by the school improvement movement, which sees a healthy school culture as central to real change for the betterment of the school (Harris, 2001; MacBeath *and* Mortimore, 2001; McMahon, 2001). This is not the place to revisit these debates, but merely to note that the culture of any organisation within the educational service, whether at school, regional office or ministry level, has a symbiotic relationship with the behaviours and actions of those working in the system: while the organisational culture itself is determined by what people do, it, in turn, provides the guidelines for how people will respond to any given sets of circumstances that arise. The organisational culture and behaviours in this way form a feedback loop for each other. Schein describes organisational culture as 'a pattern of basic assumptions— invented, discovered or developed by a given group as it learns to cope with its problems' that is 'taught to new members as the correct way to perceive, think and feel in relation to those problems' (Schein, 1985, p.9).

The recognition that 'there is a relationship between an organisation's culture and its performance' (Heller, 1997, p.229) echoes the findings of Peters and Waterman (1982): in their research into excellent organisations, they found that the stronger the organisational culture, the less need there was for policy manuals, organisation charts, or detailed procedures and rules.

While much literature focuses on the development of a healthy organisational culture, less explores the relationship between this and the national/ethnic cultures that comprise the organisation, or attempts to answer the question: which has the greater effect on the way people respond? Hofstede downplays the effect of organisational cultures, saying that they are 'often only based on statements by corporate heroes' (1991, p.183), and not much to do with value: 'at the national level cultural differences reside mostly in values, less in practices [. . . while at . . .] the organisational level, cultural differences reside mainly in practices, less in values' (p.182). He concludes that 'shared perceptions of daily practices should be considered to be the core of an organisation's culture' (pp.182–183), and that values, per se, are more likely to be linked to the nationality, age and education of employees.

Some might find this a curious view: are practices not underpinned by values? Is it inevitable that an organisation has to accept values as 'given', or can it not develop values of its own to shape a bespoke organisational culture? Cray and Mallory (1998) argue that practices in an organisation are governed to a significant extent by a combination of three factors: the mix of cultures represented in the society, an individual's own cognitive framework (i.e. their own experience and outlook), and the culture of the organisation itself. But if the latter is invisible or weak, either of the other two factors will prevail, resulting in potential dissonance in the team/organisation. So they advocate adopting a cognitive approach to organisational culture, making explicit the 'rules' and ways of working, and *deliberately* adopting them, rather than leaving it to chance and hoping that these will be learnt through practice.

Their argument is persuasive, as it involves the people in the organisation subscribing *consciously and collectively* to the way they wish to work together. Where more than one national or ethnic culture is represented, this is easier to achieve once there is an understanding of the different assumptions inherent in those cultures. The case examples that follow explore the importance of such understanding.

APPLYING CROSS-CULTURAL THEORY TO EDUCATIONAL LEADERSHIP

This section looks at two types of educational situation where cross-cultural communication and understanding are particularly challenging, and where leaders may apply the theory to help them become more effective. The first of these (see case example 1, p.28) arises where teams or whole organisations are composed of people from two or more cultures. Then it becomes important to understand the hidden 'rules' by which everyone else around them operates. A similar situation exists for anyone finding themselves working or studying in a different culture from the one they grew up with, living and working in a different part of the world.

A second type of situation (see case example 2, p.36) which is cross-culturally challenging is where inappropriate ways of working are transplanted from one place to another—whether the latter is mixed- or mono-cultural. This is particularly the case where training materials for schools, colleges, education authorities or ministries are drawn mainly from one culture, and where the other cultures represented are expected to operate by different cultural norms than the ones they were brought up with. The indiscriminate adoption of imported policy also fits into this category.

Working with mixed-culture teams, or in an 'alien' cultural setting

Where teams or whole organisations are composed of people from two or more cultures, 'the way we do things around here' is not always clear. The situation presented earlier in case example 1 demonstrated how difficult it can be for someone (John) who uproots and goes to work in a completely different culture. It was also hard for the victims of John's cultural misunderstandings. On the surface, the school environment may seem to John to be quite similar and familiar to the national schools he has worked in at home, but it is only when a critical incident occurs that a cross-cultural misunderstanding becomes apparent and forces him to question, not only his own practice, but also what is expected of him by students, parents and staff. Let's look at this more closely.

Discussion of case example 1

This situation arises because there is a basic misunderstanding between John's Australian culture and the Japanese culture about the *purposes of education* and what is expected of a 'teacher' in that society. Noriko's parents may have chosen to send their child to this school for several reasons: international schools frequently represent to parents—in all parts of the world—a way of helping their child to acquire an English-medium education, or to give them an educational advantage in getting to the university of their choice (Shaw, 2001a). Parents do not *necessarily* subscribe to the style of teaching at the school—and may not even be aware of it when they enrol their offspring. The broad purpose of education is often *assumed* to be understood by both staff and parents, and not explained fully when parents sign up.

Using cross-cultural theory to examine what was going here, Hofstede's values (1991) for the relevant nationalities indicate that:

- Australia is quite individualistic, while Japan ranks low on individualism (i.e. is relatively collectivist);
- Australia ranks a little lower in power distance than Japan;
- Japan is ranked considerably higher in uncertainty avoidance than Australia.

These differences have practical implications.

While collectivist societies may tend to place much educational emphasis on learning facts (Hofstede, 1991, p.63), more individualistic societies, such as Australia, may be inclined to assume that, as well as acquiring knowledge and good exam results, education is also about preparation for unknown future situations, and thus it focuses on *learning how to learn* for life, encouraging investigation—which is what John was doing here.

As Noriko comes from a high uncertainty avoidance (UA) culture, she is more likely to want to extract a single right answer from her teacher, as she expects teachers to hold all the knowledge. In this case, when answers were not given, this was taken by the parents to be a sign of weakness.

While John *assumes* that the student will develop best through finding out, and has developed his pedagogy along the lines of active learning, Noriko's parents *assume* that his response means that the teacher does not know his subject. The parents therefore make a *fundamental attribution error* (Ross, 1977): they form an incorrect judgement about the teacher's motives for asking Noriko to find out for herself.

John is confused. Not only is a previously successful teaching strategy brought into question by parents, but he makes a fundamental attribution error of his own in assuming that Noriko's parents have gone directly to the Principal in order to embarrass him, or get him into trouble. This is not their intention. Coming from a higher power distance culture than John, they feel that the correct protocol is to go to the more senior person, not directly to the teacher.

The Principal is caught between the two sets of expectations, and needs to reconcile them. On the one hand, she needs to be explicit to these parents, and to others in the future, about the educational values of the school, and the related pedagogies, so that they know what to expect, and can understand the practices of the teachers. At the same time, she will be working with her staff on increasing the profile of an appropriate school culture—developed within the context of the national cultures represented in the school community—and the appropriate pedagogies.

Of course, this is all supposition: this exposition is made on stereotypically cultural lines, and must remain suspect, as we know nothing about the individual characters in the story! However, the main point is that, while there may be many reasons for misunderstandings, not all connected with culture, where there *are* cross-cultural encounters, it is at least worth taking the theory into account—it can sometimes help when analysing such situations.

The transfer of theories and ways of working from one culture into another

The last case examined a critical incident where inter-personal cross-cultural practices were misunderstood because they were viewed through the different cultural lenses of the people in a school community. But even where a group of colleagues may be mono-cultural, cross-cultural misunderstandings can still occur. Case example 2 explores such a situation which is extremely common and which, if not recognised, can smack of cultural imperialism—albeit inadvertent. Educational ministries in the parts of the developing world are frequently partners in aid projects which are funded and led by richer countries. Management trainers and consultants bring with them training materials or policies developed elsewhere in the world, usually modelled on theories which evolved in the West, as described earlier. If the consultant is not sensitive to the local culture, it can appear that the participants are expected to operate to cultural norms different from the ones they are brought up with.

This situation is compounded by the fact that aid funding is tightly linked to values reflecting those of government policy in the donor's country (e.g. humanitarian objectives such as equality of opportunity, or a focus on female education). Indeed, it is not unknown for the conditions set out by the donor to influence policy formulation in the recipient country if this might increase the likelihood of getting project funding. This trade-off can be quite open: 'in order to encourage democracy, international agencies increasingly attach political strings to loans and aid—no democracy, no money' (Harber, 1995, p.2).

Rodwell's categories (1998) of materials as either being 'internationalised' (i.e. they are expected to be applicable to all cultures) or 'indigenised' (i.e. made suitable for the local culture) are useful, but she points out that the former is more likely because of time pressure. This point is reinforced by Arthur and Preston (1995) who found in their research that, however well-intentioned consultants may be, with the current increased time and financial pressures on international consultancies, materials are more likely to be recycled around the world.

Case example 2 examines what happens when an educational policy is imported wholesale.

Case Example 2

The public service sector of a recently unified, post-conflict country (which is high on both power distance and uncertainty avoidance) has introduced a policy of decentralisation throughout all its departments. A United States aid agency consultant has been supporting the Ministry of Education in a project to reorganise its services so that more decisions are made at lower levels (i.e. at school and district levels) instead of at central Ministry level.

The policy of decentralisation and its implementation were modelled on the way it was successfully introduced in the USA. In effect, this means showing leaders at *all* levels how to delegate, apportioning tasks, and expecting those at school and district level to take more responsibility than they had previously done.

Two years into the project, however, it is clear that the decentralisation process is not working as intended. Although they now have the power to make decisions and take action, people continue to defer to those above them rather than trust their own judgement. In parallel with this, post-holders in the central ministry find it hard to let go their previous power to those below them in the hierarchy. They tend to supervise closely, as before, preventing leaders at lower levels from either increasing their management capacity or becoming empowered.

The outcome for the whole education service is that:

- decisions are slow to reach the districts, as they are waiting for central answers;
- when decisions *are* made, they are not always sensitive to local conditions;
- the people in the most senior central positions are becoming stressed with all the work being handed back up the line to them;
- the leaders at district and school levels are deprived of the professional development they should be receiving.

In other words, nothing much has changed, except that people feel guilty that they are not performing as expected under the USA 'rules' of decentralisation.

Reflection 1

Before reading on, consider how cross-cultural theory helps us to understand the problem here.

Discussion of case example 2

In common with many education services, this country is moving towards a greater degree of site-based management, which should help people at lower levels to gain confidence in leadership and management. Once established, this system should improve the standard of service, as decisions will be made closer to the need. In addition, those at top levels will be freed up to concentrate on more strategic issues. This is not the place to discuss the many forms of decentralisation, but all involve taking on responsibility at lower levels. Bullock and Thomas (1997) expand further on the principles of site-based management/decentralisation, as does Chapter 4 in this volume.

In this case, where a policy has been imported from one culture into quite a different culture, it has been introduced without consideration of what might (or might not) work. Making decisions and taking action always involves a degree of risk, and people like to know what will happen if they fail, or if things go wrong. High uncertainly avoidance (UA) would tend to make it harder for people to take this sort of responsibility in the first instance: it feels safer to continue to check upwards as before. In addition, the country is a post-conflict one, where trust may well be fragile across the population—another reason for not wishing to get anything wrong.

In a high power distance (PD) culture, there is also the expectation that those in power will continue to make decisions and take action, and that middle and junior managers will wait to do as they are told (Hofstede, 1991). Additionally, it is not unusual for post-conflict countries to be fairly centralised, operating—at least in the first instance—through directive rather than participative leadership styles.

The situation in this case is not uncommon in countries which are still developing their systems. The initial problem lies with unrealistic expectations, and the impetus for the initiative can come from either the donor or the aided country: practices that have been recognised as successful in the West—in their own cultural environment, and at that particular stage in the evolution of the educational service—are often considered to be suitable for use elsewhere, regardless of the national cultures, the history of the educational system, or the organisational culture of the ministry or team itself.

This section has discussed two examples of how false assumptions, partly due to cultural differences, can interfere with the processes of education. It illustrates the need for an enhanced cross-cultural understanding. Without it, not only do initiatives themselves fail, but the hegemony—albeit inadvertent—of the West (or the North) is reinforced by behaviours exhibited, potentially demonstrating yet another twist to cultural imperialism.

Reflection 2

Have you encountered other examples of situations where inter-cultural communication has failed one of the parties? Can you use the theory to illuminate the reasons?

THEORY-INTERROGATION FROM A CROSS-CULTURAL PERSPECTIVE

The central purpose of this chapter is to demonstrate that, while educational praxis can mis-apply under different cultural conditions, it is possible to interrogate it in order to be more relevant. This section, then, re-examines a well-known theoretical model through the eyes of a different culture than the one in which it evolved. After reminding the reader of the theory in question, a new model designed to help to transfer theory into a different culture is introduced, and this is finally applied to the theory in the illustration.

A well-known leadership theory

This theory has been chosen with the situation in case example 2 in mind, as it has been commonly used in the West to help leaders delegate. The Situational Leadership model of Hersey (1985), in essence, gives managers a structured approach to flexible leadership tailored to each member of their team, depending on the level of readiness or development of each individual. The leader is encouraged to provide the right *style of leadership* for a *specific individual*, for a *specific* task.

The 'readiness level' is found by analysing the relative combination of competence (knowledge and skills) and commitment (confidence and motivation). The most appropriate leadership style (telling, selling, participating, or delegating) is then selected *for that individual for the task in question*. For example, in Figure. 2.1, if someone's readiness level is identified as R1, for a certain task (i.e. they are enthusiastic, but naïve about how to perform), they would need a lot of help from the leader to do this task: the most appropriate style to use with *this person*, for *this task* would be the directive style of 'telling'.

Applied judiciously by educational managers, this model has been found to be flexible and successful in helping them to analyse their team composition and their own leadership behaviour. By careful deployment of successive leadership styles (moving from telling, through selling (coaching) and participating (supporting) to, eventually, delegating), leaders can let go incrementally so that individual members of the team can gradually develop by improving their development levels from R1, through R2 and R3 to R4 for various tasks. The benefits are universal: a better sharing of tasks by the leader, an improved chance of success in task-completion due to stronger ownership in the team, and the team members also develop their professional skills in a natural and work-based environment.

However, it was 'made in the USA', and this has serious implications for those intending to use it in an environment with different cultural norms.

A model to aid in adapting this—or any other theoretical model—for use in other cultures is discussed next.

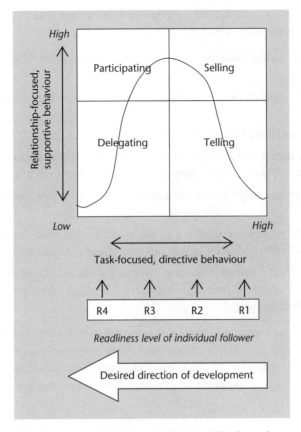

Figure 2.1 Situational Leadership Model (adapted from Hersey, 1985)

Reflection 3

Before reading on, consider some of the implications of using this model unadapted in a culture with a high power distance index, a fairly low individualism index (i.e. one which is collectivist), and a high uncertainty avoidance index.

Theory-interrogation model

Any reader who has studied educational management in a Western university, or been a recipient of aid-funded management training from a Western donor country, might well have questioned the relevance of the resources they are receiving to their own situation if this is significantly different. Perceptive educationalists or consultants, when they start to really tune in to the way a different culture thinks, might start to question their own perceptions about their 'standard' offerings, e.g.

- How does change-management theory apply in cultures which have a high uncertainty index?

- Is it reasonable to expect a woman in a traditional society to behave assertively to her male colleagues?

- Is a linear analytical model useful in a holistic society?

- How feasible, in a high power distance culture, is it that a ministry employee who does not fully understand how to do the job might ask for help from his or her line manager?

- Can the line manager above admit not knowing the answer to a question without losing face?

- Can performance appraisal be used as a professional development tool in a national or organisational culture which is largely bureaucratic and/or punitive?

- Is it realistic to expect a manager working in a particularist culture to support, coach or mentor a junior colleague from an out-group (i.e. a group which is not part of the manager's closely-knit group)?

Such questions generate further questions, and eventually a more logical and systematic line of questioning, which is more practical than the opportunistic approach, evolves. A general 'theory-interrogation' process might follow a sequence, such as that given in Box 2.2, which helps us to understand, and to adapt, theories as they are used in different cultures.

Box 2.2 A Theory-Interrogation Model (Shaw, 2001b)

i) In *which culture* did this model/theory originate?

ii) What are the stereotypical *characteristics* of this culture (e.g. Hofstede's analysis, 1991)?

iii) What are the *cultural assumptions* that the model makes? (e.g. stress on the success of the individual or the group, what counts as appropriate behaviour in given circumstances, when it is OK to ask for advice from those above, tolerance of mistakes in the interests of professional development)

iv) *What is known* about the culture(s) where the management development is to be carried out? (e.g. Hofstede's research again, 1991)

v) How do the *cultural norms match or differ from* those of the model's culture? Is a wide range of cultural norms represented in the client group?

vi) What, then, might the *misunderstandings* (e.g. Ross' fundamental attribution error, 1977) be in using this model in a different cultural context?

vii) Under the circumstances, then, is the model *likely to be useful or not*?

If useful, does the theory/model need *adapting, or presenting in a different way*? If so, how? (e.g. more emphasis on one part, omission of another part, altering part of it, etc.)

The principles in this model can be applied broadly to a range of theory and practice, as illustrated in the following section, which considers how the Western model in Figure 2.1. might be analysed through the eyes of a quite different culture.

Applying the theory-interrogation model

This example takes the case of a developing country which is keen to adopt the practices in Situational Leadership; an analysis might look like this (using the numbering of the model in Box 2.2):

i. *In* which culture *did this model/theory originate?*
North American.

ii. *What are the stereotypical* characteristics *of this culture?*
Using just a few characteristics as an illustration: the USA has a very high individualism index, a relatively low power distance index, and a very low uncertainty avoidance index (Hofstede, 1991).

iii. What are the *cultural assumptions* that the model makes?
The culturally based implicit assumptions in this model are that close interpersonal interaction is possible between the manager and *each* team member, that both praise and frank feedback are acceptable in the culture, that team members expect to be treated as individuals, that communication is open and two-way, and that team members feel relatively at ease with team leaders (e.g. able to ask questions when an individual is uncertain).

iv. What *is known* about the culture(s) where the management development is to be carried out?
In order to illustrate the argument, let us define that the culture of the country where the management development is to be carried out is high on power distance, fairly low on individualism (i.e. is collectivist), and very high on uncertainty avoidance.

v. How do the cultural norms *match* or *differ* from those of the model's culture?

Table 2.1

	Culture of target country	Culture of model/theory
Power Distance	*High*	*Fairly low*
Individualism	*Low*	*High*
Uncertainty Avoidance	*Very high*	*Very low*

Clearly, the culture of the target country is quite a contrast to that of the USA in several important ways, many of which impact on the way that people work with each other (just a few selected here).

vi. What, then, might the *misunderstandings* be in using this model in a different cultural context?

In teams of high power distance culture, where status is highly revered, the interpersonal interaction between leader and team member is likely to be restricted. It can easily be more possible for a leader to issue instructions and to supervise, or to hand something over entirely, than to enter the closer relationship required for the selling (coaching) and participating (supporting) styles. Team members collude with this: they can find it more difficult than their counterparts in a lower power distance culture to ask for advice or help from a superior in performing a task. They expect that all managerial tasks will continue to be carried out by those in managerial positions, as that is what they are paid to do. They also fear failure if they, the mere team members, get it wrong. In such cultures, leaders tend to use the directing and delegating styles far more than the coaching and supporting styles—and this suits everyone's comfort level (Shaw, 2001b).

The situation is compounded if introduced to a mixed-culture team of collectivists, where people are more likely to perceive greater differences between their own group and others than those who have a more individualistic culture (Hofstede, 1991). It is, again, easier for collectivists to tell people from a different group what to do than to enter into more productive dialogue: after all, selling and participating styles need close cooperation, empathy and understanding of what the other is thinking. Furthermore, these styles also require a degree of determination to help

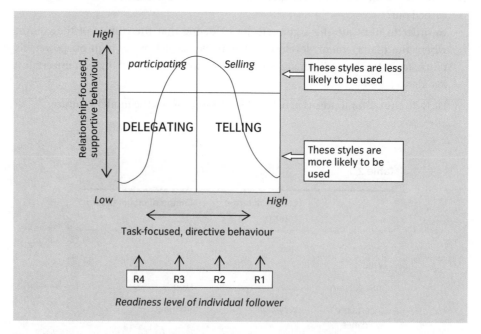

Figure 2.2 Likely corruption of the Situational Leadership® Model if introduced into a high power distance, collectivist and high uncertainty avoidance culture

the other succeed—not an automatic response when working with someone who is distinctly from another group (Fadil, 1995, p.199).

This situation may be made even more complex in ex-colonial countries, where a management style of 'tell and blame' has often been inherited from the civil service of the colonising power. As a result, the processes by which the countries' public services operate may be quite rigid. Such organisational cultures are not conducive either to participative leadership styles, or to employees volunteering for new responsibilities.

In summary, few, if any, of the cultural assumptions given in (iii) above pertain here, and if this model is applied in the normal 'Western' manner, it is largely a waste of time, as nothing is likely to change.

vii. Under the circumstances, then, is the model *likely to be useful or not?*

If applied indiscriminately and used without training, it is unlikely to be very helpful, and could be positively harmful. Figure 2.2 (page 42) shows the sort of outcome that might occur under these circumstances.

The problem here is that the transition from one style to another is interrupted: if the telling and participating styles cannot happen, there is no smooth pathway for an employee to progress from R1, through R2 and R3 to R4. It tries to leap from R1 to R4 without much linking them, and employees are frustrated that the Western model they have been given simply does not work:

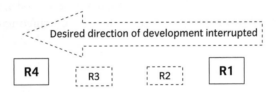

Not only is the model disappointingly unsuccessful, but it may also be damaging, as it increases inequalities, and potentially upsets established relationships.

If it is adapted, however, or introduced in a more culture-sensitive manner, the model does have some value, as shown next.

viii. If useful, does the theory/model need *adapting*, or presenting in a different way?

Once a theory or model has been thoroughly interrogated, specific adaptations may be made which make it useful to specific circumstances. In the case of the situational leadership model, such adaptations might include the following, though there can be no blueprint—each step or move would depend on the previous one:

- Discussion with the whole staff in more depth about what is involved in each style, opening the possibility for real choice.
- Open discussion of the suitability of each of these styles *inside this culture*, evolving into a broader discussion about barriers preventing these styles being used in *this* team.
- If appropriate from the previous step, exploration with all concerned of specific behaviours that are needed for successful telling and participating, examining the degree to which they might be appropriate *inside this culture*.

- If appropriate, a focus on the culturally acceptable leadership behaviours which might enable real upwards communication inside the team. This needs to be mutually agreed: it is a paper exercise if leaders do not genuinely want it to happen, or if they themselves feel vulnerable or threatened by team members' questions/suggestions. (One reality of workshop discussions is that participants often agree to things in the sanctity of the workshop environment that they have little intention of recognising outside it.)

- Keeping open the possibility that, collectively, the members of the team (or whole organisation) might exert some influence on the team culture themselves if they so wished (while remaining within the cultural framework of society).

  The above process may result in whole-team agreements about explicit *'rules of procedure'* by which the team wishes to operate in future, encouraging choice of style, limiting overuse of the two extremes and contributing towards a mutually agreed organisational climate. The key to success is helping people make small changes sequentially, ensuring that comfort zones are not challenged too much. In this way, confidence is built up in a new way of working and, over time, the organisational climate will gradually shift.

This section has gone into some detail to deconstruct a well-known leadership model, and to re-examine it through the eyes of a different culture, using a 'theory-interrogation' model that emerged from research. The combination of this model, together with the body of cross-cultural theory, might provide a tool for interpreting other theories for suitability.

CONCLUSION

This chapter has examined issues of leadership and management through the lens of cross-cultural literature. The research is fast-growing, immensely complex, and sometimes controversial. Nevertheless, the discipline of cross-cultural research is constantly evolving, as problems with the research in this sensitive area become apparent. The direction is progressing, albeit slowly, from the direct comparison of nation states with each other, where characteristics of indigenous peoples are identified by complex Western research tools, towards a more sensitive and organisationally focused approach, using research tools elaborated in mixed-culture teams. This is helpful because it recognises that, once the assumptions behind the different cultures represented are understood, organisations (or teams within those organisations) need not be passive victims of their national components, but can cognitively and collectively construct the organisational culture they want.

The current worldwide tendency for site-based management demands a new set of capacity-increasing skills to enable managers to encourage a degree of responsibility and risk-taking at lower levels, but the origin of these skills—and manner of their acquisition— needs to be examined. This chapter has aimed to show that, despite sometimes unequal power-relationships, a degree of both challenge and education may be needed if, in the attempt to share expertise and *not* constantly to be re-inventing the wheel, praxis from elsewhere is used. The warning bell sounds to those who, in the interests of uniformity, convenience or speed, are prepared to import wholesale—or to accept—models and theories inappropriately from different cultures.

The topic raises huge issues which extend well beyond the boundaries of this chapter. Education is the cradle for the values of the next generation, and educational leaders consequently bear a tremendous responsibility (Harber, 1995; 1998; Harber and Davies, 1997). A framework for democratic, inclusive and transparent leadership and management practices has been set for us by the Universal Declaration of Human Rights—but nailing a set of rules to the wall does not automatically change practice over night. And it cannot be forced: brutal imposition of another's values is cultural imperialism. On the other hand, educational development can be stifled if we are so culturally relativistic that culture is allowed to be an excuse to leave things as they are. It is a fine line, as all of us are culture-centric. While the study of cross-cultural interactions is both exciting and illuminating, none of us likes to feel stereotyped: any changes that challenge cultural thinking demand utmost sensitivity.

SUMMARY

This chapter has opened up some of the issues that emerge in applying Western theories of leadership and management in non-Western settings. Some of the theories relating to cross-cultural research were introduced. In the latter part of the chapter a 'theory interrogation' model was outlined and applied to an example of theory. This model can be used to interpret theories of leadership and management in different cultural contexts.

RECOMMENDED FURTHER READING

Hofstede's book, *Culture's Consequences* (1980) explains how his research was carried out. However, his later book, *Cultures and Organizations* (1991) is recommended as more readable. If you are interested in index values for specific countries, the tables for all Hofstede's dimensions can be found in this later book.

If you wish to read further critiques of Hofstede's work, the following may be helpful.

Søndergaard, M. (1994) 'Research note: Hofstede's consequences: A study of reviews, citations and replications', *Organization Studies*, 15(3) 447–456. This paper does what the title suggests: it summarises and analyses the literature regarding other people using Hofstede's research.

Trompenaars' book, *Riding the Waves of Culture* (1993) discusses seven aspects of cultural difference, and gives findings for (mainly European) cultures, though not as extensive as Hofstede's.

Brislin's book, *Understanding Culture's Influence on Behaviour* (1993) is a general and very readable book on a whole range of issues surrounding culture.

If you wish to test your own degree of cross-cultural understanding, you can do so in *Intercultural Interactions* (1986) by Brislin et al. They present 100 mini case studies and invite you to choose the real reason for the misunderstandings from four possible reasons given (multiple choice questions). They discuss all the cases fully, which helps you with your analysis. These cases do tend, however, to focus on the differences between the USA, Latin America, Europe and the Far East; other parts of the world are nearly absent.

Cray and Mallory's book, *Making Sense of Managing Culture* (1998), shows how organisations can override national cultures in order to create their own organisational culture.

Although none of these are specific to education, they all make very interesting reading.

Further case studies of cross-cultural misunderstandings when managing mixed-culture teams in international schools can be found in Shaw (2001a).

3

Organisations: Power, Structure and Culture

Marianne Coleman

INTRODUCTION AND LEARNING OUTCOMES

This chapter will consider power in the organisation and the related areas of structures and cultures of organisations. Before considering these concepts, the context of the organisation and some aspects of organisational theory will be introduced.

By the end of this chapter you should be able to:

- conceptualise the organisation and comment on its levels and its relationship with the environment;
- recognise the ways in which power in the organisation can be exercised;
- critically engage with the idea of power within the organisation;
- relate the wider concept of power to equity issues;
- summarise the concepts of structure and culture and how they inter-relate;
- reflect on the nature of your organisation and how the concepts of structure, culture and power can be applied there.

WHAT IS AN ORGANISATION?

So far in this book you have been concerned mainly with theoretical concepts of leadership and with broad aspects of national culture. You have engaged with the fact that leadership and management should be considered within the context of varying national cultures. The focus is now turning to the organisation, to look at leadership and management mainly in the institutional context.

Within an organisation such as a school (unit) there are levels (sub-units), e.g. departments and classes, and outside the unit there is a larger organisational structure relating to the region and to the national government. There are also subsidiary levels or sub-units within a regional or national educational organisation.

The school or college can be seen as a system with levels:

1. the individual;
2. the face-to-face teams;
3. the inter-departmental group—integrating the work of the teams so that they have a commitment to the whole;
4. the organisational level which establishes the unit in its own external environment.

(Tuohy and Coghlan, 1997, p.66)

These four levels are inter-locking systems with each level having an effect on the other levels and the organisation as a whole. For example, an individual who is unhappy and potentially unreliable may have an impact on team development, which in turn may lead to difficulties in coordination of teams and contribute to a negative climate in the organisation as a whole. This is similar to seeing the whole organisation as a system and this way of looking at the whole organisation as a system, or 'systems thinking' as Senge (1990) called it, is an important concept for educational managers and leaders. The organisation seen in this way is a complex system with inter-relating subsystems and the flow of information through the organisation will impact on the way that individuals operate.

Some organisations may be more cohesive than others. Weick (1976) developed the idea of 'loosely coupled' systems, and this idea is appropriate for schools and colleges where, for example, staff may operate within a department according to their professional norms, and the departments then make up a loose collection of subsystems within the organisation as a whole.

In such ways of thinking schools or colleges are envisaged as basically functional and rational systems with goals. An alternative critical perspective is that of the conflict approach seeing organisations including schools and colleges based on conflicting interests which can only be resolved by the exercise of power. The conflict can be internal, or can be related to the response to external demands such as the imposition of performance tables on schools.

A radical philosophical stance rejects the importance of the organisation or system entirely and stresses the importance of the individual, taking the view that there is no single social reality, only the view of the individual so that the reality of a particular school for you will be different from the reality perceived by me. This view should be contrasted with the potential reification of the system. For example, some treatments of the concept of the learning organisation attribute to it a kind of 'objective' reality of its own rather than seeing it made up of the subjective realities of the people who constitute its members.

For most of this chapter the dominant stance is that of the school or college as a system, normally this is envisaged as an open system, i.e. one which interacts with its environment. This theory of your organisation places it in an environment which has regional, national and international levels.

Features of open organisations

Hanna (1997) refers to organisations as open systems which can react in different ways with their larger environment. He sees organisations as having the following:

1. boundaries (which may allow for openings to the wider system);
2. purpose/goals;
3. inputs such as money and people;
4. transformation or throughput as the inputs are transformed through the work performed;
5. outputs or products;
6. feedback;
7. environment, with which the organisation interacts.

Reflection 1

Take a few moments to reflect on the nature of the organisation where you work and the extent to which you can identify Hanna's seven aspects of organisations as they relate to your situation. Each of the seven aspects are considered in turn below.

---

1. Boundaries It may seem obvious that there are boundaries to a school, college or university, but the physical boundaries of educational institutions are now challenged by the opening up of education to encompass lifelong learning, and by the idea of the learning community. These new ways of looking at education have implications for existing structures and raise questions about those that might emerge in the future.

The idea that learning takes place *only* in schools and colleges must be challenged: for example, learning certainly does take place in the home and at work. Parents and other members of the community have a role in educating children. A student does not have to be physically placed inside a particular building that is designated as a school or university in order to be a student. In particular, the development of information technology and of flexible and distance learning, does question the traditional nature of schools and colleges even challenging the relevance of national frontiers, at least for students in higher education.

The issue of boundaries also has implications for the status and roles of the people who relate to the institution. In respect of a school or college, who is inside the boundaries and who is outside? If you think of the various stakeholders: students; teachers; support staff; parents; governors; it is clear that pupils, teachers and support staff are inside the boundaries, but where are the parents and governors placed? Are they inside, outside or actually on the boundary?

2. Purpose/goals All organisations have purposes or goals even if these are not articulated. Many educational organisations, schools, colleges and departments of education have purposes which may be couched as mission statements, for example the statement of purpose for the Education Service in Singapore is:

to mould the future of the nation, by moulding the people who will determine the future of the nation. The Service will provide our children with a balanced and well-rounded education, develop them to their full potential, and nurture them into good citizens, conscious of their responsibilities to family, society and country. (Singapore Ministry of Education, 1997–98)

The purpose of education may be seen as improving examination results, i.e. narrowly focused on measurable academic achievement, or it may be seen as a wider purpose as the preparation of students for all aspects of their lives; or the inculcation of the idea of life-long learning. More consideration will be given to the implications of these two differing purposes in Chapters 7 and 8 which cover institutional improvement and effectiveness.

3,4,5. Input, throughput and output These ideas may be more difficult to reconcile to the educational process, as they owe a lot to a model of an organisation devoted to commerce; specifically to manufacturing. However, it is possible to see students as an input of raw materials to which value is added by a school or college before the output (the educated student) is fed out to the wider society.

This is a very narrow and simplistic version of what education is and does, and many people would find it unusual if not offensive to consider students at the end of their school life as no more than an 'output' or product. There is also an implicit assumption in the input/output model that the throughput is a simple rational/technical process. In reality there are many other ways in which an educational institution or process can be understood (see below).

6. Feedback Schools, colleges and universities are subject to some form of evaluation or inspection. This may come from students, parents, government inspectors or from self-evaluation or evaluation of peers. Feedback may be positive or negative, it may be formative (helpful in development) or summative (judgemental). It may be intended to help the institution improve, or it may be that the feedback comes in the form of a judgement that is part of the accountability process to which an educational institution is subject. More will be said on the subject of evaluation and feedback in Chapter 9.

7. Environment In reality, no organisation is a closed system. Schools, colleges and universities interact with their environment, for example responding to government initiatives. In countries where there is more institutional autonomy and competition between educational institutions, schools, colleges and universities have to be aware of the market in which they are operating and may have to be responsive to the needs and demands of their potential students.

Ways of conceptualising organisations

So we have considered the organisation and some of the aspects that may be common to all organisations. However, organisations are complex and one of the ways in which theorists have tried to understand and analyse them has been through the use of metaphors. For example, the metaphor of 'machine' is often used in relation to an organisation, particularly one which is hierarchically structured (Morgan, 1998) and this might lend itself to the input/output view we have considered above. Hanna (1997) also uses the idea of an organism as a metaphor in his exploration of institutions and their relationships with their environment. Some of the other images used by Morgan (1998, p.11) are:

- the organisation as a brain—stressing the importance of information processing and learning;
- the organisation having a culture with its own values, beliefs and rituals;
- the organisation as a political system shaped by power and conflict.

Bolman and Deal (1997, p.15) prefer to think of organisations as being viewed through alternative 'frames'or 'lenses'. Again they make use of metaphors to increase our understanding of their analysis; the frames they identify are structural (factory or machine), human resource (family), political (jungle) and symbolic (temple or theatre).

During the rest of this chapter you will be concerned with three over-arching dimensions of organisations which relate to the analyses of Bolman and Deal and Morgan. The dimensions or frames that will be considered are those of:

power;

structure; and

culture.

The human resource 'frame' is the context of Chapter 11.

POWER AND THE ORGANISATION

It has already been recognised that if an organisation is regarded as open it is affected by its environment. For example research on decentralisation in Malawi (Nsaliwa and Ratsoy, 1998) shows that despite reform, control over many educational decisions is still perceived to be at Ministry level, although heads of schools are also seen to have control in many types of decisions. The extent to which power is devolved is very variable and there are many countries where education is tightly controlled from the centre. South Korea, with its colonial and post-colonial inheritance is one such example. In a study of democracy and human rights education in the country, Kang (2002, p.322) states that:

> Korean schools are either publicly or privately funded, but all are subject to government control. No school can decide what kind of education to offer. All teachers must follow the national teaching guidelines. They cannot decide what or how to teach.

The issue of the distribution of power between national, regional and institutional levels will be looked at in detail in Chapter 4, so for now the focus is mainly on the ways in which power operates and is distributed inside an educational organisation. However, the section on power will also include brief consideration of the relationship of power to equity issues particularly in terms of implications for educational leaders.

One useful differentiation of types of power is that of Hales (1997) who sees power as:

1. physical power resources;
2. economic power resources;
3. knowledge power resources, including administrative knowledge about how an institution works, or technical knowledge concerned with how tasks are performed;
4. normative power resources, for example, personal qualities, or the 'aura of office'

(Hales, 1997, p.25)

Quite a similar list differentiating sources of power is quoted by Hoyle (1986, p.74):

- structural: power as a property of a person's office or structural position;
- personality: power as a function of personal characteristics, such as charisma or leadership qualities;
- expertise: power as a function of specialised knowledge or skill or access to information;
- opportunity: power as a function of the occupancy of roles which even though they may rank low in the hierarchy, provide the opportunity to exert power through the control of information, or key organisational tasks.

It is helpful to differentiate power as a concept, from the two related concepts of authority and influence. Power is over-arching, but authority relates to the legal or statutory right to exert power, whilst influence relates to the more informal power that individuals may have. In schools for example, the headteacher or principal may exercise power with authority because of his or her status, whilst individual members of staff may exercise the more unofficial aspect of power which is influence, which could be linked to personal charisma. Our understanding of the analysis of power and authority is based on the work of Max Weber (Gerth and Wright Mills, 1947).

Reflection 2

If you are in a school or college, consider what makes the position of the headteacher or principal particularly powerful. Are there others who also wield large amounts of power? If so, identify on what basis.

Physical power is unlikely to be an element in the management and leadership of schools by the headteacher or principal, but the head may have economic power, particularly if financial devolution has occurred. Knowledge and expertise in relation to professional matters and management skills are likely to be in the hands of the head/principal. Not all heads/principals will necessarily wield power through charisma or strength of personality, but it is quite likely that they might do so. A recent conceptualisation of power has differentiated the ideas of 'power with' and 'power over'. This differentiation has been articulated particularly in relation to the ways that women use power. For example in this description of an Australian woman school principal:

> Yet she did not feel comfortable with the notion of having power *over* others. Power was a 'male way of doing things', and professionally and ethically questionable. She redefined her power as power through and with others—shared leadership—'being at the centre of the spokes of a wheel rather than out in front pulling the wagon'. (Blackmore, 1999, pp.160–161.)

A headteacher/principal is leading a group of professionals. Although the headteacher has authority, they may decide to cede some of their power and share it with the teachers in the school in a collegial manner (power with), or they may operate in a more formal hierarchical structure where they are at the top and others are subject to rules and regulations imposed from the top. Alternatively, power in the form of influence may mean that power is exercised unofficially in a micro-political way.

The following sections are concerned with these three models of the exercise of power. However, they do not exist independently and it is usually possible to identify elements of all of the three: collegiality, bureaucracy and micro-politics operating side by side, although one style may predominate.

Collegiality

In much of the writing on educational leadership and management, the model of collegiality is regarded as desirable. Bush (1995) lists the major features of collegiality as:

1. it tends to be normative, i.e. thought to be the 'best' way of managing and advocated as such;
2. it is seen as particularly appropriate to organisations where staff are professionals (like teachers);
3. a common set of values is assumed;
4. it may work best in small organisations, or else a system of democratic representation may be used;
5. decisions are reached by consensus.

The following example from England, illustrates aspects of collegiality.

In a sample of 21 secondary schools in the north west of England (Brown, Boyle and Boyle, 1999), headteachers and middle managers were interviewed and a typology of three types of decision-making by middle managers emerged. Type A schools could be regarded as broadly collegial in style, Type B as less so and Type C schools were certainly not collegial, but it would be hard to say from the evidence presented what the dominant form of management style actually was. What is certain is that power was held in the top echelons of the management structure of these schools, rather than being distributed.

Type A schools showed:

- a commitment to regular formal opportunities for collaboration with other heads of department and colleagues from different subject areas;
- their departmental priorities correlated closely with the School Development Plan and with themes and issues agreed collectively;

- heads of department were actively involved and consulted in whole-school policy and decision-making;
- the headteacher saw them as having a wider whole-school management role.

Type B schools showed:

- less frequent formal opportunities for collaboration with other heads of department;
- heads of department believed that they were viewed by the headteacher as having whole-school management roles and involvement in whole-school policy decisions;
- some involvement in the School Development Plan beyond their own department.

Type C schools showed:

- little formal collaboration between heads of department;
- little or no cooperative working with other staff colleagues;
- a wide divide between the role of the headteacher and the heads of department in decision-making;
- little evidence of whole-school committees for curriculum and management;
- no whole-school decision-making role for heads of department;
- no consultation on whole-school decisions for heads of department.

These three types of decision-making processes observed in the English schools can be set alongside the conclusion of the researchers that: 'In general, heads of department want bureaucratic approaches to leadership to be replaced by distributed leadership throughout the school' (Boyle et al, 1999, pp.328–329). However, they also state that despite the general approval of the collegial model, it remains difficult to attain the more cooperative horizontal type of decision-making.

Research undertaken in Tasmania, Australia (Mulford et al, 2001) on perceptions of the decision-making process indicated amongst other findings that:

- the role of the school council (including lay people) in decision-making was limited, particularly in the primary schools;
- the level of involvement in decision-making is linked to the position in the hierarchy;
- between 40 and 60 per cent of teachers perceived overall management style to be top-down and were dissatisfied with decision-making processes.

Another research project on decision-making in Australia (Wildy and Louden, 2000) showed that the principals felt that:

> efficiency takes a high priority. Making decisions alone takes less time than setting up structures and processes to involve staff or parents. Efficiency, in terms of time, is valued above collaboration (p.181).

They may aspire to collegiality, but in reality are torn by the demands on them to be strong and efficient as leaders and to keep power centralised within the school and to not 'waste' teacher's time.

In a New Zealand school, teachers were engaged in trying to improve the academic performance of a minority group of Samoan students (Timperley and Robinson, 2000). Research showed how: 'The problem of workload was compounded by a norm of collegiality which precluded public criticism of practices which were privately judged inadequate' (p.49). The supportive element of collegiality tended to mute any potentially constructive criticism.

Reflection 3

Even though collegiality is generally favoured as a way of sharing power, what are the difficulties that you have observed through reading the four examples above?

There are problems associated with collegiality such as:

- the development of appropriate structures;
- the time taken to come to decisions;
- conflict with external demands for efficiency;
- apparently supportive collegial values leading to uncritical acceptance of practice.

There may also be reluctance on the part of senior managers and other educational leaders to distribute and share power which would otherwise remain vested largely in them.

Perhaps arising from an attempt to deal with the difficulties identified above, collegiality is subject to the criticism of being 'contrived' (Hargreaves, 1991). An example is drawn from the work of Franziska Vogt (2002) who compares collegial practices in England and Switzerland in relation to joint planning in primary schools. She found in the English schools that:

> The policy of joint planning is in this case not the result of a process of organisational development but rather has been introduced top down, by the head teacher responding to wider policy changes. The power of policy changes has led to a coercive teamwork in the school which illustrates elements of what Hargreaves termed 'contrived collegiality'. Joint planning is a highly coercive strategy, as it is endorsed by the system with general legislation (directed time) and practices of inspection (Ofsted report), demanded and controlled by persons in positions of power (head teacher and senior management), builds on defined technology (planning sheets) and is sponsored by an ideology (working together is good) (p.10).

In the Swiss schools although teamwork is strongly encouraged, the teachers are still in control of how much they plan together and there is no direct pressure to introduce joint planning. A conclusion is drawn that relates to the wider power structure of the two societies:

> Teamwork can be pushed through in an all encompassing way in an English school because of the powerful demands of policy makers in central government through league tables, a national curriculum, literacy and numeracy hours and inspection, and because of the powerful position of the English head teacher. Such powers do not exist

nor are they assumed by either Cantonal government or head teachers in Swiss schools and are not part of the structure of the education system even after the new managerial reform (Vogt, 2002, p.13).

In the examples of collegiality above, there is a tacit comparison with a model of power sharing which vests power and authority in the leader and senior management team who are at the top of a pyramid of authority. Power is taken to be formally vested in the leader and decreases lower down the hierarchy.

Bureaucratic or formal models

The main features of bureaucratic or formal models are:

1. a hierarchical authority structure with formal chains of command;
2. goals of the organisation are important, the assumption is of a rational technical process;
3. a division of labour with staff specialising, e.g. in departments in a secondary school;
4. decisions are governed by rules and regulations;
5. neutral and impersonal relations between staff are a feature;
6. recruitment and progress are determined on merit.

(Based on Bush, 2003)

Although the term 'bureaucratic' is identified with red tape, delays and unnecessary complexities, in its original formulation of an ideal type, Weber saw bureaucracy as: 'a form of organisation which strives continuously for maximum efficiency through rationally defined structures and processes' (Harling, 1989, p.21). Some element of the model of layers of authority arranged in a hierarchy where rational behaviour is paramount is present in our conceptualisations of the vast majority of educational organisations. However, the trend is for the pyramid to have become a flatter model with less layers and more distribution of power.

Many of the aspects of a rather traditional bureaucratic model can be seen in the following brief case example of a description of how infringements of discipline are dealt with in one Israeli school. This style of leadership and management may be typical of schools in many countries, where a more collegial style has not been accepted as an aspirational norm.

Case Example 1   Bureaucracy in an Israeli middle school

The middle school deals with discipline difficulties in a typical bureaucratic manner. The school has very detailed written rules, which exactly specify how students and teachers are expected to behave. Sanctions are attached to each kind of violation and a clear sequence of reactions is defined. For example, once a student violates a rule (e.g. coming late), the teacher talks with him and the violation is registered in the student's file. If tardiness is maintained then a letter is sent to the parents and later they are invited to a serious talk with the educator and the grade-level leader. If the student continues to violate the rules more than five times then he or she is suspended for one day from school. The rules, which are written by the principal and some senior teachers, are distributed to everyone before the beginning of the school year. One of the secretaries is charged to keep all the records in the personal files.

There is a clear chain of command regarding who deals with discipline problems. Teachers are expected to calm down rude behaviour. When a student severely misbehaves the grade-level leader is asked to intervene (sometimes together with the grade-level counsellor). The next step in the ladder is referral to one of the two vice-principals who is responsible for issues of discipline. Very few problems are referred to the principal. On a broader perspective, the middle school is well-organised with clear definitions of who needs to do what.

(Eliezer Yariv, unpublished)

In organisations like the one described here, the formality protects the individuals in the organisation from being arbitrarily treated. However, in an organisation where power is wielded micro-politically there are not the same safeguards.

Micro-political models

The major feature of a micro-political style of management is the use of influence to further the interests of individuals or groups within the organisation.

1. there is a focus on the group rather than the organisation as a whole. For example in secondary schools, there may be conflict and a struggle for power between subject departments;

2. there may be differences in values and aims between interest groups within the organisation;

3. there is a stress on conflict in the organisation;

4. there tend to be a variety of goals, linked to the interests of groups rather than agreement on goals for the organisation as a whole;

5. decisions are made through negotiation and bargaining;

6. power is the key, with decisions being made on the basis of who is holding power.

(Based on Bush, 2003)

However, as Busher (2001, p.79) has pointed out, a micro-political perspective actually 'offers explanations for how people co-operate in educational institutions, as well as giving insights into how people handle conflict'.

There is a relationship between micro-political activity and the conflict model of the organisation identified earlier. In particular, micro-politics engages with overt and covert conflict within the organisation and it may also be affected by the operation of power outside the institution which rebounds on the relationships within it. Where power has been devolved to schools from central government, the increase in the nature and amount of decision-making in the school has opened up further the possibilities for micro-political activity. For example in the ' Schools of the Future' initiative introduced in the Australian state of Victoria, power was shifted away from the state to the level of the school. In research carried out by Bishop and Mulford (1999) principals were having to ensure that a common curriculum was introduced in the schools and classrooms. In a case study school, the principal, who was generally liked and trusted, was faced with opposition and resistance from her staff which revealed underlying distrust about the use of power:

> I'm not necessarily convinced that the principal acts in the teachers' best interests. Often I think there is a hidden agenda, so that when we are sometimes asked to discuss an issue, I feel that the result is basically predetermined. I think it is often a case of the . . . [head office of the Department of Education] wanting something a certain way and the principal then having to manipulate enough staff in order to achieve that. (Teacher quoted, p.184)

The conclusions of the researchers were that:

> there was a disparity between the view of the government and the views of the teachers about the reforms;

> there was an intensification of micro political processes and structures in schools as a result of the changes: 'teachers' perception of principal co-option in implementing a key change which they did not support, qualified their trust of the principal, increased teacher alienation, and heightened the use of resistance strategies'. (p.185)

This research shows how external initiatives, or macro initiatives can impact on micro-political processes within the school.

Micro-political theory also focuses on the interaction of groups both formal and informal. West (1999) identifies how there may be formal groups or teams formed within a school, for example departmental teams or the senior management team. However, there may also be informal groupings which cut across the more formal teams. These could be defined as 'cliques' with their own norms and ways of behaving. You can see how such groups could be defined as sub-cultures within the dominant culture of the organisation. Such groups, formal and informal, sustain their own members giving support and encouragement and also providing them with a sense of power. However, the existence of groups can promote competition and conflict with potential hostility between groups. These clashes can occur within cliques in the staff room, or between the powerful groups of academic departments in secondary schools referred to by Ball (1987, p.221) as 'baronial politics', where there is competition over access to resources. These clashes may be most vividly experienced in relation to bidding over finance.

Reflection 4

Can you identify an experience in your professional life where you have been aware of conflict between groups which has been an expression of the power and influence of the groups? Was it the protagonist who had the most power who was successful, or was it the one who might be seen to be 'right' by a neutral observer?

In a school, the decision about what is 'right' is a normative one, but powerful groups distort a bargaining process. West (1999, p.195) suggests ways by which leaders in schools might limit the harmful effects of micro-political behaviour.

- Emphasizing overall effectiveness, rather than departmental excellence, and recognising/rewarding groups for their contribution to the whole, rather than their individual achievement.

- Engineering frequent interaction and communication between groups, providing opportunities for groups to collaborate and reinforcing/rewarding assistance provided between groups.

- Avoid win-lose situations, by not placing groups in positions where they need to compete for resources or are rewarded according to 'success'—place emphasis on pooling and sharing of resources to maximise commitment and involvement.

- Rotate members between groups, to de-stabilise, to increase mutual understanding, to minimise the strength of individual-group identification.

We have been considering the ways in which power is dispersed, or held by an individual or group within the organisation. This might be through:

- a collegial approach where power is shared;
- a formal or bureaucratic approach where power is held at the top and linked to official position in the hierarchy; or
- through micro-political activities and conflict.

There have also been references to the way in which political decisions outside the organisation can impact on the decision-making and power structure inside the organisation.

The dimension of power transcends the institution and its policy context, since power in society tends to lie in the hands of certain groups and to be denied to others. One aspect of power that has not so far been considered is equity in relation to the access to power. Access is influenced by issues of gender, class, race and ethnicity and religion. All of these factors will help to determine who actually obtains power in a society or its institutions. Access to power is not gained on grounds of merit alone. In schools, and in the wider system, women and members of ethnic minorities, possibly members of certain religions or classes are likely to have difficulties in gaining access to more senior positions or posts. In contrast men, particularly if they come from the dominant ethnic and religious group and from a high status class background, are more likely to be in positions of leadership and power.

Power and equity issues

It can be argued that at any time and in any place, there are groups of people who are less powerful simply by virtue of characteristics over which they have no control. For example, Connell (1987, p.183) talks about the concept of male hegemony, 'the global dominance of men over women'. Ethnicity, religion and class also impact on access to power. The issue of equity is one for society as a whole, but it is also one which has implications for existing leaders and managers in schools and colleges who have a responsibility to ensure that they promote equity and equality of opportunity.

Specific issues of equity will differ from one society to another, but gender, race and class are likely to be important. Where gender and race are linked the difficulties can be compounded. Referring to her work in higher education in a South African university, a woman of mixed ethnicity comments:

> I never quite feel I'm one of them . . . I sometimes wonder which one it is, is it because I'm Black or is it because I'm a woman, that no one takes me seriously . . . Maybe if I was a White female it would be easier to know, or if I was a Black male. But being both Black and female I'm not sure why they see me as so different. (Walker, 1998, p.349)

After surveying all of the female and a sample of the male secondary headteachers in England and Wales the conclusion was that:

> One of the most striking outcomes of my research was that despite many similarities in the ways in which they worked and perceived themselves as leaders, the majority of the women were conscious of the tension between their sex and their power role. This was related to the 'natural' leadership status of men and the association of women with the private sphere of home and family. The consequence of this assumption was that women were less likely to be appointed as heads, had particular difficulties in the appointment process and could find their leadership contested once they were in post. (Coleman, 2003, p.326)

Research in China indicated that:

> Despite the promotion of equality for women in the public sphere since the 1950s, management and leadership appear to be firmly identified with the male role in society, and the achievement of a management role as an indicator of male success. (Coleman et al, 1998, p.152)

The social structure and culture of society then impact on who has power. Leaders and managers in education should be aware of this and the messages that are given through their management of curriculum, staff and students. They can work on the culture of the organisation to ensure clear leadership in terms of the values that are promoted. They can take practical action in the development of a policy of equal opportunities. In management of the other adults in the school or college they can ensure that women and minorities are encouraged to apply for promotion and can then be role models for other staff and for the students. Equal opportunities and inclusion can be seen as the keystone of the management of the curriculum.

Having considered in some detail the ways in which power can be conceptualised in the organisation, and more briefly the relationship between equity and power, we will now move on to consider the two other dimensions of organisations that are themes of this chapter: the structure and the institutional culture of the organisation.

ORGANISATIONAL STRUCTURES

Structures exist in any organisation in order to facilitate the coordination of work and workers and in order to provide control over the people and activities within the organisation. Structures may therefore support power relationships, indicate the allocation of responsibility and the lines of command and coordination as well as titles and job descriptions which help to designate the individual's location, and their formal role in the structures. For the purposes of management the usual structure involves some sort of hierarchy that is most often illustrated by an organisation chart. The norm will be some sort of hierarchy which usually supports a type of bureaucratic organisation. However, in British schools there has been a move towards a flattened pyramidal structure, with a large group of middle managers having delegated authority, this structure supports a more collegial exercise of power.

Reflection 5

Does your organisation have a chart designating roles of responsibility and lines of management responsibility? If so, does it reflect the reality of the structures?

Although schools usually include an aspect of hierarchy, they are staffed by professionals. Fidler (1997) discusses Mintzberg's (1983) 'professional bureaucracy', a hybrid model where there is a basic hierarchy but there are 'professional workers in managerial positions and a participative mode of operation' (p.59). In such a professional bureaucracy there could be five component groups:

- strategic apex—those who lead the organisation;
- middle line—middle managers who control the operating core;
- operating core—those that directly deliver a service to clients;
- technostructure—those not in the main work flow, e.g. those who plan, or evaluate;
- support staff—those providing vital but indirect support, such as canteen staff.

In schools the operating core are the body of teachers and the technostructure and support staff serve the operating core, who are providing the key service of the school.

Bolman and Deal (1997, pp.41–42) see structure as operating in two ways:

vertically, through top-down devices, and *laterally* through meetings, committees, coordinating roles, or network structures.

This implies a potentially more complex matrix structure where, for example, possibly conflicting dimensions of academic and pastoral responsibilities can be reconciled through staff being grouped by academic specialism into departments but also contributing to interdisciplinary groups, e.g. for pastoral responsibilities (Fidler, 1997).

The following case example includes extracts from Bush et al (1998, pp.186–187) where the structures of two secondary schools in an area of Shaanxi Province China are outlined.

Case Example 2

The administrative structure of secondary schools follows the pattern set out by Lewin *et al* (1994) . . .
- the principal's office;
- the teaching affairs section, responsible for the organisation of teaching;
- the general affairs section, responsible for infrastructure;
- school factories or farms.

There are also teaching and research groups (jiaoyanzu) which are usually organised by subjects. (Within them teachers discuss their subject related work.)

The management of the schools rests with the Committee of School Management (CSM) which comprises the principal (chair), the vice-principal, teaching deans, the director of the general affairs section, teacher representatives and the secretary of the school branch of the Communist party. There is also an Administrative Committee, subordinate to the CSM, which comprises the principal, vice principal, deans and support services, to deal with routine matters.

School 98 (a district junior secondary school in a large city with 1141 students and 72 teachers) has a principal, vice principal, three deans and 11 heads of department. The CSM has eight members, the principal, vice principal, the three deans and three representatives of teachers. The principal is also the Party secretary.

Qian Ling (a small rural junior secondary school with 249 pupils and 21 teachers) has a principal, a teaching dean who is also the ideological director, and a director of logistics. These three senior staff and two staff representatives comprise the CSM. Unusually, there is no Party secretary or Party branch at this school. The relative lack of hierarchy suggests that a flat structure may be appropriate for smaller schools.

In these schools, the structures mentioned include:

- a form of bureaucratic hierarchy with the principal at the top working within the key management committees;
- a collegial structure (the jiaoyanzu);
- differing spans of control (managers control different numbers of subordinates);
- the professional as administrator (the superior position of the principal);
- grouping of tasks (in this case into the principal's office, the teaching affairs office, the general affairs office and the farm or factory);
- Mintzberg's five basic parts to an organisation, i.e. the operating core of teachers, strategic apex of the principal's office and CSM, the techno-structure of the general affairs office. There are also support staff, not actually mentioned in the cases above but including staff such as a doorman and a nurse or doctor.

The relationship between structure and culture

All organisations have structures of some sort and structures may be regarded as 'the physical manifestation of the culture of the organisation' (Bush, 1998, p.36). For example, a rigid, hierarchical structure will imply formal relations and a change in the structure and roles will have an impact on the culture of a school. In one example (Hannay and Ross, 1999) two Canadian secondary schools were told that they had to abandon their existing structure of middle management based on academic departments and find an alternative more suitable for site-based management. In one school, although they had loyalty to the subject-based structure, gradually they began to question if it really met their needs. One comment illustrates how the change in structure resulted in a change in culture:

> I think as things progressed it was just obvious that there's no point in holding back any longer. It's got to be swept away . . . So it just kept getting closer and closer to the edge and boom, finally . . . it was put over (and the staff disbanded the department head structure) (p.349).

As a result of the change in structures, teachers began to talk more and collaborate with staff from different subject backgrounds, and communication improved. There was a growing willingness to consider issues that previously had been thought 'non-negotiable' and the staff began to focus on generic issues of learning and teaching rather than being subject specific.

ORGANISATIONAL CULTURE

The whole of Chapter 2 was devoted to the analysis of the idea of macro, or national culture in relation to leadership and management theory. The type of culture discussed in this chapter is micro or institutional culture. Although the culture of each organisation will be affected by the national or societal culture in which it operates, each institution will have its own unique culture most often captured in the much repeated phrase: 'the way we do things around here' (Deal and Kennedy, 1982) which encapsulates the subtle differences between working in one organisation and another.

> Organisational culture is the characteristic spirit and belief of an organisation, demonstrated, for example in the norms and values that are generally held about how people should treat each other, the nature of the working relationships that should be developed and attitudes to change. These norms are deep, taken-for-granted assumptions that are not always expressed, and are often known without being understood (Torrington and Weightman, 1993, p.45).

Culture is a difficult concept to capture, but it is helpful to try and analyse its components. O'Neill (1994, p.107) identified four interdependent elements of organisational activities which contribute to the culture:

- purpose—both the declared purpose and the interpretation of the purpose by people working in the school;

- symbolism—the messages which pedagogy, management structure and styles and rituals convey;
- networks—the ways in which people communicate, meet and work together;
- integration—the extent to which areas and people are brought together and are able to share in a unified culture.

Some of the important elements of culture can be identified through the values that are commonly held in the organisations, the behaviour of those within it and the visual symbols and the rituals that are important within the organisation. For example, a formal school, with traditional uniforms for the students, a regular morning assembly of students and teachers, and trophies on display in the entrance hall epitomises one sort of culture. A school where there is no uniform, no bells marking the end of a lesson and where students and teachers eat together and even call each other by their first names indicates a very different sort of organisational culture.

Reflection 6

Stop here for a moment and consider the culture of your organisation. What are the key values that are commonly held? Are there visual signals that indicate the type of culture that prevails? For example, what is the main entrance hall like? Is it welcoming to the visitor? Do the members of the organisation habitually greet each other in the morning and if so is this done formally or informally?

Answers to these questions will give an idea of the culture of the organisation, but it is possible that, particularly in a large organisation there may be sub-cultures, where different values and attitudes to that of the larger organisation are held (remember the loosely coupled organisation referred to earlier). Detert et al (2001, p.206) talking about schools in the USA, go so far as to say: 'In fact, most educational organisations seem to have two or more subcultures operating at any given point in time. Subcultures in schools may be comprised of educators in different roles, departments, or grade levels'.

The culture of a school, college or other organisation affects everything that occurs within it, but it is particularly relevant to management and leadership and can be a key to the improvement and effectiveness of the organisation (see Chapters 7 and 8). There is a two-way process, with culture being affected by the style and nature of leadership, and leadership and management being impeded or supported by the prevailing culture.

SUMMARY

In this chapter we have considered the conceptualisation of organisations and then focused on three inter-locking dimensions of organisations: power, structure and culture. A large part of the chapter was devoted to power and its sub-concepts of authority and influence as they might be exercised collegially, bureaucratically or micro-politically. In addition, we briefly considered the issue of how access to power is constructed in the wider society and the implications of that for educational institutions and their leaders.

Consideration was then given to the types of structures that might be found in schools and colleges and how structures and institutional culture relate to and influence each other. Power, structure and culture are three dimensions of organisations, and it is possible to see any of the three as dominant. For example, in a staff room the existence of a group of people who always sit in the same corner together to drink coffee could be seen in structural terms as the maths department (for example), in cultural terms as a sub-culture who share the same values and norms, or in power terms as a group which has a lot of influence because of the importance of the subject and the fact that the deputy head of the school is also a member of that department.

RECOMMENDED FURTHER READING

A clear exposition of the school as a social system is given in Hoy, W.K. and Miskel, C.G. (2001) *Educational Administration* (6th edn.) New York: McGraw-Hill. This book also covers the other areas of this chapter, including power and politics, culture and structure. Refer to Morgan, G. (1997) *Images of Organisation*, London: Sage Publications, for detail on metaphors for organisations.

For a greater understanding of micro-politics and power, read Hoyle, E. (1986) *The Politics of School Management*, London: Hodder and Stoughton, Chapter 1, 'Understanding Schools as Organisations'.

Power, politics and culture are discussed in Wallace, M. and Hall, V. (1997) 'Towards a cultural and political perspective' Chapter 9 in Harris A., Bennett, N. and Preedy, M. (eds.) *Organisational Effectiveness and Improvement in Education*, Buckingham: Open University Press.

Fidler, B. (1997) 'Organisational structure and organisational effectiveness' in Harris, A., Bennett, N. and Preedy, M. (eds.) *Organisational Effectiveness and Improvement in Education*, Buckingham: Open University Press. This chapter provides a clear account of structures in organisations.

For an overview of equity as it relates to leadership and management, read Coleman, M. (2002b) 'Managing for equal opportunities' in Bush, T. and Bell, L. (eds.) *The Principles and Practice of Educational Management*, London: Paul Chapman Publishing.

4

Decentralization, Autonomy and School Improvement

Lesley Anderson

INTRODUCTION AND LEARNING OUTCOMES

Decentralization has been on the political agenda as a strategy for education in countries around the world for the past two decades or more (Fullan and Watson, 2000, p.453). Davies et al (2003, p.139) describe it as 'something of a panacea or even mantra in global discussions of "good governance" or more effective forms of decision-making' and, according to Calloids (1999, p.9), it is 'one of the most important phenomena to have affected educational planning in the last fifteen years'. It is evident in both developing (World Bank, 1995) and Western societies (Rondinelli et al, 1983) although, as Hanson (1998, p.111) points out, the motives, strategies and outcomes are as different as the countries themselves. For example, in Nicaragua, decentralization has been used to empower local educators and parents through increased state school autonomy and in Pakistan the aim is to increase educational participation of children from low income families. In Western countries such as Australia, New Zealand, the Netherlands, the UK and the USA, decentralization is a main strand of systematic educational reform as the country seeks to raise educational achievement as part of a drive to ensure competitiveness in the new global economy.

This chapter investigates the decentralization phenomenon and the way in which educational decision-making and the power associated with it shifts within a system. In doing this it introduces the reader to a number of concepts and processes that relate to decentralization and considers the implications for educational leaders and managers, particularly in relation to school improvement.

By the end of this chapter you should be able to:

- understand what is meant by decentralization, autonomy and the variety of other terms associated with these concepts;
- appreciate the implications for educational leaders and managers working at all levels within a system—government, regional, district or in a school or college—of

the movement of educational decision-making and the power associated with it from the centre to 'lower' levels;

- understand decentralization in practice through the identification and consideration of different international case studies;

- debate the relationship between institutional autonomy and school improvement.

The first of these objectives flags up a major challenge when considering decentralization: the variety of terms that are intrinsically linked to it. In the next section, some of this terminology is identified and discussed.

TERMINOLOGY

A cursory glance at the literature reveals different terms used to describe the movement of decision-making from one level of authority to another within systems as well as the resulting conditions for individual organisations from these dynamics. Some writers use one or other term without detailed attention to precise meanings with the outcome that they may be used interchangeably. For example, in the context of the UK, the following can be found:

- self-management/school-based management (Davies and Anderson, 1992; Sherratt, 1994; Caldwell and Spinks, 1988; 1992; 1998; Fidler et al, 1997);

- self-governance (Halpin et al, 1993; Feintuck, 1994; Atkinson, 1997);

- autonomy (Bush et al, 1993; Fitz et al, 1993; Simkins, 1997);

- decentralization (Bullock and Thomas, 1997);

- delegation (Thomas and Martin, 1996);

- incorporation (Ainley and Bailey, 1997).

Internationally, the situation is even more confusing. Smyth (1993, p.1) talks about the bewildering array of terms like 'school-based management', 'devolution', 'site-based decision-making' and 'school-centred forms of education' in the introduction to his edited collection on self-managing schools. Karstanje (1999) adds 'deregulation' to the list in the context of Europe.

Unfortunately, acknowledging the variety of terms used is not enough. As Whitty et al (1998) point out, there is still a problem with terminology as different meanings can be associated with just one of these terms—for example, to some school/college-based management is concerned with decentralization and deregulation of school or college control, while to the others it is about shared decision-making *within* the school or college. They conclude that none of the terms 'lend themselves to precise definition' (p.9) and are 'open to semantic slippage' (p.10), a view that is also expressed by Thomas and Martin (1996, p.18).

However, focusing on self-managing and self-governing schools, a clear and important distinction has, in more recent times, been made by Caldwell (2001; 2002). Caldwell and

Spinks are famous for their triad of books on self-managing schools (Caldwell and Spinks, 1988; 1992; 1998) and, as Caldwell (2001) points out, he and his fellow author have used the term consistently since the publication of the first in the series. Their use of the expression *self-managing schools* refers to schools where there has been significant delegation or devolution of decision-making, particularly over resources but which operate within a centrally determined framework of standards and accountability. (The latter is discussed later in the chapter.) Self-governing schools, however, do not operate within such a framework, making private (non-government) schools in most systems a good example of self-governance.

It is evident from these examples that care is necessary in the interpretation of the various concepts, processes and ideas associated with different levels of decision-making within an educational system. However, in order to understand the issues, we start by focusing on the concept that is core to this chapter: decentralization.

Reflection 1

Which of the terms mentioned above have you come across in your professional experience? What was their impact on your professional activities?

DECENTRALIZATION

Defining the term

A definition is a useful starting point although, in this case, it is not straightforward. According to Karlsen (2000), decentralization has 'no precise meaning'. It is, however, closely connected with other concepts such as deregulation, delegation, devolution and deconcentration (Smith, 1985). The prefix 'de' in all of these terms (which are defined later) is used to indicate actions such as *removal* and *reversal*. Thus, they suggest a sense of separation from some thing or point. In addition, they all describe a dimensional relationship that relates the centre with the periphery. In other words, they can be seen as ends of a continuum (Mintzberg, 1983) which, in turn, means that they are relative concepts. What is considered decentralized at one level can easily be seen as centralized at another. Hanson (1998) and Karstanje (1999) both define the decentralization of a system as the process whereby decision-making authority for particular functions and the power that is associated with it are shifted from a certain location to one that is less central or 'lower'. Hence, there is a sense of a changing power-base linked to the concept of decentralization.

It does not necessarily follow, however, that decentralization implies power being shifted to the 'lowest' unit which, in the case of education, is generally taken to be the school or college. Additionally, within the individual school or college, power may be kept by the principal with no power being devolved to others in the institution. Green (1999) points out that 'decentralization has variously meant devolving power to the regions, the regional outposts of central government, the local authorities, the social partners and the institutions themselves' (p.61). In other words, decentralization can be to any 'lower' level. Green's definition also highlights the difficulty of terminology. *Devolution* is a permanent arrangement relating to the transfer of decision-making to a lower level as opposed to *delegation* when the central authority can still readily re-appropriate some or all of the power to make decisions (Office for Official Publications of the European Communities, 2001, p.180). However, there is another option, that of extending the scope of decision-making at institutional level and this is likely to involve *deregulation*, the process by which the number and extent of regulations that constrain what, in this case, the school or college can do, is reduced (Levačić, 2002). *Deconcentration* describes the territorial sense of decentralization as tasks and power are moved from central to local bodies. Thus, it is concerned with the locus of authority and power over formal rights to educational decision-making (Levin and Young, 1994).

Karstanje (1999, p.29) distinguishes between decentralization and deregulation in his discussion about trends in Europe. He argues that the former is associated with Central and Eastern European countries while the latter tends to dominate in the West. However, in drawing up a conceptual framework relating major tasks in school management and different grades of autonomy, he puts the two processes together and indicates different levels of combined centralization/decentralization and regulation/deregulation. This, then, is another example of the 'loose' way the terminology is used.

Centralization and decentralization

The centre-periphery definition means that if decentralization is possible then centralization must also be an option. Various arguments for centralization are given. Brooke (1984, p.170) includes the need for central control, particularly when strategies may not be seen to be in the interest of lower units, as well as lack of confidence. On the latter, Brown (1990, p.33) comments that it is similar to Simon's (1957) view that '(centralization) feels safer' (p.235). The principal arguments for educational centralization as put forward by both Winkler (1993) and Welier (1993) are listed by Hanson (1998):

- financial, to benefit through economies of scale as well as the equitable allocation of resources to reduce regional economic disparities;
- policy and programmatic uniformity, to establish consistency in quality, programmes and activities (for example, curriculum, hiring, examinations, delivery of administrative services);
- central placement of scarce human resources, to place strategically the scarce, skilled human resources at those points in the institution where their impact can reach across the entire educational system;
- the diffusion of innovation, to spread changes more rapidly through the entire system;
- improved teaching-learning, a tightly controlled curriculum can be one policy response to the problem of poorly qualified teachers.

Hanson (1986) provides a useful illustration of a situation where a policy of centralization dramatically improved the organisation and management of the educational system.

His example is about Colombia from 1968 to the late 1980s. Prior to 1968, the departments (similar to provinces or states) existed in a condition of semi-anarchy. According to Hanson, they were 'highly politicised, rarely hesitant to use educational funds for other purposes, generally disorganised, very inefficient and quite capable of routinely ignoring national educational policy whenever it proved convenient'. He points out that as a result of a shift to increased centralization in 1968 the educational system improved.

Centralization and decentralization are then intrinsically linked through the swings that are observed from one to the other and back (Brown, 1990, p.37). Changes between them, however, are seldom total (Lundgren and Mattsson, 1996, p.141) and, as Papagiannis et al (1998) point out, empowering one party through decentralization often means strengthening the supervision on another. Caldwell (1993), in discussing the shifting pattern of governance in education internationally, highlights the current trend to centralize in terms of goal-setting, establishing priorities and frameworks for accountability and to decentralize authority and responsibility for key functions to school level. He writes about a 'centralization-decentralization continuum' and suggests the shifts in either direction which are occurring simultaneously or in rapid succession are responsible for 'much uncertainty' (p.159). This view is also supported by other writers (for example, Angus, 1993, p.15; Gibton et al, 2000, p.193).

An international trend

As has already been highlighted, the trend is evident around the world, for example, in the USA (*Elmore*, 1993; *Weiler*, 1993), Canada (*Hallak*, 1991) and England and Wales (*Levačić*, 1995). In respect to England and Wales, it is exemplified by the 1988 Education Reform Act (ERA). This Act introduced a national curriculum, standardised assessment, local management of schools and grant maintained status for schools. As a result of this single piece of legislation, aspects of policy, the curriculum and assessment were centralized, while practice and management responsibility for human and physical resources were decentralized. Although the Conservative Government responsible for the ERA promoted the legislation on the basis of autonomy, choice and diversity, in other words, concepts connected with decentralization, the Act did, in fact, centralize many significant powers to the Secretary of State for Education. With respect to the ERA, Whitty (1990) takes a particular ideological view and argues that 'the rhetoric of decentralization is a cover for centralization' (p.22) while other writers (for example, Thomas, 1993; Levačić, 1995) also comment on the polarisation of aspects of education policy and practice within the reforms introduced through this Act.

A case example of decentralization in Brazil provides another example.

Case Example 1   Decentralization in Brazil in the 1990s

Gorostiaga Derqui (2001) explores these policies in Brazil where the quality of education was considered low in comparison to other Latin American countries and access was a problem in the poorest regions. The 1988 Constitution decentralized to municipal education systems and from 1985 onwards, some states allowed the creation of school councils including teachers, administrators, students and parents. These make administrative decisions and, in some cases, select the principal. Moreover, some states and municipalities have been moving towards the inclusion of budget and personnel administration within the responsibilities of school councils (*Plank et al*, 1996).

Alongside these changes, in 1991, the national government began implementing a centralized system of evaluation although with other initiatives it seemed that integration of the system was intended (Souza, 1997; de la Fuente et al, 1998). A ten-year federal plan was approved in 1993 with the goals of establishing minimum curricular contents and standards for educational management while in 1996, the Congress passed an educational law that encouraged school autonomy although it also ensured an active role for the federal government.

Krawczyk (1999) analyses school management policies in 11 Brazilian municipalities and observes a trend towards schools able to make their own decisions, organizing tasks around institutional projects, administering resources and selecting procedures within limits set and controlled by the municipality. Although these policies were intended to improve the quality of education, two of the less helpful consequences are the fragmentation of the system as schools are left to their own fate (*ibid*, p.145) and the adoption of management models that originate from the commercial world (*ibid*, p.146).

Reflection 2

Consider, again, your own experience of educational reforms which shift power from one level of authority to another. What was the impact on your work with pupils and their learning?

Why decentralization?

In the previous section the connection between decentralization and centralization was explored and some arguments for centralization offered. However, as already stated, in recent times it is decentralization that is the main focus of interest and the next section considers the case for decentralization and why it has become a central post of educational reform.

Rhoten (2000) considers decentralization to be an outcome of globalisation and explains that:

> by the early 1980s, it was believed that philosophies and practices promoting the institutional centrality of the national Welfare state were incompatible with neo-liberalism and economic globalisation. This supranational paradigm shift resulted in several national policy moves in which administrations around the world . . . rearranged the roles, relation and responsibilities of state, market and society via policies like deregulation, privatization and decentralization. Because of this paradigm-policy shift . . . the provision of domestic public services—like education—was passed to sub-national states (p.594).

She goes on to comment that the most common approaches to the analysis of educational decentralization in the literature are either technical or political. The former are concerned with inputs and financial, organisational or pedagogical outcomes and the effects of decentralization are assessed in terms of cost-effectiveness as measured by rates of student promotion, graduation and/or assessment relative to the resources expended per student (see Carnoy, 1998; King and Osler, 1998). Thus, the technical approach focuses on cost-effectiveness and school improvement. The latter, the political approach to the analysis of decentralization, looks mainly at tensions and negotiations between governments, large education bureaucracies and/or interest groups in situations where decentralization of power is part of the national democratisation process rather than concern with school improvement.

Hanson (1998), however, argues that educational decentralization reforms 'typically have their roots in the political arena' (p.3). He describes decentralization as an 'almost natural outcome' (p.3) as nations make the transition from autocratic to democratic forms of government and attempt to establish citizen participation in government. Example of such countries include Nicaragua, Venezuela, Spain, Argentina, Columbia, Chile, Mexico as well as the ex-communist countries of Central and Eastern Europe. Hanson also points out that there are many different, but often related, goals that drive decentralization initiatives. These include:

- increased economic development through institutional modernization, e.g. Venezuela in the late 1960s and 1970s (Hanson, 1976);

- increased management efficiency, e.g. Venezuela in the 1990s (Cruz, 1992);

- redistribution of financial responsibility, e.g. Argentina (primary education 1978 and secondary 1991) (Fernandez Lamarra and Vitar, 1991);

- increased democratization, e.g. Spain in the late 1970s, Columbia in the early 1990s;

- neutralization of competing centres of power, e.g. in Chile and Mexico (Cortina, 1995; McGinn and Street, 1986; Nunez et al, 1993);

- improved quality of education (Winkler, 1993, p.66).

Karstanje (1999) describes the motivation behind decentralization as usually twofold: 'shortening the distance between the government and the organisation in charge of implementation (school); and shifting the financial risks to a lower level' (p.29). Having distinguished deregulation as a separate process, he explains that deregulation 'stems from the view that the central authorities which are situated at some distance from the educational institutions are not capable of taking stock of specific situations at institutions' (p.30). Karstanje also clarifies that 'it is often better if the institution itself makes decisions within the parameters set by the government' (p.30). His argument is that decisions made close to the point of implementation and those that carry financial responsibility are likely to be better decisions, particularly in terms of school and college improvement.

The following case study explores the arguments for decentralization in one European country. It illustrates the swings between decentralization and centralization and the associated shifting power.

Case Example 2   Arguments for Decentralization in Norway

According to Karlsen (2000, pp.526–527) decentralization in Norway has been on the agenda since the late 1960s. Although the emphasis in the arguments for it has varied at different times, there have been four main strands:

- to strengthen democracy by transferring power from central to local bodies;
- to bring about innovation and school development;
- to strengthen local culture, local business and the local community as a whole;
- to achieve rationalization and efficiency.

During this time, legislation had been enacted to bring about decentralization and the intended aims for it. As early as 1969, the Educational Law for Primary and Lower Secondary Schools gave the community and students the right to participate in decision-making at school level. The 1974 Curriculum Guidelines and, particularly, the Revised Guidelines in 1987, provided more flexibility and freedom for schools and teachers. For example, the 1987 Guidelines gave schools the opportunity to develop local curricula and to adapt the guidelines to local needs and conditions. In particular, they opened up the curriculum to include local knowledge and local culture. However, the 1997 Curriculum Guidelines reversed this endeavour and were more concerned to achieve standardisation and stress the need for academic and skill-orientated education. As Karlsen points out 'even though this bottom-up strategy is still the accepted rhetoric, there has been a shift towards a more traditional top-down strategy in the 1990s. The new Curriculum Guidelines in Norway, put into effect in 1997, are mainly the result of a central initiative bringing back the top-down strategy' (p.527).

At the same time, the focus for decentralization in the 1990s was about the accountability and efficiency of schools as a result of reduction in public spending generally following the oil crises. The argument was that local authorities and individual schools were best placed to use the existing funding more efficiently as well as endeavour to obtain new resources. Thus, decentralization was understood in a more market-oriented way. Schools should have more autonomy and independence and operate in the market place like other businesses. Karlsen describes the more recent approach to decentralization as 'characterized as a strategy for a more privatized and commercialized school' (p.528).

In addition to providing an example of the processes of decentralization and centralization, this case study highlights the breadth of the arguments for the former including issues of accountability, efficiency and markets. These are discussed in more detail later in the chapter. Before this, however, discussion about decentralization would be incomplete without considering the closely related concepts of autonomy.

AUTONOMY IN EDUCATION

Autonomy is defined as the right of self-government. In other words, an autonomous organisation is responsible for making decisions about a pre-determined set of issues relating to its governance and mode of operation. Autonomy may be an outcome of decentralization although it is important to point out that decentralization does not necessarily lead to autonomy. Like decentralization, increased autonomy at one level may lead to reduced autonomy at another (Bullock and Thomas, 1997). This means that, as before, decision-making and power are shifted along the centre-periphery dimension. In classifying Australian schools over a 20-year period, Sharpe (1994) describes a continuum from total external control to total self-management. He identifies four sub-continua that describe 'over what' the schools have autonomy: *input* variables, such as finance, staff and students; *structure* variables such as decisions about the pattern of provision; *process* variables such as the management of the curriculum; and *environment* variables which are concerned with reporting and marketing.

In their examination of decentralization in 11 countries, Bullock and Thomas (1997) also use four dimensions. They categorise the degree of educational decentralization, or the areas over which the lower units enjoy some degree of autonomy in broad terms as: *curriculum and assessment, human and physical resources, finance and access* (pupil admissions). Simkins (1997, p.20) explores similar issues in his discussion about autonomy but adds another: under what forms of *control* and *constraint* must these powers be exercised? This question highlights the relative nature of autonomy and the paradox that autonomous organisations may be subject to more central control and constraint. Developing his argument, he distinguishes between *criteria power* which is concerned with determining purposes and frameworks and *operational power* concerned with service delivery. Karlsen's (2000) analysis of educational governance in Norway and British Columbia, Canada is also relevant here. He comments: 'We are looking at a decentralization dynamic in which initiating is a central task, but in which implementation and accountability are local duties' (p.531).

Levačić (2002, p.188) discusses the forms of school autonomy in terms of decision-making which may be at a school's discretion. Based on her own work (Levačić, 1995) and that of Karstanje (1999) she suggests five domains:

- school organisation: structure, differentiation, decision-making processes, capacity class size;

- curriculum: (guidelines, content, hours, textbooks), teaching methods and assessment;

- staff: regulations on qualifications, appointment and dismissal, in-service training, appraisal, pay and conditions of service, including methods of performance management;

- financial and resource management: spending decisions; size of staffing establishment, premises, information systems, financial assets and liabilities;

- external relations: admissions policies, pupil recruitment, relationships with other organisations (e.g. trade unions).

She points out that within each domain some decisions can be assigned to schools and others to higher levels. The form of school autonomy and the governance structure of the school system depend on the different domains and the extent of delegation to schools within each domain.

Although it is evident that, like decentralization, consideration of autonomy is problematic, especially in respect of the variation in the terminology used, Levačić's classifications are helpful as they enable comparisons about the degree of decentralization within different educational systems, for example, the Organisation for Economic Co-operation and Development's (OECD, 2000) indicators.

Reflection 3

Consider your own professional situation. Using Levačić's five domains, identify the areas over which the organisation where you work has some degree of autonomy, or more. If the control lies outside your domain, where does it lie? What controls and constraints are imposed by higher level organisations?

ACCOUNTABILITY

Earlier in this chapter, it was noted that Caldwell and Spinks draw on accountability in defining the operational framework of a self-managing school. Moreover, the case study on decentralization in Norway highlights accountability and efficiency as one justification for decentralization. In this context, the argument is that leaders and managers close to the delivery of education are more able to make effective and efficient decisions about the service. Hence, decentralization is considered to improve efficiency. However, it is also clear that in order for the system to succeed, those exercising the decision-making power must be open to scrutiny and, if necessary, effective challenge and sanction in order to ensure that the exercise of power is within the prescribed limits. Accountability, then, can be regarded as the counterpart of greater freedom at institutional level as demands are made to demonstrate how greater freedom is being used. Kogan (1986) describes it as 'a condition' applied to 'individual role holders' (p.25).

Other reasons for accountability include:

- *Economic competitiveness*—in recent times, nations have become increasingly concerned about their international competitiveness in business and commerce and the performance of the educational system is seen as a way to prepare students to become economically productive.

- *Financial stringency*—increasing demands on public expenditure in may countries has led to concern to obtain value for money for whatever is spent on the educational system.

- *Equity of opportunity*—on the basis that all citizens in a democracy receive equal access to public services, there is increasing concern that certain groups either have not profited from their educational opportunities or have dropped out. These groups have particularly included the socially disadvantaged and ethnic minorities.

Accountability is yet another complex issue. In a 'pure' and literal form, accountability from one party (A) to another (B) requires three things. First, there is an expectation that A will act in ways which are consistent with the legitimate requirements of B. Second, that A will render some form of account to B. Third, that B may exercise sanctions over A if A fails to conform to B's expectations (Simkins, 1997, p.22). However, in practice accountability is enacted in different ways and various models are offered in the literature. At the macro level, four dimensions of accountability can be identified:

- *Political*—in a system that is supported by public funds, the institution is accountable for the best use of those funds and the government has a right and even a duty to ensure that the institution is contributing fully to the economic development, social progress, cultural conservation, individual fulfilment and other goals which enjoy widespread support.

- *Market*—the institution is accountable to its customers, partners and stakeholders and choice and efficiency are emphasized. The customer, partners and stakeholders are all 'free' to withdraw their custom or support if the institution does not provide what is required in a way that satisfies demand.

- *Professional*—each institution, school, college, district, regional or central authority is accountable for maintaining the highest possible standards of the educational service. This accountability is represented by the norms that are self-imposed by educational professionals and are embodied in professional codes of practice and sets of values.

- *Cultural*—education can be considered as fostering new insights, knowledge and understanding and it can be a force for change in society. This means that an institution that has little regard for such responsibilities cannot be considered responsive and hence not accountable. In this way, education's 'external utility is rooted in its internal validity, its private integrity' (Scott, 1989, p.2).

Accountability is an intrinsic part of management, both within an organisation and across the system. Educational reforms around the world such as decentralization and increased autonomy at the level of the school or college have placed greater emphasis on the first two mechanisms for accountability listed above. One of them, the market, is now considered in more detail.

MARKETS, CHOICE AND EQUITY IN EDUCATION

The restructuring of education around the world in recent years is characterised not only by the shift to decentralize systems but also by the introduction of choice for the consumer (Gewirtz et al, 1995; Glatter et al, 1997). This means that, in principle, parents and students have the right to select a school or college, rather than being allocated according to where they live although other factors may reduce or even eliminate this choice. (Schools and colleges usually have admissions criteria that have to be satisfied before a pupil/student is offered a place, assuming one is available.) Such choice means that schools and colleges compete to attract and recruit pupils and students and are accountable to them, their parents and employers for the quality of education they provide. This choice and market accountability implies the creation of 'markets' within publicly funded education systems (Levačić, 1995, p.2; Whitty et al, 1998, p.3).

The term 'market' is borrowed from the commercial world and applied there to the exchange of products and services on the assumption that the aim of the supplier is to maximise profits and that of the consumer is to minimise costs. In addition to choice, markets are also about competition, supply, demand and price, terms which create immediate difficulty when applied to education. The providers, or suppliers, of publicly funded education are not traditionally concerned with 'profit', nor are the schools in question privately owned. Furthermore, in some situations, total demand at one time may be regarded as fixed by assuming movement in and out of the private sector is ignored. For these reasons, the term *quasimarket* has been used to describe the changes in education (Le Grand and Bartlett, 1993).

As indicated above, competition is also about market share. The marketing of schools in an attempt to attract more pupils and, thereby, maximise its market 'share', has become a standard school management process, particularly in English-speaking countries. Although school managers are not interested in 'profit', the formula-funding mechanisms of systems like local management of schools (LMS) in the UK are designed to encourage schools to compete for pupils and the funding they bring with them. Additionally, in some countries, for example, in South Africa, pupils attending publicly funded schools are also expected to pay school fees. This means that schools want to ensure that they recruit their full quota of pupils who are able to pay school fees or attract government funding.

The introduction of the market mechanism into education has provoked considerable controversy. For some it is a good thing. Its advocates argue that it is the key to improving schools because 'consumers influence schools by their choices' (Ranson, 1996, p.216). The theory is that choice creates competition between schools. Good schools prosper and failing schools are forced out of the 'market'. Hence, school leaders and managers are held accountable and the 'market' provides the incentive for school improvement.

For other commentators it is not as straightforward as it may appear. Alongside the theory that the individual school and the individual parent are free to make decisions about the education 'supplied' or 'purchased', other factors, such as self-interest, come into play and schools and parents do not enjoy these 'freedoms'. Issues of equity are of major concern in a market situation and Stinette (1992, p.6) outlines the kind of effect a policy which is too decentralized is likely to have for disadvantaged students:

> . . . decentralization is designed to bring decision-making closer to the student and the learning environment of the classroom. However, decentralization brings with it the possibility of extreme inequalities—the possibility that local communities, including parents and educators, may not have the knowledge and resources to adequately protect the quality of education provided to their children. Just as centralization has failed as a full guarantee of the rights of all, so may decentralization prove inadequate to the same task.

Examples of groups that are likely to be excluded include girls in some settings where school fees are charged (such as South Africa as indicated above) and pupils with special educational needs where pupils' results of achievement are used as a marketing tool for future intakes. From their research, Van Langen and Dekkers (2001, p.382) found that market forces acted against the cooperation between schools that would benefit disadvantaged students and the alignment of education with other services like health, welfare, the police and social provisions was not possible without coordination by local authorities.

Having considered decentralization and a number of related concepts and processes, the final two sections of this chapter focus on the vital issue of the impact of the various ways in which decision-making power is distributed throughout a system. On the basis that the purpose of any educational structure and reforms to it is to enable the highest level of learning and overall school and college improvement, it is most significant and important that the impact and outcomes are brought to the forefront. Hence, the matters of leading and managing in a decentralized system and the relationship between autonomy and school improvement are now discussed.

LEADING AND MANAGING IN A DECENTRALIZED SYSTEM

Decentralization impacts on leaders' and managers' work at all levels within an educational system. As indicated previously, the counterpart to increased autonomy is usually increased accountability. Thus, although decentralization may provide school principals and governors with decision-making authority, it can also result in more complex accountability mechanisms being established from and to a 'higher' level.

Additionally, it is evident that issues of policy relating to the structure of systems differ from the process of change within, and the culture of, an organisation. Fullan (1993, p.49) explains 'to restructure is not to re-culture . . . changing formal structures is not the same as changing norms, habits, skills and beliefs'. Hanson (1998) also comments on this theme:

> Decentralization clearly does not come with the passing of laws or the signing of decrees. Like most types of reform, it is built rather than created. It happens slowly because the organisational culture (e.g. 'the way we've always done things around here') must be transformed, new roles learned, leadership styles altered . . . , communication patterns reversed . . . (p.121).

Reflection 4

Reflect on the implications of a decentralized system for leaders and managers in schools and colleges as well as those working at district, regional and national levels. If you have the opportunity, discuss the issue with colleagues working both within your organisation and with others who operate at different levels within the overall educational system. How do their views vary?

The following case example shows the impact of working in a decentralized system.

Case Example 3   Malawi

Davies et al (2003) report on research on educational decentralization which the Government of Malawi intend as a means to improve the management of education through greater decentralization of educational decision-making (p.142). The research was concerned with decentralization to district level that was introduced after democratic elections in 1994 following a period of autocratic rule. It focused on one particular district where the British Department for International Development has designed and implemented an initiative aimed at school and managerial improvement. Extra resources were provided to the District Office with a view to enabling the desired change in educational provision. Davies et al (pp.143–144) describe the initiative as 'holistic and exploratory in nature and ... intended to see how affordable, equitable, good quality and replicable community-based primary education might be delivered in a single district operating in a context of increasingly decentralized administrative responsibility'.

The change envisaged as part of the initiative included: provision of specialist staff in the district education office, training for new and existing staff in new roles and systems, the expansion of existing office space, the provision of extra supplies and equipment, new accounting and budgetary procedures, the introduction of a computerised education management information system and strengthening the district's monitoring and evaluation systems. However, as Davies et al point out such changes inevitably cause other changes in work culture, for example in relation to goal-setting, equity and accountability. Their research, therefore, focused on the nature and process of change within district-level governance of education.

Using a grounded theory approach, these researchers identified five key areas whereby 'the understanding of their interplay is necessary to understand fully the impact of an intervention to assist decentralization' (p.146). These areas are:

- work culture: for example, the practice of low salaries being supplemented by allowances and expenses, hierarchies and changes in roles, development of individual initiative;

- accountability: for example, job descriptions, wider participation in decision-making;

- information: for example, availability, accuracy;

- resources: for example, the appropriate levels of human and physical resources required to enable the local office and district to function effectively as well as their control;

- sustainability: for example, necessity to address the four areas above in order to sustain the initiative and decentralization.

Like many other studies, Davies et al's research confirms the importance of understanding the local context in the management of change in education. In addition and importantly, they describe the process of decentralized change as 'highly complex, unpredictable and non-linear ... because it is also intensively political and linked to power relationships within and between cultural frameworks' (p.146). (See also Chapter 2.)

In addition to responsibility for strategic and financial management and leadership of, and relationships with, the local community that may result from school autonomy, several writers comment on teachers' lack of commitment to decentralization (Gorostiagi Derqui, 2001; Nir, 2002). Van Zanten (2002, p.291) also raises the impact on teachers and other groups as power relationships are altered. She argues that teachers may lose part of the influence they had at the national level through union actions and become 'more exposed to individualised and more immediate pressures from the administration, headteachers or parents at local level' (p.291). Such situations could create tension between the senior managers and the teachers which, in turn, has implications for the leadership and management of the school in terms of personnel function.

Reflection 5

What is your experience of teachers' response to increased autonomy at school level and on other groups as power relationships are altered? If you have no or little experience, can you predict possible outcomes?

AUTONOMOUS SCHOOLS AND SCHOOL IMPROVEMENT

In this section links between autonomy and educational improvement are explored briefly. As stated previously, it is reasonable to assume that the main purpose of any educational organisation is to achieve the 'best' possible educational and social outcomes for its students and that such organisations are continually striving for improvement. Thus, if the concepts and processes that have been discussed so far in this chapter are worthwhile, it is likely that they contribute to improving educational outcomes.

Levačić (2002, pp.198–202) discusses the empirical evidence relating to decentralization and autonomous schools and school improvement. She cautions that it is difficult to establish causal links because the research is applied to different school systems and uses different methods although, nevertheless, puts forwards some conclusions. Levačić's determination to evaluate the impact of decentralization and the autonomous schools that result from it is both relevant and brave. It is relevant because the fundamental purpose of any educational system must be about providing effective teaching and learning and it follows that changes to the system should be designed to contribute to overall improvement. As discussed earlier, the educational argument for decentralization is that decisions made at a local level, along with the involvement of parents and the local community, are more likely to be effective and bring about improvement than those made at a distance by a bureaucratic government department. Her determination is also brave because few researchers working in this area attempt to link their findings directly to the impact on pupils and learning. This said, the chapter closes with a summary of research that attempts to explore the connection between school autonomy and school improvement.

Dempster (2000) examines the impact and effects of what he describes as 'site-based management' in schools using a framework developed by Canadian researchers, Sackney and Dibski (1994). He starts from the assertion that school-based management leads to improved student learning outcomes although his findings do not support it. However, he goes on to claim that there is indicative data which imply that aspects of school-based management related to planning and communication help 'shape some of the conditions which indirectly influence classroom practice' (p.56). His work in Australia (with Logan and Sachs) indicated that teachers reported that school development planning (required of self-managing schools) had a much lower impact on classroom activity and student learning than that perceived by principals. He also draws on Wylie's (1996) work in New Zealand in which she is inconclusive as to whether school-based management had any impact on students' learning although she observed that School Boards, which were expected to focus on learning, spent most of their time on decisions relating to property and finance.

Studies of school effectiveness in Australia, have found differences in performance between schools under school-based management. Blackmore et al (1996) comment on fundamental changes in teachers' work which impedes good teaching and learning if teachers perceive that the value of the work they do goes unrecognised. The most productive schools tend to be those with motivation and commitment within their School Councils and with resources available to support new initiatives (Gammage et al, 1996); and those which have used devolved management processes in implementing school-based management (Wildy, 1991).

Babyegeya (2000, p.6) describes decentralization in Tanzania which is aimed at making the public school system more effective. He highlights a project designed to make local school communities responsible for the development of their school. However, although the intention of this project is that each stakeholder, the community members, the teachers, the village council, the district authority and the Ministry of Education and Culture, has certain responsibilities, Babyegeya is concerned that the focus of the work is on improving school facilities, enrolment and attendance. He acknowledges that poor facilities and declining enrolment are a major problem in Tanzania although argues that improving them is not sufficient to make schools more effective and efficient. He supports Lockheed and Verspoor (1991, p.1) viewpoint that it is meaningless to improve enrolment and attendance without considering the organisational structure of the school and the teaching-learning process.

Finally, Caldwell (2000) maps what he describes as third generation studies of potential links between local management and learning outcomes. Optimistically, he concludes that:

> while there is still much uncertain about the nature of and impact of school reform, it is evident that the means are at hand to create a system of public schools that will provide a high quality of education for all students and that will be professionally rewarding for teachers and other professionals. The challenge is how to put the pieces together (p.37).

SUMMARY

In many countries around the world, a process of educational decentralization has enacted in recent years. There are many and varied reasons. Indeed, in some situations, it is countered by increased centralization in some aspects of educational policy. Moreover, as a concept, decentralization is not straightforward and is interpreted in different ways in different situations. Alongside decentralization, educational organisation may find increased autonomy which is also countered by increased accountability. Decentralization impacts on leaders and managers at all levels within the educational system although its effects on school improvement are still uncertain.

RECOMMENDED FURTHER READING

If you are interested in finding out more about the topics covered in this chapter, then you may like to read some or all of the following chapters and articles. Brian Caldwell and Ron Glatter each contribute relevant and useful chapters to Bush and Bell's 2002 edited collection entitled *The Principles and Practice of Educational Management*. Berka writes about the legal and philosophical meaning of autonomy in education in the book he edited with Groof and Penneman in 2000, and Mulford, Kendall and Kendall discuss if local school management makes a difference in their chapter in Wallace and Poulson's (2003) edited volume. Finally, Michael Fullan and Nancy Watson consider the fundamental issue as to how school-based management, in whatever form, impacts on pupil learning and can be harnessed for school improvement. The full details of these publications are found below.

Berka, W. (2000) 'The legal and philosophical meaning of autonomy in education' in W. Berka, J. De Groof and H. Penneman (eds), *Autonomy in Education: Yearbook of European Association for Education Law and Policy,* Vol. III, The Hague: Kluwer Law International.

Caldwell, B. (2002) 'Autonomy and self-management: concepts and evidence' in T. Bush and L. Bell (eds) *The Principles and Practice of Educational Management*, London: Paul Chapman Publishing.

Fullan, M. and Watson, N. (2000) 'School-based management: Reconceptualizing to improve learning outcomes', *School Effectiveness and School Improvement*, 11(4), 453–473.

Glatter, R. (2002) 'Governance, autonomy and accountability in education' in T. Bush and L. Bell (eds) *The Principles and Practice of Educational Management*, London: Paul Chapman Publishing.

Mulford, B., Kendall, L. and Kendall, D. (2003) 'Local school management: does it make a difference?' in M. Wallace and L. Poulson (eds) *Learning to read critically in Educational Leadership and Management*, London: Sage.

5

Learning and the External Environment

Philip Woods

INTRODUCTION AND LEARNING OUTCOMES

The external environment is the source of social, political, economic and cultural influences which both constrain and open opportunities for education. This context shapes the purposes of education and its governance, and knowledge and understanding of this context is vital for leaders and managers in education. The first section of this chapter examines purpose and governance as important aspects of educational institutions' relationships with this context.

The external environment can also be looked at in terms of social organisation and institutions that comprise it, including families of current and prospective students, local communities, other educational institutions, employers and the businesses community, and government (central, regional and local). The second section of the chapter concentrates on relations with families and communities, as these are most immediately and directly concerned with education, and home and community have been shown to be key influences on students' learning, educational progress and well-being (Wolfendale and Bastiani, 2000; Gelsthorpe, 2003; West-Burnham, 2003).

By the end of this chapter you should be able to:

- appreciate the place of education in its economic, political and social context;
- analyse the range of different forms that the governance of education can take, and the ideas that underpin them;
- reflect on the position of educational professionals and leaders;
- note the challenges in establishing democratic governing bodies;
- appreciate the diversity of families and communities and how they are active shapers of individual identity and social and educational careers;
- understand the importance of participation in education by families and communities;
- reflect on the idea of 'learning communities' as a conceptual framework, extending to families and communities.

EDUCATION IN CONTEXT

Purpose

What does the community want education to do? Some of the main types of educational purpose are summarised in Figure 5.1. Any actual education system is probably seen as striving for more than one of these, and within complex systems purposes may differ amongst educational institutions or local education systems.

Cultural transmission is concerned with passing on the values, knowledge and beliefs that represent the culture of a particular community or society. One example is schooling which nurtures students into a particular religious tradition, the traditional function of Catholic schools (McClelland, 1996). A secular example is Israel's use of education as one of its means of nation-building. A unified national curriculum aimed to assimilate new immigrants by simultaneously emphasizing Israel as a 'melting pot' of cultures and constructing 'a new Israeli-Jew through a standardized . . . canon of curricular content' (Benavot and Resh, 2003, p.178). Education may also be conceived as contributing to *liberal emancipation*—by developing or nurturing in students the skills, aptitudes and attitudes that enable individuals to make choices and think for themselves and to be, to some degree, autonomous. This is especially associated with the idea that education is most essentially about developing people's ability to reason and know themselves so they are able to decide what kind of person they wish to become (Ungoed-Thomas, 1997).

A third purpose which a community or society may determine as important for education is *improvement*. One aspect of this is *personal and social* improvement: for example, '. . . much of the thinking that has guided definitions of a good education in many cultures has been about the relationship of education to the acquisition of virtue' (Lawton and Cowen, 2001, p.18). A group advising the UK Government set out a number of desirable 'values and dispositions' to be encouraged amongst students, including concern for the common good, concern to resolve conflicts, tolerance, and a determination to act justly (Advisory Group on Citizenship, 1998, p.44). Improvement may be conceived in predominantly *economic* terms, where the community or society seeks,

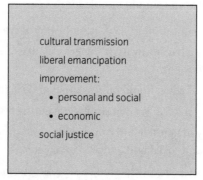

cultural transmission

liberal emancipation

improvement:

- personal and social

- economic

social justice

Figure 5.1 Some socially conceived purposes of education

through education, to improve a nation's or local area's economic performance and individual students' employability. This is sometimes seen as making education subservient to economic and market interests (Gewirtz, 2000; Woods, 2002).

A further ambition that education may be seen as serving is that of *social justice*. In this perspective education helps to redress social and economic inequalities by offering educational opportunities and learning that benefit all, whatever their socio-economic and cultural characteristics. It is especially important in this perspective that the education system effectively works towards eliminating the gap between advantaged and disadvantaged families and communities in terms of learning, enriching educational experience and formal qualifications.

Reflection 1

Take a few minutes at this point to consider what the main purposes of education are that your school or college is expected to fulfil by your society or local community, or what your education system expects of educational institutions. Is there a consensus about the aims of education, or are there significant differences of view?

A study of a coastal fishing village in Papua New Guinea illustrates how differing interests and perspectives may exist within the community served by schools. Demerath (1999) describes the complex issues that face the islanders in coming to grips with the modern world. From the mid-twentieth century there was an increasing tendency to value Western goods and the Western way of life, and education was seen as a means to attaining these. In other words, education was valued for its contribution to economic improvement (Figure 5.1). But in the 1990s, with opportunities in the economy more limited, interest in gaining a formal education fell as the time and resources it required seemed to be a poor investment. Villagers' evaluation of the worth of education was adjusted accordingly and more attention was given to the traditional (communal) way of life which did not require formal education. One might conclude (not a conclusion that Demerath draws) that the local education system is failing to be responsive to the local community's changing emphasis concerning the purpose of education: from Western-style economic improvement to cultural transmission. However, the care which is needed in interpreting local perspectives on the purpose of education is illustrated by Demerath's observations on students.

> Community school students themselves had a variety of aspirations and approaches to school. While some truly did aspire to subsistence lives in the village, others hid their aspirations to possible futures involving high school and jobs in the cash sector so they would not appear to betray the valorized traditionality being constructed by their parents, relatives and friends (p.191).

Having considered some of the overall purposes of education, we now move on to examine issues of governance and accountability of schools and colleges to the wider environment.

GOVERNANCE

Schools and colleges have to be coordinated as a sector of society, and held accountable—i.e. role holders made 'liable to review and the application of sanctions if their actions fail to satisfy those with whom they are in a relationship of accountability . . .' (Kogan, 1986, p.18). The form this takes, and how educational institutions relate to each other and to stakeholders, differs according to the culture and governance arrangements of a society.

The discussion on governance is intended to provide some of the conceptual materials which enable analysis of the governance environment for education in different countries or regions, and how these may be changing. First, a typology of governance models is considered before, secondly, turning to some broader ideas that justify and legitimise governance and influence how governance arrangements are devised. Thirdly, the multiple accountabilities of the education profession are highlighted. Fourthly, the discussion concludes by looking at governance at the level of the institution and considering issues in democratic school governance.

Models of governance

Glatter (2003) proposes four models of governance which can be used to analyse the governance of educational institutions in different national contexts:

- *competitive market*—educational institutions are likened to firms in a commercial market-place and funded according to their success in the education market;
- *institutional empowerment*—stakeholders in individual institutions are empowered to make decisions—'The focus is more on the institution itself and the way it is run than on its competitive activities "against" other institutions' (p.49);
- *local empowerment*—control and responsibility are devolved to 'the locality as a social and educational unit' (p.50), specifically to local and municipal authorities and to groups or 'families' of educational institutions;
- *quality control*—educational institutions are conceived as the 'point of delivery'. Higher authorities at national or regional level lay down rules and establish targets, evaluation criteria and monitoring arrangements with the aim of ensuring education is 'effectively' delivered.

Legitimacies of coordination

Running through models such as these are broader ideas of how educational institutions should be coordinated with each other and stakeholders—ideas that legitimise different approaches to organising the coordination of educational institutions. Woods (2003) identifies five legitimacies of coordination (Figure 5.2) which can be related to Glatter's models.

Bureaucracy or hierarchy involves direction and oversight of education through a hierarchically ordered system of organisations, posts and rules. This sort of direction can include what is sometimes called 'steering from a distance', which means that government is not necessarily always the service provider, but uses various levers to encourage other organisations to contribute to service provision (Osborne *and* Gaebler, 1993). Glatter's

bureaucracy (hierarchy)

exchange:

- markets

- networks

interior authority

community

democracy

Figure 5.2 Legitimacies of coordination

quality control model entails direct intervention by higher authorities, which may be done by requiring educational institutions to follow a national curriculum, as in England or Israel. Some degree of hierarchical control is usually evident with actual forms of the institutional empowerment, local empowerment and competitive market models.

Exchange is about governance through reciprocal compensation (give-and-take) based on negotiations between educational institutions, and possibly other local and national agencies. *Economic markets* are the clearest example of systems based on exchange relationships. Hence they are integral to the competitive market model. Governance through *networks*—now seen as important as markets and hierarchy for understanding contemporary society (Rhodes, 1999)—is also based on exchange relationships. With networks, the emphasis is on cooperation, partnerships and horizontal relationships, as opposed to hierarchical or vertical authority relationships (Frances et al, 1991). They are often seen as having advantages in coping with complexity and promoting social order (by overcoming the rigidities of bureaucratic hierarchies and the anonymous relations of markets). Exchange through networks has a part to play in each of the models.

Interior authority is where governance comes from inside the person. The concept highlights trends in contemporary governance which involve dispersal of authority and personal responsibility and placing greater emphasis on employees and others acting as 'self-regulating subjects' (Newman, 2001, p.94). Some see this as being done in such a way as to create 'a culture of self-discipline or self-surveillance' (Gewirtz, 2000, p.152), often accompanying moves to make schools and colleges more like players in the competitive market model or to increase institutional or local empowerment. In many countries it may seem that changing contexts are giving leaders and managers of educational institutions, and other local stakeholders, more freedom through devolution of budgets and managerial responsibilities. But to what extent does such an emphasis on interior authority involve genuine empowerment, and to what extent does it reduce autonomy in practice if professional educators are conditioned to internalize—i.e. take on as their own—certain values and attitudes favoured by higher political and administrative authorities?

Community refers to communal forms of governance. These are significant where educational institutions draw their legitimacy from strong ties to community identities, cultural authorities or educational philosophies viewed as being especially compelling or inspirational. Such ties may be important in versions of the local empowerment model, where, for example, loyalties to a geographical community are strong motivators for education. Educational institutions may also be expressions of other types of community, like the supplementary schools established by and for the Black community outside the state system in the UK (Mirza and Reay, 2000) and schools and colleges which derive their identity and purpose from particular traditions, such as a religious denomination, or a founding idea, such as that of Summerhill school in England (Neill, 1990).

Democracy refers to democratic legitimation, where the main emphasis is on everyone with a stake in education having the opportunity to participate in its governance and on educational institutions being responsive to stakeholders' values and preferences. Democratic governance can operate at a number of levels: national, regional, local, institutional. Below, democracy at the level of the educational institution is addressed, through consideration of South Africa as a distinctive case.

In considering actual education systems more than one of these broad legitimating ideas can be seen as applicable, though one may be dominant. Benavot and Resh's (2003) study of the Israeli education system illustrates this complexity.

Israeli education is a centralised, hierarchical system which embraces both Jewish and Arab schools. However whilst some degree of uniformity is evident as a result, there are variations between the Jewish and Arab sectors. School leaders have different degrees of potential for discretion in their schooling. Compared with those in the Jewish sector, schools in the Arab sector, according to Benavot and Resh's study, give more time to core subjects and less to social science, the humanities and arts and social education. Why is this so in what is a highly centralised and hierarchical system? Part of the reason is the different local circumstances and contexts of schools in the two sectors. Jewish schools are able to access funds to supplement state funding, from local community institutions. Thinking in terms of the governance concepts discussed above, schools in the Jewish sector benefit from informal local empowerment so giving them access to material support from local organisations. Arab schools on the other hand lack that local empowerment. On top of this, Arab schools are further limited by communal ties. Benavot and Resh suggest that recruitment of teachers is constrained by family ties and extended family networks which remain strong in local communities, and leads to fewer innovative teachers being taken on. In consequence, with fewer resources and a more conservative teaching staff, Arab principals concentrate much more on the core subjects, which are highly valued because success in these is the passport to universities. But this is at the expense of less instrumentally valuable curriculum areas.

Reflection 2

Which of Glatter's models comes nearest to describing the environment of your school or college, or your education system? Which of the legitimacies of coordination (bureaucratic, markets, networks, communal, democratic, interior authority) are helpful in understanding the governance of educational institutions in your country or region? If governance is changing, how do you consider it is affecting how leaders and managers view the purpose of education?

Multiple accountabilities of the education profession

The education profession contributes to the governance of education as a community of experts which, within limits, is able to regulate itself and exercise its own interior authority—as custodians of expert knowledge and accumulated experience orientated to a sense of professional duty and ethical principles. To a point education professionals are able, therefore, to exercise professional accountability, i.e. accountability to the profession's own community and standards.

At the same time, teachers and school leaders are embedded in the governance arrangements that characterise schools, colleges and education systems. The profession, therefore, has multiple accountabilities, to:

- hierarchies in which it is embedded—which require it to follow mandated curricula for example;
- the market—in so far as educational institutions are required to compete against each other for survival;
- networks—where educational institutions collaborate amongst themselves and with other agencies;
- interior authority—as a professional exercising his or her own informed judgement;
- communal ties—to the profession as a community, or to the traditions and values of a community sponsoring an educational institution;
- democratic values and democratically expressed views and preferences—where educators see themselves as democratic professionals, responsive to clients as part of their professionalism (Whitty, 2002).

Institutional governing bodies

Governing bodies and councils of educational institutions are expressions of democratic and communal legitimacy. At the same time they are hierarchically mandated. South Africa probably makes the strongest explicit connection between democracy and school governance (Bush and Heystek, 2003).

Case Example 1 Democratising school governance: the case of South Africa

South Africa introduces an overt commitment to democratization to its version of Glatter's local empowerment model. Addressing school governors, the Department of Education explains that:

> Just like the country has a government, the school that your child and other children in the community attend needs a 'government' to serve the school and the school community.
> (Cited in Bush and Heystek, 2003, p.127.)

It goes on:

> The democratization of education includes the idea that stakeholders such as parents, teachers, learners and other people (such as members of the community near your school) must participate in the activities of the school. (Cited in Bush and Heystek, 2003, p.128.)

South African governing bodies include students (in secondary schools). Bush and Heystek (2003) draw attention to how South Africa's emphasis on the democratic governance of schools is a reaction to apartheid. As Sayed explains (1999, p.143) the notion of grassroots community participation was constituted in the context of a state which was oppressive and where the state itself was the primary apparatus of oppression. Thus, grassroots community control was the antithesis of state control. Power to the people as opposed to that of the state reflected a strong commitment to participatory democracy and the decentralization of state control.

South African government policy on democratic school governance assumes, suggest Bush and Heystek (2003, p.129), 'a "harmony" model of operation, which would be optimistic even without the background of tension and conflict which affects many schools'. The Department of Education sets out a vision of how governing bodies are to work:

> Meetings of the governing bodies . . . will be the place for calm discussion about how the school should be run, how problems must be solved and where important decisions are made. Since many interest groups are represented on the governing body, everyone involved must learn how to respect the opinions of others and how to make decisions together . . . the talents of many will be combined to make the best decision for the school. (Cited in Bush and Heystek, 2003, p.129.)

There are many problems and challenges facing development of effective democratic school governance as envisaged in South Africa. Similar challenges would arise anywhere. They include:

- *Understanding the policy context.* For example the motives behind pushing forward devolution can affect the policy's implications. Some see cynical motives behind devolving power to governing bodies, interpreting it as a means by which national authorities transfer to others responsibility for intractable problems (Bush and Heystek, 2003).

- *Tackling inequalities between schools.* Both Bush and Heystek (2003) and the case of Jewish and Arab schools discussed above show how disparities can be exacerbated by differences in locally available support and the consequent differential empowerment of institutions. Local communities do not have equal leadership capacities to involve themselves in governance, nor equal access to material resources. Hence there are limits to what governing bodies can achieve. Availability of external support and facilitation, from national authorities, is essential in addressing inequalities and enabling family and community representatives to contribute to improving educational opportunities locally.

- *Achieving representativeness.* There are problems in ensuring governing bodies are genuinely representative. The community may in fact be made up of very different communities or groups. Children's perspectives may differ from their parents and other adults in the community. Those who share membership of a particular social or ethnic group do not necessarily possess views or behaviours in common, as will be highlighted in a later section. Communities and their representatives may be distant from each other: for example, Suzuki (2002, p.252), in a study of primary school governing bodies in Uganda, found that the 'distance' as perceived by parents between themselves and local leaders on the parent-teacher association and the domination of governance positions by the local elite meant that 'ordinary parents are reluctant to ask questions that challenge their leaders' (p.252). This is a phenomenon found in developing countries too (see, for example, Deem et al, 1995). Middle class parents tend to be more involved in school forums for participation than poorer, disadvantaged families (Vincent and Martin, 2002), although, as will be seen below, there are suggestions from some research that this is not always so.

- *Attending to power imbalances*. Participation can be a device by which to assimilate and thereby weaken 'possible dissenting voices' (*Brehony*, 1992) and may result in extending institutionalisation (a process by which an organisation infuses in its members its own set of values—Abrahamsson, 1977) to the community. Suzuki (2002, p.252), in the Uganda study, found:

  > an evident power imbalance between parents and headteacher that hinders parents from accessing the information they need . . . Many parents are . . . concerned about the school but feel intimidated when asking questions to the headteacher or even to the ordinary teachers . . . Overall, headteachers tend to dominate the school governance and manipulate the work of the SMC [school management committee], particularly in rural areas where other members of the SMC are often semi-illiterate.

- *Facilitating open dialogue*. Bound up with power imbalances is the challenge to ensure open dialogue, to which parent and community representatives feel able to contribute. Vincent and Martin (2003, p.18) suggest that creating protected spaces for disadvantaged groups is a way of helping parents to contribute to open dialogue. These spaces provide opportunities for members of a subordinate social group to talk and exchange ideas amongst themselves and develop an agenda 'away from the gaze of the dominant group'. Who might be the subordinate group differs in different contexts. It may be parents as a group; it may be a certain community (such as newly arrived refugees) within a local area. Effort and commitment are required by school and college leaders to guard against professional domination and to realise the potential of parents and community representatives to be involved in decision-making processes.

- *Creating trust*. In order to reach the harmonious consensus envisaged in the South African case, relationships of trust amongst professionals and governors need to be established.

In the second part of this chapter, the focus moves from purpose and principles of governance to the role of the family and community in learning.

FAMILIES AND COMMUNITIES: DIVERSITY AND THE CULTURAL 'WORK' IN COMMUNITIES

Parents and their communities are not monolithic social groups. Families have diverse needs and preferences, and varying economic and cultural resources, affected by factors such as social class, ethnicity and gender. Rose (2003, p.49) highlights the care which needs to be taken with the idea of community:

> A community implies a network of shared interests and concerns, with communities categorised in a variety of ways, for example in relation to geographic areas (e.g. villages), ethnic and racial groups, religious groups, and school communities such as Parent–Teacher Associations. In reality, however, a community is not necessarily a homogenous group of people with a common voice and shared set of views and, by emphasizing common knowledge, it can fail to acknowledge the ways in which local power is reinforced.

Reflection 3

Take a few minutes to consider what community or communities are served by your school or college, or education system. Are they homogeneous in character, or are there significant differences within them? Does it make sense, in view of Rose's definition, to describe them as communities at all?

There has long been awareness of differences between middle class and working class parents regarding education (Ball, 2003; Power et al, 2003). Some research suggests that ethnicity and gender are becoming more significant. However, on the basis of a study of parents with children at secondary school in disadvantaged contexts in England, Martin (1999) challenges some of the assumptions concerning relations between families and schools.

First, she argues that contrary to the conventional assumptions, parents at disadvantaged schools are keen to have greater involvement in the education of their children. According to her findings, less advantaged parents are becoming 'more assertive and challenging' (p.59) and 'it may be that working-class parents are "repositioning" themselves as more active partners in their children's education' (p.60).

Secondly, Martin points to how conventional assumptions about gender and ethnicity are challenged by her findings:

- More men appear to be taking an active role in their children's education. (The type of involvement may be influenced by gender, however. For example, men are more likely to attend public meetings {the 'male' public sphere} than meetings about their own child {the 'female' sphere of home-school liaison}.)

- Black, Asian and other minority ethnic groups were found to be 'more positive [about involving themselves with their child's school] and surprisingly assertive given their traditional experience of marginalisation' (p.60).

Reflection 4

Pause here to compare both of these sets of conclusions from Martin's study with parents of students at your own school or college, or generally in your education system. Do you find parallels in your area, or do the more conventional assumptions hold? What evidence are your conclusions based on?

Martin's findings are unlikely to be replicated everywhere. It is more than likely that in many areas of the world—within a developed country such as the United Kingdom as well as developing countries—being disadvantaged, working class or in an ethnic minority is often associated with being disaffected by or distanced from formal education. Educational opportunities for parents such as these are often adversely affected by the social and education systems. Reay and Lucy (2003) conclude from their research in an urban area in England that certain schools are demonised by local communities and that working class children are more likely to be the ones attending those demonised schools. Reay and Lucy emphasize that it is not only the institution that is demonised, but people are too. Middle class children view the demonised children as different and 'other'. This 'pathologised otherness' can be especially marked for refugees and other ethnic minority children.

Race, social class and gender interact in various ways. With regard to aspirational black families for example:

A number of Afro Caribbean mothers stressed the structural difficulties facing black people in their struggle for social mobility. These mothers were as aware as white professional middle class parents that the type of secondary school their children went to would be a key factor in their children's economic, social and personal futures. In this way, they were very much concerned not only with who their children were, but who they would become (Lucy and Reay, 2002, p.21).

These parents are seeking, through education, both improvement and social justice (Figure 5.1) at an individual level for their children. But in doing this by avoiding demonised schools with large ethnic minority student populations, they recognise that it may conflict with other aims of social justice—i.e. having more aspirational black families in those disadvantaged, demonised schools.

Another example relates to white working class boys, who have to struggle with emotional pulls which Reay (2002) illustrates through the story of a 'hard working, well behaved, poor, white, working class boy trying to achieve academically in a "sink" inner city boys' comprehensive school whilst simultaneously trying to maintain his standing within the male peer group culture'. She suggests that this struggle:

raises questions about the possibilities of bringing together white, working class masculinities with educational success in inner city working class schooling . . . . to combine the two generates heavy psychic costs, involving young men not only in an enormous amount of academic labour but also an intolerable burden of psychic reparative work.

There are limits to what educational institutions in themselves can achieve.

> Until social processes of male gender socialisation move away from the imperative of privileging the masculine and allow boys to stay in touch with their feminine qualities the problem of 'failing boys' will remain despite the best efforts of teachers and researchers.

This also illustrates that a socially required responsibility to exercise interior authority (Figure 5.2) is not only a phenomenon affecting staff in education systems. Individuals and families in communities have to be active shapers of their identity and social and educational lives. Educational leaders need to appreciate and understand the complexities of this cultural 'work', which is going on amongst families and communities. And this applies to widely differing contexts. For example, it can be seen amongst the Papua New Guinea villagers studied by Demerath (1999), mentioned earlier:

> . . . as the relational links that provided the basis for 'traditional' identities have been weakened by the Western model of economic self-interest, local people have been presented with the problem of fashioning an identity without precedent—of having increased responsibility for self-creation (p.175).

PARTICIPATION

Some orientating ideas

How educational leaders and managers can and should respond to the variability, diversity and complexity of the families and communities served by schools and colleges depends in part on the ideas driving participation. Parents and other adults responsible for children can be conceived in different ways, which are not necessarily mutually exclusive. They may be seen as:

- *customers*—particularly in the context of the competitive market model;
- *citizens*—with rights and responsibilities expressed through local empowerment (through participation in school governance for example) or quality assurance models (educational institutions being held to account on behalf of parents as citizens);
- *clients*—who are offered the professional expertise of educators dedicated to service to others (Macbeth, 1989), which may be in the context of any of the governance models;
- *first educators*—recognising the social and biological closeness of parents to the child in which daily experiences of an educational nature are embedded and which is a reality to be acknowledged by all governance models;
- *partners*—which implies professionals and adults working together with some degree of equality in the relationship and perhaps fits best with a democratised local empowerment model.

Many educationalists are drawn to the idea of parents as partners. However, deciding what it involves and putting it into practice are very challenging tasks. Bastiani (1993, p.105), on the basis of much practical experience in home-school links, proposes the following as components of partnership:

- sharing of power, responsibility and ownership;
- mutuality, which begins with the process of listening to each other and incorporates responsive dialogue and 'give and take' on both sides;
- shared aims and goals, based on common ground, but which also acknowledge important differences;
- commitment to joint action, in which parents, pupils and professionals work together to get things done.

Because governance contexts usually have features of more than one idealised model, hybrid conceptions of the parent are conceivable. Woods (1993; 1995), for example, has suggested that in some contexts parents act as *consumer-citizens:* parents as consumer-citizens display dimensions of consumer activity—such as making choices, exercising rights to access and information and creatively adapting services—but embedded in a framework of democratic citizenship which enables participation in the governance of education.

Another variable is institutional focus. School-community relationships can be driven by an *inward focus*, orientated to the institution and its values and educational priorities, or by an *outward focus* concerned to empower the community. Martin et al (1999) highlight the tension between two traditions. Inward focus—the 'professional tradition' (p.63) as Martin and colleagues call it—emphasizes the potential of the community to enrich the school curriculum and of parental participation for improving student motivation, behaviour and attainment. The school reaches out to the community in order to 'enhance traditional goals of pupils' progress and performance but the institution remains the source of the educative value and process' (p.63). By contrast, what is referred to here as outward focus aims to serve the learning needs of the community:

> The task of educating individuals and groups in the community is defined as serving the wider purposes of empowering the community to regenerate its own social, economic and cultural development. From this perspective, boundaries are perceived as permeable in order to achieve the flexibility required to support learning where it is most appropriately located (Martin et al, 1999, p.63).

Schools serving the Papua New Guinea villagers, mentioned earlier, can be seen as being more inward than outward focused. A study by Muskin (1999), of community schools in Mali, highlights the potential for educational institutions to incorporate the different needs and preferences in the local community. He suggests that his work shows the value of 'an evaluation approach that combines conventional systemic indicators of school quality—academic performance and school efficiency—with measures of local knowledge attainment and use'. It takes into account the local aspirations of parents and children to live, work and evolve in their home village as well as achieve literacy, numeracy and other capabilities.

Elements of participation

Participation by families and communities covers different types of involvement and concerns. It can:

be individual (involving an individual parent or family) or collective (where parents, families and the community act together either as a group or through representatives);

be focused on the particular (meaning a child of a particular parent and family, usually through the individual involvement of the parent and family) or the general (meaning broad matters of policy, including purposes of education and curricular and pedagogical matters);

involve different activities, each having an inward and outward focus and framed by the values which the educational institution and families and communities consider most important:

- Communicating—this is two-way and includes the information sent by the school or college to the home/community, and vice versa. It includes how information is communicated and the signals, welcoming or otherwise, conveyed by staff and the institution when meeting and communicating with families and the local community.

- Educating—family and community have an educational influence on the child out of school, and can give time in schools to assist teachers in the classroom. They can collectively support educational activities too, through organising educational visits and raising funds. In the other direction, where there is an outward focus, family and community can be offered and enabled to take up learning opportunities by the school or college.

- Exercising influence—parents for example may do this individually in relation to their own child's teaching arrangements or homework, or collectively through governance structures when they comment on or make decisions on policy matters. In the other direction, schools and colleges may seek to influence families and communities about their attitudes to education.

Thinking critically about participation

In considering what is involved in helping to facilitate genuine, more outwardly focused participation, it is important to reflect critically on the appropriateness and benefits of participation, and to consider whether it is always inevitably positive in its effects. Amongst the factors highlighted in a study by Rose (2003), which distinguishes between pseudo and genuine participation, is the importance of enabling leadership by local people in communities. The implication is that leadership of schools and colleges must complement or be shared with leadership within the community. So the ideas involved in distributed leadership or shared leadership (as noted in Chapter 1) are highly relevant to community participation. Communities need to have dispersed within them a capacity for leadership in order to take advantage of opportunities to participate.

Rose points to the reliance that community participation has on the resources—economic, social and cultural—in the community and to the fact that those with the greatest educational needs are the poorest, with least resources to enable their participation. She concludes that participation may not operate in the interests of equality and equal access to educational opportunities. This links back to the point made earlier in discussing the aim of democratic school governance in South Africa, concerning inequalities between schools. Rose suggests that what might be better is, in effect, a version of the quality assurance model, namely an increased state capacity to 'deliver quality education efficiently and effectively' (p.62). This is not to advocate central, hierarchical control as the answer generally, but it is to underline the necessity for careful evaluations of the negative and positive effects of participation in practice.

Improving participation

The elements of participation outlined above need to be given practical substance. They can be seen in the key activities set out in a practical framework, aimed at all kinds of schools, developed by the London Borough of Tower Hamlets and authored by John Bastiani (2002). The framework is based on local examples of successful practice as well as the growing body of literature and research on home-school links. The key activities are summarised in Figure 5.3 and can be used as a frame for auditing a school's or college's relationship with families and the community. The framework advocates a whole-school approach in which a consensus is sought about the value of good home-school relations. One of the important ingredients for success is leadership which is committed to and actively working for the improvement of home-school links.

Reflection 5

Take some time now to consider the strengths, weaknesses and challenges concerning effective participation in your school or college, or your education system. How could it be improved and what are the main issues in doing this?

You will need to consider the various elements of participation explained earlier;

(a) individual participation focused on the particular child. Consider each activity: communicating, educating, and exercising influence;

(b) collective participation focused on general matters of policy, curriculum and teaching in relation to each activity: communicating, educating (collective support for educational activities), and exercising influence.

There is a range of factors and issues which influences participation and which school leaders need to attend to and be aware of when seeking to improve participation. Drawing from the discussion in this chapter so far, these can be summarised under three headings: 1. the community; 2. power; and, 3. policy context, support and facilitation.

The key activities covered by the framework comprise:

- *establishing key values*—which include inclusion, working together and democracy and empowerment;
- *developing a welcoming school*—when children join the school (this includes attending to special cultural and linguistic needs of families), when parents have a concern, and in all contacts between staff and families (this includes supporting staff, through training for example, to do this);
- *supporting children's learning at home*, by giving families practical ideas and materials and supporting children and families under pressure;
- *treating parents as partners in children's learning*, by ensuring effective communication with all parents, providing regular, honest and accessible information about the progress of individual pupils, seeking families' help in and around the school, obtaining feedback from families, and using ICT wherever it helps communication;
- *ensuring parents have a voice*:
- *collectively*, by making 'serious and continuing efforts . . . to seek, and respond to, the views of parents as a whole' (especially before making significant changes of policy, curriculum and organisation), giving parents a collective voice at different levels in the school (class, year group, etc.) and through an association or council, and working to make the contribution of parent governors as effective as possible;
- *individually*, by ensuring there are arrangements, suitable for all parents, to discuss regularly their children's welfare, progress and development;
- *supporting parents' own learning and development*, by considering what courses or other support the school might offer parents and the community (in areas such as literacy, ICT, etc.) and by having working links with other educational partners in lifelong learning so that it can facilitate parents and community members taking advantage of courses and opportunities elsewhere;
- *drawing on local culture and communities to enrich the life and work of the school*, based on an 'informed up-to-date and systematic working knowledge of local cultural and community life';
- *developing an agreed home-school policy* that includes an understanding of what the school is trying to do and why, an audit of existing arrangements and practices, and a detailed outline of principles, plans and priorities.

Figure 5.3   A practical framework for the review and development of home-school work: Tower Hamlets, London

1. The community

- *Diversity and difference*. This requires awareness, sensitivity and responsiveness on the part of school leaders. High diversity may make it harder for families and communities to influence schools and colleges collectively and requires the sort of open dialogue that enables agreement to be achieved despite differences. Diversity may also lead to markedly different patterns of individual participation.

- *Resources.* Included here are economic, social and cultural resources and, related to these, the imbalances in leadership capacity and power between and within local communities. It is important that such imbalances are recognised and addressed.

- *Relationships and representativeness.* Trust and responsiveness need to be developed and sustained between parents and community members and their representatives.

- *Information and understanding.* How aware are parents and the community about opportunities for participation? This is a crucial factor in being enabled to utilise opportunities. Is communication from the school or college the most effective for all the parents and community it wants to reach?

2. Power

- *Formal levers of influence.* The type and nature of available options and sanctions affect the degree to which families and communities are enabled to participate in and influence educational institutions.

     individually—whether they have rights to information (reports on children's progress for example) and access (meetings with the child's teacher for example) and to choice of school;

     collectively—the powers of representative bodies: some are purely advisory (as in Scotland); some have statutory powers and duties, as in England and South Africa.

- *Professional influence and attitudes.* Formal rights are mediated by everyday social relationships and differences. In particular, professional dominance of the language and exchange of views and information about education restricts the capacity for parents and other community members to participate (Bacon, 1978; Field, 1993).

3. Policy context, support and facilitation

- *National and regional.* The chances for genuine participation are enhanced if the national and regional context of schools, colleges and communities is one in which:
  i.   expectations of participation are high;
  ii. effective support and training for participation are available;
  iii. inequalities between educational institutions and between communities are addressed.

- *Local and institutional.* In the end it is at the level of the locality and institution that opportunities, encouragement and a climate for participation is made. The case study above, of Tower Hamlet's practical framework, is an example of a local authority or district bringing together ideas on successful practices and key principles, which helps the educational institution itself to review and improve its policy and practice.

Learning communities

Underpinning the goal of improving participation is a question which has an importance beyond specific strategies and tactics of involving families and communities.

Is learning something to be delivered, or is it to be regarded 'more as an unfolding learning process which is adapted continuously to suit the needs of particular individuals' (Ranson, 1990, p.15)? The different answers to this question are implicated particularly in two of the legitimacies of coordination (Figure 5.2).

With relationships predominantly justified in terms of *exchange*, the emphasis is on an instrumental approach to education. The usefulness of tasks, people and resources is judged according to their utility in achieving ends such as achievements in tests, examinations and other performance criteria, employability and contribution to the economy. This perspective also opens the way for families to be seen as potential customers, especially in the competitive market model.

With relationships justified in *communal* terms, certain activities, people and learning are valued in themselves, regardless of their utility as measured by outcomes or productivity. A commitment to a communal perspective is represented in much contemporary literature on education and educational leadership (Furman, 2002; Rose, 2003; Sergiovanni, 2000). In this spirit, Martin and colleagues, in their analysis of case studies in home-school and community links, commend the idea of 'learning communities where all partners can contribute their distinctive knowledge and skills' (Martin et al, 1999, p.73). (See also Chapter 12.)

Community participation, as noted, is not automatically positive in all its effects. Furman (2002) warns that the research evidence for its proclaimed benefits is thin. Implementation and practice of community participation therefore calls for continual critical examination and evaluation. For educational leaders, clarity on what community participation is intended to achieve and the collection and scrutiny of evidence from differing perspectives on its operation in practice over time are essential. In other words, community participation is not the enactment of technical procedures, with known consequences if effected correctly. Rather, it is a process of reflective change in which values choices and power imbalances are inherent in its day-to-day activity.

SUMMARY

This chapter has drawn attention to some of the issues that educational leaders need to consider in reflecting on the role of educational institutions in relation to their external environment. It has sought to highlight the way in which socially conceived purposes of education are bound up in that context and aimed to encourage critical reflection on broad ideas about models of governance and coordinating education as part of society. The discussion of governance also highlighted the multiple accountabilities of teachers and educational leaders, and raised issues to do with governing bodies, especially if they are intended to be democratic.

The chapter also underlines the diversity of families and communities. The implications of this diversity carry over into addressing participation. It has highlighted different elements of participation and encouraged critical thinking about the benefits, and possible disadvantages, of participation. The point of this has been to provide a basis for considering how participation might be improved in any particular situation. In summary, conditions for effective participative relationships between educational institutions and their families and communities include:

- commitment to communal relations in which the intrinsic worth and rights of all are respected, and a *dominating* instrumental approach to people and communities avoided;
- awareness of diversity and difference amongst communities and the cultural 'work' they engage in, as part of an outward focus towards their learning needs;
- strategies for inclusive participation in light of this diversity and difference;
- strategies, nationally and regionally, to tackle inequalities between educational institutions and between communities;
- strategies to reduce power imbalances between parents/communities and
  - i. professional educators
  - ii. representatives of those parents/communities;
- strategies to facilitate open dialogue;
- supportive national and local policy contexts which facilitate the above;
- critical evaluation of positive and negative impact of participation.

RECOMMENDED FURTHER READING

You will be able to take some of the ideas in this chapter further by reading the following:

Gelsthorpe, T. and West-Burnham, J. (2003) *Educational Leadership and the Community*, Harlow: Pearson. Perspectives from a number of countries are offered in this volume. Chapter 2, Gelsthorpe, T. 'Engaging communities and schools' provides a useful overview.

Gleeson, D. and Husbands, C. (eds) (2001) *The Performing School*, London: Routledge Falmer, particularly Chapter 13, by Ball, S., which gives a more critical perspective on the place of education in the wider society and Chapter 8, by Smyth, J.

Griffiths, M. (2003) *Action for Social Justice in Education*, Maidenhead: Open University Press includes responses and stories from a variety of perspectives.

Lingard, B., Hayes, D., Mills, M. and Christie, P. (2003) *Leading Learning*, Maidenhead: Open University Press. Chapter 4, 'Leading the field' reports research on case study schools in Australia covering approaches to community participation.

Earley, P. (2003) 'Leaders or followers? Governing bodies and their role in school leadership', *Educational Management and Administration*, 31(4), 353–367, reports results of recent research and discusses some of the challenges for governing bodies in exercising leadership.

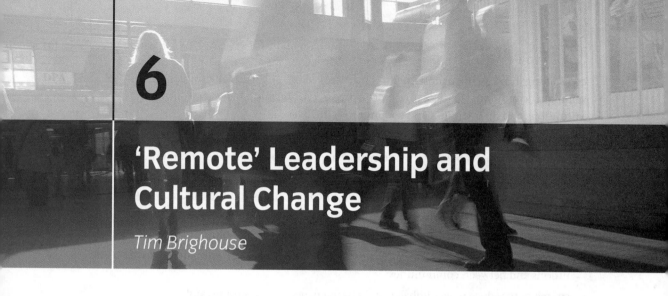

6

'Remote' Leadership and Cultural Change

Tim Brighouse

INTRODUCTION AND LEARNING OUTCOMES

This chapter considers the importance of context for educational institutions, particularly those in urban areas. It is written from the point of view of the Chief Education Officer of a large Local Educational Authority in England and therefore the context is that of a system influenced by political and economic factors which must be moderated by the 'remote' leader on behalf of the schools and colleges in it. The chapter reflects on a time of change, and benefits from the author's experience of leading educational reform in the large conurbation of Birmingham. In itself the chapter is a kind of case study of change and improvement of systems and institutions in an urban environment, but it draws on examples from individual schools within the area showing how school leaders can effect cultural change.

By the end of this chapter you should be able to:

- conceptualise your regional system and reflect on the political will and resources that are made available to improve education;
- reflect on the interplay of culture and leadership in your institution;
- understand the importance of communication, particularly communicating the vision;
- reflect on being a leader of change;
- understand that attention to detail, time management and delegation are essential skills for leaders, including remote ones.

BIRMINGHAM: ITS CONTEXT FOR EDUCATIONAL LEADERSHIP

Leading Birmingham's education service with more than 450 schools and pre-school provisions and a budget of £600m+ was an exercise in remote leadership. Remote leaders, such as those in large distributed organisations operating on different sites at different levels and with different but allied functions, need all the same qualities, characteristics, behaviours and competencies as leaders in more compact and focused settings such as single site schools or offices. But they need to understand them more thoroughly; for remote leaders need to be especially aware of their context. For example, contact with stakeholders will necessarily be sporadic: one wrong note struck can resonate for a long time.

Cosmopolitan Birmingham involves a million inhabitants drawn from all quarters of the United Kingdom and the world but especially from Ireland, Pakistan, India, Bangladesh, the Caribbean, Africa and more recently in smaller numbers, central and eastern Europe and China.

Moreover, leading the Local Education Authority is shaped and influenced by the City's past, present and future ambitions. Birmingham is the UK's second city with a culture based on manufacturing. In the seventies and early eighties it had suffered like all the UK's industrial revolution cities from all its habits, rationale and infrastructure being rooted in an industrial age which was beyond its twilight period. So Birmingham's pride in being a 'metal-bashing' city of a 'thousand trades', which had been so attractive to the tens of thousands of recently arrived economic migrants was suddenly a liability. These same economic migrants could have encountered a confused civic leadership unsure of the direction to take a city down on its economic luck. However, in the mid-eighties as a response to the economic changes, there was a seminar of all the movers, shakers and creative thinkers of the area at Highbury—a stately home bequeathed by Joe Chamberlain, a nineteenth century industrialist turned city mayor, who a hundred years earlier had municipalised gas, electricity and water and laid the foundations of the modern industrial city before embarking on a distinguished national political career.

However, it was 'Highbury One' (as it became known) which created the vision and laid down the strategic direction for the first stage of the city's late twentieth century economic recovery. The city leaders decided they would take whatever European funds were available for the remodelling of a comparatively small area near the Council House. This involved the creation of three closely linked and beautifully reconstructed modern European-style squares and the building of an International Convention Centre incorporating a Symphony Hall and the National Indoor Arena. Both ensured the generation of jobs. The city worked closely with the private sector—never a difficulty for the pragmatic Labour party leaders—in attracting developers to start a programme of inner city expensive private housing allied to commercial development of shops, offices and hotels which would surround and punctuate the squares. Simultaneously the city shifted its spending priorities and practices, relocated the Birmingham Symphony Orchestra to the magnificent Symphony Hall within the International Convention Centre and invested in the arts. The city council sponsored the Birmingham Royal Ballet, supported the Rep and attracted a young conductor, Simon Rattle, to put Birmingham's music on the world stage.

Indeed an international as well as a national reputation for achieving bold ventures has always been a part of Birmingham's ambition. After all it had been the 'manufacturing heart' of the 'workshop of the world'. So it was natural to want to 'market' itself in its new shape.

But such necessary single mindedness was not painless, especially at a time when central government was systematically squeezing public expenditure. Servicing the debts on the infrastructure projects denied resources to other services. 'Place marketing'—for that was the purpose of Birmingham's strategic development—came at a cost of ignoring 'place making'. So expenditure on education was squeezed to levels below government published guidelines. The schools' fabric was tired and getting worse through neglect. Those who worked in them felt they were working in an unsupportive climate of too little professional leadership which itself was being undermined by undue political interference. Birmingham's education was becoming a byword for low aspiration and of low standards of provision and outcome.

So it was that 'context' which presented itself to the author on being offered the job of Chief Education Officer in the spring of 1993. But it is not the whole story. For the same civic leaders who at 'Highbury One' had laid the blueprint for this economic revival were realising that 'place marketing' was not enough. 'Place making' was at last necessary. They needed a good education service—or at least one that began to deliver sufficient youngsters to satisfy the appetite of inward investors and companies relocating in search of workers with higher levels of education and training than those required by metal bashers. Behind closed doors the ruling group tired of what the leader of the council called 'those bloody people in Margaret Street' (the Education Department's main office). They debated whether to take advantage of the Conservative government's push to schools to abandon local authorities and opt for grant maintained status by positively encouraging rather than discouraging schools along that route. This was a pragmatic move, as grant maintained schools obtained their funds directly from central government, and particularly in the early years of the reform received comparatively generous funding which was seen by many as divisive to cooperation between schools (Bush et al, 1993). However, going grant maintained was an attractive argument for it would absolve the council of much of its educational responsibility for standards in schools—a responsibility which it knew it was not discharging with any distinction—and simultaneously allow it to focus on what it did well: economic regeneration and the revival of sport, culture and the arts together with its often two main struggling services—housing and social services. To their credit the city's political leaders decided to have one last effort at reviving education because it could see it was a matter of civic pride and vital to the health of its population as well as its economic future.

So it set up a commission chaired by Professor Ted Wragg of Exeter University to take evidence from the stakeholders, the public, community groups, the churches, the schools which had gone grant-maintained and the media. His subsequent report published in November 1993, two months after the new Chief Education Officer had started, helped set the scene for Birmingham's educational revival.

Assuming the role of 'remote' leader—advantages

So that was the general context of the new Chief Education Officer assuming the role of a remote leader of a very large local education authority. But it's a broad-brush description only. It doesn't describe the inheritance—of the usual but particular balance of brilliant, creative or competent officers, advisers, heads, teachers and governors who made up Birmingham's education service. The first task of a leader is to ascertain the balance and set about tipping it in favour of the brilliant, creative and solidly competent and reliable. Nor does the description of the general context acknowledge three extra-ordinary advantages.

- First, there existed a data base and a set of accurate information which enabled there to be a clear and very precisely focused analysis of where the schools were in terms of performance over time and comparatively, as well as the state of their buildings and their finances. Having good data is vital in terms of informing leadership and management. Professionals in education in the UK and elsewhere are being encouraged to ensure that their practice is informed by the use of evidence and data (Anderson and Bennett, 2003).

- Secondly, the political leadership of the education service was to shift from a party journeyman (who would only some few years later defect from Labour to the Liberal Democrats) to a brilliant eccentric and very intelligent and influential young Labour politician, Andy Howell.

- Thirdly, the council decided to back the education service at least for a couple of years with a positive budgetary financial shift. Although marginal—say one per cent increase in real terms—it occurred at a time when the Government's theoretical level of spend for education in Birmingham was reduced so that suddenly the council moved from being a major under-spender on schools to one which appeared comparatively generous.

So far I have been describing (albeit generally) the context of place and to some extent of time so far as my 'remote leadership' is concerned. I've called it 'remote' because in a sense I was seen by others to be just one, albeit an important one, of the educational professional leaders of Birmingham. That is to say the leader of 30,000 staff distributed in 450 schools and other work places pursuing different if allied disciplines. But I was also the remote (the headteacher and the teacher being the more immediate) leader of upwards of 350,000 parents and their 200,000 children. Context is therefore not merely the place and time you perceive but also their perception of it too.

Reflection 1

From your knowledge and experience, can you identify any 'remote' leaders of education who have been faced with similar challenging circumstances?

TIME AND GEOGRAPHY: THE DIFFERENCE BETWEEN THE LEA AND THE SCHOOL

Contrast this 'remote' leadership of a 'schooling system' with similar leadership exercised at the level of the school. There are similar constraints of inherited cultures of people, time and place. But they can be shifted more dramatically—sometimes very dramatically in a school, in a way not possible in the LEA or school district.

For the school still has the potential to win an almost impenetrable mystique in the minds of those who encounter it. Let me give you a true example of how a school rolled back the influence of the contemporary age and established a distinctive culture (references to examples of changing cultures are in the further reading section at the end of the chapter).

When I started my career it was a much more deferential and less participative age: what was possible then in a school and a public service—and I guess the professions and the business world—was heavily influenced by the conventions of the time. Not merely did we not use first names but we knew when to speak, how to address those we regarded as our superiors and we had a habit of language which was effortlessly sexist and racist. In those days there were few students of what we now call 'body language' and a glance at the library would reveal how little had been written about management and leadership. Not all schools had telephones and the only advice on the primary curriculum had appeared in the form of a booklet called 'Story of a School' published in 1949 and re-issued in 1953. That's how it was when I started my career in 1961. Nor is it sufficient to reflect on the accelerating speed of life and the shrinking of the world driven principally by electronic communication, speed of travel and the media—important though they are. But as I have implied, schools can defy those pressures in ways less insulated organisations cannot. There are now exceptions, oases of a bygone age even in the hurly burly of the present. I visited a school the other day—a blackboard jungle 15 years ago—in London where a strong-minded leader had pushed back the clock. Consider the case example below.

Case Example 1

The boy was probably 14 and at a sign we were led by him ringing an ancient school hand-bell. The considerable hubbub of the assembled 600 pupils fell instantly silent as they rose to watch the headmaster (for so he is called) with flowing gown approach the dais. Three phalanxes of pupils—one facing the dais, two at right angles facing each other. Some general remarks are followed by the ritual lighting of the peace candles—a commemoration of September 11th.

We witness some seasonal hand bell performers play out 'We Three Kings' and the Chaplain explains about myrrh and connects with the students' lives in the modern world: we contemplate and pray. We depart. The school falls silent as it goes about its business: the only sounds are those of the teachers' voices as they 'whole class' teach and sit at their desks. For all the world it reminded me of nothing so much as the Nottingham grammar school where I did my teaching practice in 1961. I remember it astonishing me then just as it does now.

The head had achieved this remarkable time warp with a style reminiscent of his youth. I listened to his tale of the difficult inheritance—the story of going grant maintained, the change in admissions criteria, the 'sorting out' (as he calls it) of the staff (only two of whom were there when he arrived). I could only be impressed by the sheer determination—against all the odds of the time he's lived through—which has enabled him to impose his will on the context. And of course leadership by others in that school is heavily circumscribed by the *micro climate* he created. So the case examples story makes the point about micro climates or cultures but also that the issue of *time* is more complex than it first appears. The candle commemorating September 11th illustrated that the school is very alive to present circumstances. Indeed most of the context and approach to the appearance and trappings of its very rigid assembly and tutorial practice relates much more particularly to the present day than do those of some other schools. So gangs, guns and drugs are frequently the subject of whole-school debate in a way which other more contemporarily organised schools are not. Nevertheless the school is the exception. Not many leaders can roll back the participative un-deferential present: the world is too intrusive to do that. In remote leaders in complex organisations in the public gaze such creations of time-warps are not possible. But let the cameo of the school make another point about context—namely that of place.

Leadership in the inner city schools is very different from suburban and rural schools. The first context (the inner city) is likely to be much more challenging with the culture of the street and disadvantage intruding both physically (most urban schools are not surrounded by a moat of green with what constitutes a drawbridge of a main drive to the school) and metaphorically. In these circumstances so many of the youngsters bring the baggage of their disrupted and challenged lives into the classroom where there is in consequence more challenge to get them ready for learning. And then in our multi-racial, multi-faith, multi-lingual cities there is the complexity and depth of greater knowledge about those issues for staff to understand, internalise and then make sense of those they are leading whether in the classroom, the school as a whole or the larger administrative system. Stoll and Fink (1996) drawing on the work of others (e.g. Rosenholtz, 1989; Fullan, 1992) have established that schools can be 'moving', that is improving in difficult circumstances whilst schools in leafy suburbs that appear to be successful, may actually be 'stuck' and not adding value to what the pupils bring to the school.

The city too is capable at one and the same time of being very different. Gated communities, selective schools, and violent estates—all exist side by side in the inner city. The schools too reflect these differences.

There are further complications. London inner-city is very different from Birmingham inner-city—and both from Sheffield. What will work in one will not in the others, even though the deprivation and the social and racial mix is apparently very similar. The places and the relationship (or their lack of it) with their different communities, together with history and tradition bring in another factor.

Finally, so far as context is concerned, there are the prevailing circumstances. Is the school or the organisation dysfunctional—as the school I illustrated had been—or is it successful? One of the most difficult and important features of a type and circumstances of leadership is to take over from a highly successful predecessor of a really successful organisation, especially in challenging circumstances. That's when promotion from within is a wise move, provided the successor is a relative newcomer with the eye still uncluttered by the cataracts which can come with staying in one place a long time. The newcomer—as leader—has to have extraordinary insight and qualities to lead wisely in such circumstances.

According to how far the organisation is dysfunctional—and most have some dysfunctionality—or how far it's being successful or whether it is suddenly in crisis, it will require a different mix of leadership (see Chapter 1 for a discussion of different types of leadership styles).

Reflection 2

Before you move on to the next part of the chapter reflect on the culture of your institution. How would you define the prevailing culture? Has it changed as a result of a change in leadership?

So much for context with all its variations of time, place, content and their combinations.

LEADERSHIP—THE ROLE OF HISTORIAN AND FUTUROLOGIST AND THE NEED TO COMMUNICATE

As we have seen Birmingham's education service in 1993 presented a particular combination—a widely shared perception of dysfunctionality but with features, for example a data and information base, political leadership, thirst for improvement of the Wragg report and history allied to civic pride which could be harnessed to advantage. As it turned out there was one more significant advantage—the quality of the staff and leadership of its schools. Of course like any leader one seeks to find luck—and the luck of one's inheritance is powerfully influenced by how one accurately describes it but in a discriminating and selective manner. Leaders need to continue to seek to talk—at least in public—about the good things they inherit because they know they are seeking to 'create energy'. So they look for and remark on the 'energy creator' in the system—that is to say the optimistic realists who ask 'how they could' rather than assert 'why they can't'—the 'silver linings' rather than the 'clouds', half full rather than half empty—people who ask 'what if?' instead of saying something's been tried before, 'didn't work then and won't work now'.

They are *historians*. That is to say they tell stories with vivid images often of the previous success of their organisations to fill people's pockets with confidence and pride. They are *futurologists* too in the sense that they see wider and further than those they lead. Importantly however, they don't see wider and further about the discrete parts of the organisation. The mathematician for example will know more about the maths curriculum and associated teaching developments than the head, as will the English leader about English, but the head pieces them and many other aspects of school and community life together to see further and wider than the others. That's why successful leaders often say they know nothing about much of what goes on but they have colleagues who do.

So in Birmingham it was necessary for me as Chief Education Officer not merely to remark on these two roles (historian and futurologist) among successful headteachers, heads of department, etc. but to display them too in what I did as an example. So whenever speaking to large audiences or writing in the local papers or in the half termly magazine for schools or in the termly personalised letter to heads, I was conscious of the need to be a historian and a futurologist to parents, councillors, staff and the media. Improvement whether in ever better results in primary schools (at Key Stage 2) or in secondary schools (GCSE exam results) could be pitched presently, historically, prospectively and by comparison with Birmingham's changing role in an information and learning age. They needed to be linked always to the city's national and international ambition.

Just as a head—or for that matter a teacher with their pupils—knows that what they say, what they do and who they are, have to ring true to win the confidence of their stakeholders, so too do the actions, words and character of the remote educational leader of the LEA in England or a School District in the USA, Africa or elsewhere. Leadership in a large and remote authority demands extra attention and effort in terms of *communication*. The headteacher describes and keeps describing the defining theme. For example, it might be 'learning' or 'our school stands for achievement' or 'we are a "can do" school—that means that all of us can succeed'. Sometimes school leaders have a little voice in their heads mocking them for going on so persistently and repetitively about the same theme but they know they have to do it. So it is with remote leaders. The importance of leaders having a vision is well documented, again further readings on vision and mission are recommended at the end of the chapter.

In Birmingham communicating the 'vision' meant frequent references to its past internationally acclaimed achievements when it had wanted to put its mind to a task. It meant frequent reminders of our determination to be a world learning city and therefore to have good schools with international links to take advantage of the ICT revolution. 'Improving on previous best' as a chosen strap-line illustrated talks, slides and many articles, papers, radio and television discussions. 'The natural inventiveness and creativity of the Brummies who had come from all corners of the world to live peacefully together in the common cause of making a better future for their children' was another recurring theme which resonated with audiences of all ages as well as the media to whom one needed to be always available with a vivid quotation.

The messages while coherent and consistent are more focused and detailed when it comes to writing for or speaking to specialist audiences. So 'improving on previous best' and 'setting a learning example' have to be illustrated constantly but differently according to context. The pre-school worker with the toddler and the young infant, the primary practitioner releasing the potential of childhood, and the secondary teacher desperately trying to fill the young adolescent's pockets with the confidence that comes from early accredited success, all need to be confident that you as a leader understand, empathise and are vitally interested in their world.

As a remote leader infrequent contact means every contact is vital and needs to be supplemented by appearing to be ubiquitous—and reinforced by colleagues whom they see on a more regular basis who while having views and expertise of their own are singing broadly from the same song sheet. So finding good things and acknowledging them is important. One of the advantages of remote leaders is that they can have a system for 'acts of unexpected kindness'. So the leader of a LEA or school district or a school can have the luxury of a system which ensures that staff who have contact with workers on the front line can drop a line to the remote leader telling them of the 'beyond the call of duty' activities of various members of staff, so the leader in turn can drop a personal handwritten line of appreciation to the person concerned mentioning the colleague who had been talking of their good work thereby doubling the impact! Of course it involves hours of handwritten notes, but it acknowledges energy and commitment at the chalk face, reinforces the support workers' appreciation of their work and increases the likelihood of there being an impression of 'more good things and fewer bad things' happening which Michael Fullan (2001) had perceptively described as a characteristic of successful organisations.

Reflection 3

Can you identify occasions when you have either been in receipt of or have offered an 'act of unexpected kindness'? If so how did it affect you?

At a school level exactly the same need for acts of unexpected kindness exist but it requires much more ingenuity and variety—in short a wider range of acknowledgement if the leader is to avoid being seen as manipulative and insincere. So in this respect, as perhaps in others, the remote leader has some advantages. Nevertheless the local and more immediately available leaders at the school are seen as more remote by some of their stakeholders. In Birmingham even the core education management team operated from four offices each located some miles each from the other so they too needed attentive care.

Lessons for remote leaders

The remote leader needs to spend lots of time in 'talk shops'—occasions where groups of staff drawn from across the service (but involving everyone over time) come together to pool concerns and then will the leader accompanied by a second colleague about what's wrong. Not to become defensive in small settings is a matter of considerable self-discipline.

The electronic revolution particularly in the management and communication technologies means that everybody can have access through an organisational internet to the minutes of meetings. I certainly made sure that my personal performance management contract with the City's Chief Executive was open for all to see. In this way, every part of the network can see the leader's personal priorities and how they relate to the city's overall purpose and ambition.

Remote leaders within large organisations, just like school leaders, need strong leaders in the team that surrounds them. At first that's difficult to achieve particularly where there's been a reputation associated with dysfunctionality. Existing staff in supporting leadership positions have usually lost confidence and are in any case associated in the minds of the main stakeholders with the organisation's malaise. So it was in

Birmingham. Moreover although all such senior managers/leaders were on fixed term three-to-five-year contracts virtually all had either never been issued or renewed. It took at least 18 months to establish a team—a mixture of the existing and new staff—driven (and that's the right word) by the same sense of all-consuming urgency, purpose and values that was needed to shift a whole city. Although it's the case that in local government councillors not officers make the judgement on appointments, there were no decisions in my ten years in Birmingham in which the members chose new staff in a way with which I disagreed. Headteachers in schools ideally have a similar relationship with key members of the governing body.

The outcome in Birmingham was a team of people who 'lived the job' from Monday to Friday and beyond and who forged a sense of common purpose that was formidable. We deployed an external team coach and analysed both our individual and collective style using the Myers Briggs taxonomy (a psychometric test) as the team changed over the eight subsequent years.

Leaders are aware that they are role models for those who they lead and that *listening, speaking, reading* and *writing* are crucial elements of leadership whether by the Year 6 teacher to her pupils or the head for the staff and wider community. Of these four activities—all of which have the complex matrix of thinking and learning threading through them—the one most often forgotten is *writing*. Indeed this analysis of listening, speaking, writing and reading is why the Birmingham senior team argued it as an *alternative* to Belbin's team inventory and Myers Briggs with their taxonomy of 'developers', 'analysers', 'inspectors', 'completer/finishers', etc. when it comes to leadership. On reflection, however, it is neither one nor the other model but *both*. The correct intersection of the Belbin/Myers Briggs *and* the 'listening, speaking, teaching and writing' taxonomies is necessary for the particular leadership context. Even within any one of those activities moreover—for example speaking—there is even more subtle complexity. The balance of 'we' to 'I' of the use of the third person, knowing when to use 'you'—all are key to a leader's success. On all these matters we collectively considered our behaviour in Birmingham in order to serve better those we led.

Reflection 4

Working within a strong and dedicated team can be the key to success. Have you been in a team where the part played by each member has been analysed as part of team development? If so, was it successful? If not, can you identify the reasons?

For remote leaders as I have mentioned earlier, the images created, the repeated use of metaphor and story are crucial to the successful sharing of the vision. And 'without a vision the people will perish'. So attention to oratorical skills linked to genuine passion and values will help the remote leader to convey a lasting message.

One of the unremarked features of successful leadership is 'attention to detail' and 'anticipation'. The attention to detail manifests itself in drilling down into the organisation to discover the 'organisational arthritis'—that is to say the occasions where the 'time-honoured way we do things round here' gets in the way of the new direction of the service as a whole. Remote leaders need to be careful to ensure that they are not so out of touch with the managerial practices that they fail to spot the gaps that can open up between not just their stated purpose and direction on the one hand and the day-to-day actions of the rest of the staff on the other. One of the ever present hazards in this respect is the possibility of leaders and managers misunderstanding delegation.

The best guide to delegation I found in something used in Cheshire in the late 1980s. There they agreed for nine levels of delegation as follows:

1. Look into this problem. Give me all the facts. I will decide what to do.
2. Let me know the alternative available with the pros and cons of each. I will decide what to select.
3. Let me know the criteria for your recommendation, which alternatives you have identified, and which one appears best to you with any risk identified. I will make the decision.
4. Recommend a course of action for my approval.
5. Let me know what you intend to do. Delay action until I approve.
6. Let me know what you intend to do. Do it unless I say not to.
7. Take action. Let me know what you did. Let me know how it turns out.
8. Take action. Communicate with me only if your action is unsuccessful.
9. Take action. No further communication with me is necessary.

There are two points to be made about the list. The first is that you need to be at different points for different people according to their length of time in the job and the nature of the task, and secondly that it is important to be clear there is a mutual understanding that you are at the same point! (Nothing is more infuriating than you assuming you are at number 2 in the list when the delegate thinks she's at number 8.) So be clear and above all don't change horses mid-stream!

Time management is crucial. Allocating the right time to the right task and preferably using time twice are the keys here. Let me give one brief example—again drawn from a school.

Case Example 2

The head and two deputies organise the timetable so that they are always off teaching on Wednesdays. They then use 15 of the Wednesdays during the year to take over in rotation the Wednesday timetables of three scientists, three historians, three English specialists, etc. The teachers relieved of their timetables are encouraged to visit schools to observe other practice with a focused agenda of course. Subsequent staff meetings of faculty are attended by the head and two deputies where marking practices, the visits, the curriculum and professional development are discussed.

Doing the right thing and avoiding 'time and energy' traps are other illustrations of using time well. 'Time and energy' traps are engaging in activity which a careful and cool analysis of the likelihood of your activity leading to a wholly successful outcome would reveal as being remote. Conversely, time and energy spent on what David Hargreaves (2003) calls 'high leverage' outcomes is time well spent.

None of this should detract from the leader's need to 'give time' apparently to all legitimate stakeholders, of whom there are more if one's a remote leader in a large organisation like an LEA or School District.

If 'delegation' and the 'use of time' are essential skills of leaders so is a practical understanding of the management of change.

Experiencing the management of change

Here there are a myriad of issues and reading Michael Fullan's books seem an effective starting point (e.g. *Fullan*, 2002; 2003). All I would want to pick out for leading in exceptionally difficult circumstances is the need to understand the way in which the forces of internally generated change can be structured and harnessed rather than, as so often happens, external suggestions imposed or accepted.

Of course there's much more to understand in change—the realisation that there's an 'implementation dip' which we experienced in Birmingham in 1996 after three years of attention to school improvement—and a substantive programme of winning the hearts and minds of teachers in introducing bottom-up targets and making much of the upcoming Millennium in talk of the special generation—had yet to translate itself in a substantial rise in educational attainment outcomes at the age of 11 and 16. But the following summer 1997 it did just in time for an Ofsted inspection report.

In the first phase of reform it had been necessary to overcome some 'barnacles' which people tend to attach to the vision of reform which was set out in a report to committee in the first weeks. 'Barnacles' are those factors which opponents will throw against the hull of the ship of reform. In the case of Birmingham these were anticipated though proposing in symbolic 'guarantees' for early years, primary and secondary schools. Each contained targets of input and resource to fund the *targets of process* (expressed in the form of experiences that any teacher or parent would want for their child) with *targets of outcome* promoted from the bottom up and expressed in terms of ever better scores at age 11 and improved GCSEs at age 16.

SUMMARY

This brief reflection on leadership has attempted to reflect on how leaders, including remote leaders, can overcome dysfunctionality in an urban setting. Although I have inevitably reflected on the tasks and activities involved in achieving this in very general terms at the LEA or school district level, I have attempted to describe the processes involved in a way that will make sense at the urban school level too. On reading it through I realise that it does not analyse or seek to describe the myriad of actions and responses to the succession of buffetings which urban educational organisation encounters on an almost daily basis. Nor does it sufficiently emphasize the prime task of securing a strong and widely shared commitment to the highest common factor of the organisational purpose and values. What it seeks to do is describe *how* one wrestles with context and seeks to shift the culture. In the end the success of these efforts will lie in perceptions of stakeholders both within and outside the organisation for which one is responsible. If their answer to the question 'Are more good things and fewer bad things happening?' is in the affirmative, then one can claim some sort of limited success.

RECOMMENDED FURTHER READING

For further reading about culture and the symbols of culture see Beare, H., Caldwell, B.J. and Millikan, R.H. (1989) *Creating an Excellent School: some New Management Techniques*, London: Routledge and for an overview of research in school culture see Chapter 1 of *School Culture* (1999) by Jon Prosser.

If you would like to pursue issues relating to leadership and the communication of vision see Beare et al, and also Foreman, K. (1997) in Middlewood, D. and Lumby, J. (eds) *Strategic Management in Schools and Colleges*, London: Paul Chapman Publishing.

A standard text which summarises theories of change and change management is that of Morrison, K., *Management Theories for Educational Change*, London: Paul Chapman Publishing.

For further reading on delegation see Gold, A. and Evans, J. (1998) *Reflecting on School Management*, London: Falmer Press. There are many books on time management, one that you might like to look at is Nelson, I. (1995) *Time Management for Teachers*, London: Kogan Page.

If you would like to read more about the use of data in education you might like to look at the site of Harvey Goldstein, at http://k1.ioe.ac.uk/hgpersonal/index.html. A range of aspects of the use of data in education is covered in Anderson, L. and Bennett, N. (eds) (2003) *Developing Educational Leadership: Using Evidence for Policy and Practice*, London: Sage Publications.

7

Reform, Improvement and Change

Kathryn Riley and Anil Khamis

INTRODUCTION AND LEARNING OUTCOMES

In this chapter we explore how education reforms can be introduced which have a positive impact on the lives of children and young people, creating rights and opportunities for them. We highlight the ways in which approaches to school improvement that are linked to teachers' day-to-day concerns and practices can transform classrooms and create new learning opportunities.

We begin by introducing a framework which enables both policy-makers and practitioners to identify the problems they face in an education system; to map the choices and the decisions which they have already made; and to consider future possible courses of action. Having established this framework, we then test its relevance by drawing on three case studies: from England, the Former Yugoslavia Republic of Macedonia and Pakistan. Although the chapter mainly considers reform and improvement at a system level, our final conclusions focus on the school improvement lessons to be learned from these explorations.

By the end of this chapter you should be able to:

- identify drivers and levers for reform and change;
- recognise the ways in which change and improvement initiatives need to be made appropriate to the local context and circumstances;
- appreciate that improvement initiatives must be owned and not imposed;
- understand that the change process is a messy business and takes time.

THE IMPORTANCE OF EDUCATION

Of all the civil rights for which the world has struggled, the right to learn is the most fundamental . . . The freedom to learn has been bought by bitter sacrifice. We should fight to the last ditch to keep open the right to learn, the right to have examined in our schools not only what we believe, not only what our leaders say, but what the leaders of other countries have said. We must insist on this to give our children the fairness of a start which will equip them with such an array of facts and such an attitude towards truth that they can have a real chance to judge what the world is, and what greater minds have thought it might be. (Civil Rights Activist, W.E.B Du Bois, quoted in Darling Hammond, 1997.)

There are few certainties ahead for our children and young people. In our world of overall opulence, many remain 'unfree', not technically slaves (although some still are) but denied basic freedoms because of their poverty and their lack of access to civil liberties, health—and to education (Sen, 1999). In the global climate of uncertainty, destabilisation and refugee crisis, the right to learn, expounded with such passion by Civil Rights activist W.E.B Du Bois many decades ago—and quoted above—remains a profound one. It encompasses a number of key elements including recognition of the emancipatory nature of education—the ways in which it can spark a love of learning, a sense of belonging and a quest for knowledge which people take through their lives (Riley, 2004).

Education reform is a top political priority in many countries today. While final policy choices will depend on local context—the developmental level of the education system, as well as political priorities and cultural values—there are some core issues about teaching and learning which transcend context. The evidence suggests that successful reforms depend on three interlocking elements:

- the skills, capacity and commitment of educators within school and at the local system level;
- the enthusiasm and commitment of parents, pupils and teachers; and
- the ability of politicians to create the right legislative framework (Riley, 2000).

Getting the policy right is only part of the jigsaw. Reforms fail for a number of reasons, including what has been described as the tendency to focus on the supposed villains of the piece—'inadequate teachers, irresponsible parents, irrelevant or inadequate curricula, unmotivated students . . . and an improvement-defeating bureaucracy' (Sarason, 1990, p.13). Education reforms are more likely to work when teachers, parents, pupils and administrators are seen as part of the solution, not part of the problem.

If reforms are to succeed, much also needs to be done to reduce the barriers to learning which prevent many children and young people from benefiting from education. Those barriers include poor health and malnutrition; lack of connection between schools and communities; limited teaching styles; materials and approaches which fail to accommodate mother tongues; strategies which do not recognise that for many children schooling is not a continuous but a fragmented process; resources inequities (particularly between rural and urban communities); and the unwillingness of teachers to be stationed in remote areas. In many countries, these problems are compounded by the spread of HIV/AIDS which is having a profound impact on education and generating social upheaval.

UNDERSTANDING THE REFORM AGENDA

Embarking on education reform, and creating and sustaining significant levels of improvement are not one and the same thing. How policy-makers try to implement reform is critical to its success. Content matters, as well as the pace of change. Although approaches to reform differ between countries and also change within countries over time, reforms are culturally and context specific, shaped by ideology and history and dependent on political, structural, individual as well as social dynamics (Murphy and Adams, 1998).

Nevertheless, most reform initiatives contain many of the same ingredients (for example, curriculum or teacher education reform). To a greater or lesser degree, most acknowledge the global and technological imperatives of the twenty-first century. However, governments or states embarking on reform differ in the levers which they select to kick start, or steer the reform process, as well as the reform imperatives—the drivers used to promote reform.

Looking across developed and developing contexts, governments have used a range of 'levers'. These include:

- the introduction of standardised testing (e.g. USA);
- the development of external audit and inspection procedures and the introduction of accountability mechanisms (e.g. UK);
- the expansion of large-scale teacher development programmes (e.g. Uganda);
- the involvement of parents and communities (e.g. Columbia, Escuela Nueva); and
- the creation of school-based school improvement projects (e.g. Guinea).

These approaches are not mutually exclusive and mature education systems are likely to include all or most of these elements. However, there are likely to be distinctive differences in emphasis, in starting points and in anticipated outcomes. An understanding of what these differences are enables those involved in reform, at whatever level, to reflect on the progress of their own country and to examine options for the future.

> **Reflection 1**
>
> Consider your education system, what have been some of the levers that have been used there?

The framework provided in Figure 7.1 offers one way of reviewing the approach adopted by a country, assessing its impact and reflecting on future options.[1] The framework can be applied to an education system as a whole, to a reform initiative within a larger system, or to an individual institution or school. It has five component parts, each

---

[1]   This framework was developed by Kathryn Riley, initially as a contribution to the Macro de Aprendizagem Continua (MAC); an education network in Brazil and Uruguay.

1. **The system drivers**—The reform imperatives which motivate reform:
   - What are the major pressures for change within the system?
   - What are the social, ideological and political forces which create the climate and imperatives for reform of the system and its overall direction?
2. **The levers for change**—The mechanisms selected to kick start, or steer the reform process:
   - What are the specific mechanisms chosen to implement the changes, taking into account its economic and cultural context?

These tend to include the following:
   - Capacity building
   - Curriculum
   - Assessment
   - Evaluation (external and self-evaluation)
   - Accountability and standards agenda
   - Funding mechanisms
   - Innovations in teaching and learning and in raising achievement.

3. **The partnerships for change:**
   - Who are the major stakeholders?
   - In what ways have they been brought into the change process?

4. **The achievements:**
   - What has been achieved so far during the current cycle of reform?
   - What evidence is there to support this?

5. **The challenges:**
   - What are the current challenges?
   - What are the future ones?

Figure 7.1 Levers for change and reform: a framework for analysis and review

of which includes a number of questions. These five parts are:

- the system drivers;
- the levers for change;
- the partnerships for change;
- the achievements; and
- the challenges.

An analysis of the challenges could include a thorough diagnosis of the problems within the education system such as:

- What are the patterns of performance? What do they reveal?
- What are the obstacles that are making schools ineffective?

- What are the main barriers to learning that are getting in the way of pupils' achievements?

- What is known about school and teacher effectiveness? (Adapted from Saunders, 2000.)

Any review would also need to take into account how to develop capacity within the system and how to involve teachers in the change process.

In the next section of the chapter we explore three contrasting examples of reform initiatives designed to involve teachers in changing their thinking and practice, and apply the framework to each. The examples are a locality-based initiative in England; an expanding programme in the Former Yugoslavia Republic of Macedonia (FYRoM); and a national initiative in Pakistan.

CHANGING TEACHERS' THINKING AND PRACTICE

Cultural beliefs and aspirations combine to influence perceptions about knowledge and learning, and about the role of the teacher. The three examples presented in this section

---

Case Example 1 England—Woolwich Reach and Plumstead Pathfinder Action Zones (WRaPP)

In 1999 the United Kingdom Government introduced Education Action Zones: an initiative designed to raise standards. EAZs were to involve large groups of schools under the direction of a Partnership Forum (which included business partners, councillors, local authority officers and schools). At the same time, the Government also introduced the idea of Small Education Action Zones (EAZs), each comprising a secondary school and a number of primary schools. These zones were non-statutory and their remit was to identify the needs of the schools in the zone and to create projects and programmes that would address those needs in innovative ways.

The Woolwich Reach and Plumstead Pathfinder Action Zones (WRaPP) sprang up under this umbrella. WRaPP, which is in the London Borough of Greenwich, was set up to work with 18 schools in two small EAZs (2 nurseries, 1 infant, 1 junior, 12 primary and 2 secondary—one girls and one boys). A local headteacher, Jill Jordan, was appointed as the Project Director and the analysis presented in this chapter about WRaPP has been developed in close partnership with her.

The schools involved in WRaPP face many challenges, including significant numbers of children whose families experience complex and multiple difficulties. At the beginning of the Project, many staff were demoralised and tired and the schools typically experienced a range of staffing problems including: high turnover, large numbers of agency staff and overseas teachers on short-term placements, inexperienced teachers in middle-management roles and poor agency cover for supply teachers.

Given these staffing issues, the introduction of an effective staff development strategy was identified as being a key element in the WRaPP strategy (Riley and Jordan, 2002). The goal was to create a professional learning community through which schools could share a common set of goals and develop a vision of what constitutes a healthy, functioning school. WRaPP took to heart the evidence (from a number of countries and contexts) that both pupils and teachers thrive in communities which support their learning, and that teachers can be enthused to change their thinking and practice by a change process which inspires them to be creative (Riley 2001; Riley and Jordan, 2002). As is illustrated in Figure 7.2, WRaPP was set up to operate at three interrelated levels, through:

- targeted funding aimed at supporting schools in carrying out core tasks (e.g. improving attendance); and developing new learning opportunities for pupils (e.g. provision of out of school hours activities);

- a development strategy aimed at influencing teachers' thinking and practice (through working intensively with 'lead learners' who were to act as catalysts for change);

- a change strategy for school leaders which developed their personal, 'intrapersonal' and professional skills, building and enhancing their capacity to develop an environment that was conducive to professional learning.

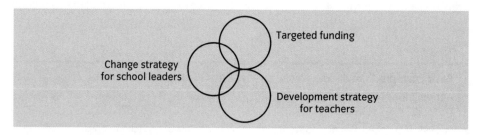

Figure 7.2 The WRaPP approach

are from contrasting education systems. Despite their distinctive contexts, there are common elements that transcend all three.

An evaluation of the impact of WRaPP concluded that the professional development opportunities on offer in WRaPP had had a strong appeal to teachers who felt frustrated and 'bogged down' by paper work, national tests and the day-to-day pressures of the job (Riley et al, 2002). Senior staff who had been on WRaPP's 'change leaders' programme spoke about it as a refreshing and invigorating opportunity which had enabled them to approach their leadership and management tasks in a new light. Teachers designated as 'lead learners' typically commented on their professional development in the following terms:

> I was a real cynic but now I'm a convert. I can see how my own behaviour can get in the way for some children. It's also given me the confidence to think about literacy and numeracy in new and creative ways. My thinking has really taken off and I'm hungry for more.

The course was amazing. It helped me to see myself as a learner and to understand the different ways in which children learn . . . . It has also given me the confidence to work with another year group.

The WRaPP evaluation included a number of classroom observations and the evaluation team reported many examples of materials and activities designed to engage pupils in the learning process, as well as teaching strategies which recognise the auditory, kinaesthetic and visual aspects of learning. Secondary school students engaged enthusiastically in science-based problem-solving activities commented:

[Our teacher is] not just doing this lesson for you. We usually do experiments like this (the senses) . . .

I like coming to science, it makes you think.

Primary students told the evaluation team:

I really like to learn . . .

I love the brain box . . .

I learn best when I can talk about things with my friends.

The first broad observation from the evaluation was that WRaPP was likely to achieve long-term gains as it:

- generated a climate of trust;
- focused its activities on changing teachers' ideas and practices;
- provided opportunities and time for collaboration and networking; and
- created a feedback mechanisms linked to evaluation and review (Riley et al, 2002).

The second observation was that changing teachers' practices within the classroom is the hardest reform goal to achieve, but the one which ultimately will have the biggest impact on pupil learning (Elmore, 1995; Louis et al, 1999; Tyack and Cuban, 1995). Evidence from the evaluation suggests that WRaPP has had a significant impact on the views and practices of those teachers most closely involved in it, and on the learning environment of the pupils with whom they work, although not all of the 18 schools had embraced the initiative with the same levels of enthusiasm.

A further observation needs to be added. The bottom-up process to reform and change which characterised the initiative's approach has been somewhat at variance with national approaches to reform and change in the UK which have been more centrally directed, requiring uniform responses to improvement. Typically, these have given practitioners limited opportunities to engage with the reform agenda, or to develop

Reflection 2

What kinds of professional development opportunities appear most likely to enthuse and inspire teachers?

Case Example 2 Interactive Learning Project—The Former Yugoslavia Republic of Macedonia

The Former Yugoslavia Republic of Macedonia (FYRoM) became an independent Republic in 1991, inheriting a traditional top-down educational system from the Federal Republic. As a new country, it faced a range of difficulties associated with transition economies which have led to a dramatic reduction in economic activity. Unemployment remains high, particularly amongst young people—44 per cent of under 30s are unemployed. Improvements in education have been impeded by a range of factors, including an over-detailed curriculum for primary and secondary schools which is heavily weighted on factual knowledge and provides few opportunities for the development of critical-thinking skills; and teacher training and teaching methods that were over reliant on rote learning (OECD, 2001).

The Interactive Learning Project (ILP) was first introduced in the early 1990s by UNICEF in a pilot scheme in four schools. The project was a response to the broad educational challenges facing Macedonia and sought to introduce more child-centred approaches in schools. By 1999, the ILP (which is supported by the Bureau of Educational Development, part of the Ministry of Education and Science) had grown to a network of 75 schools and by 2003, it was beginning to make inroads in schools across Macedonia.

The Interactive Learning Project set out to change the typical learning environment of schools in Macedonia, in ways that would encourage children to be active problem-solvers, rather than passive learners. It was supported by an extensive professional development programme which provided opportunities for teachers to work together on a regular basis; share their thinking and planning; and learn how to develop children's thinking skills and gear their classroom teaching to meet children's individual needs. Teacher mentors were appointed to support teachers' development and school pedagogues were also encouraged to play an important role.

---

their own responses to the education challenges they face, creating frustration amongst many teachers and contributing to a teacher recruitment crisis (Riley and Jordan, 2002).

Evidence from a substantial evaluation of the project leaves no doubt about its success in terms of teachers' enthusiasm. Most teachers who completed an extensive questionnaire believed that the ILP had helped them to improve their professional skills, at least to some extent, and they were working hard to realise the project's aims (Riley et al, 2003). More than 4 out of 5 of the teachers consulted thought that the project had made a difference to the ways they taught and students learnt. Typical comments from teachers were:

Children are free to express opinions and ask questions.

The pupils can integrate knowledge across subjects.

They are given skills which they can use in everyday life.

The learning environment uses all their senses.

The children are made to feel important and become a resource for ideas and input.

Box 7.1: School 'A'—Classroom Observation

Grade: 7 Physics (taught by the Director)
Topic: Velocity and weight
Grouping Strategy: Tables of 3–5
Physical Environment: Lots of pupils' work on the walls and projects out on tables. Basic equipment and OHP. Textbook adapted by IAL team. Work on display showed use of experiments, graphs and diagrams. Pupils had been on range of excursions, including the zoo to learn about animals and the conditions they live in.
Classroom Climate: Pupils were very engaged in group work, helping each other by explaining work. Activities characterised by energy and enthusiasm. Responding to questions from text books on large piece of paper and responding to prompts by the teacher.
Communication and Questioning: Open questioning by the teacher—e.g. 'What did this remind you of?' Teacher initiated friendly competition between groups. Checking previous knowledge. Asking questions of groups and class and moving from group to group. Setting a demonstration.
Pupils: Very positive about group working. 'The person who has more knowledge and better grades will help others.' Pupils elect a team leader who assigns tasks to group. 'We elected him because he was the best!'

Extract from field notes (see Riley et al, 2003)

The classroom observations carried out as part of the evaluation found evidence to support these assertions and to indicate that the project had changed classroom practices and relationships, and widened learning opportunities for pupils. Pupils, as their teachers, were enthusiastic about the ILP and welcomed the new opportunities to work together in groups and to collaborate with their peers. Box 7.1 gives one example of 34 classroom observations carried out as part of the evaluation.

The evaluation also found that teachers who had been engaged in the ILP the longest were often the most positive about the project, and also the most likely to implement key classroom strategies. The longer teachers had participated in the project, the more likely they were to say that the ILP had made a real difference to student learning and teacher effectiveness. Confidence clearly increased in relation to the length of time teachers were involved in the project.

Inevitably, there are tensions and problems in a project of this scale and the evaluation observed, for example, that some teachers had an inflated view of what they and the school had achieved and that teachers in urban areas had felt much more engaged than their rural counterparts. There were practical issues too about the change process. A heavy reliance on the workshop approach had contributed to a view that the only way

---

Reflection 3

What experience have you had of teachers changing their classroom practices? How was this achieved?

Case Example 3 Pakistan—The Aga Khan University Institute for Educational Development (AKU-IED)—The 'Professional Development Teachers' Initiative

The goals of the educational reform agenda in Pakistan can be traced to its founding in 1947. At the First Educational Conference in November 1947, the leader of the Pakistan Movement, Muhammad Ali Jinnah, urged the nation to take a critical look at the aims of education:

'If we are to make real, speedy and substantial progress we must earnestly . . . bring our educational policy and programme on the lines suited to the genius of our people, consonant with our history and culture and having regards to the modern conditions and extensive developments that have taken place all over the world. . . . There is immediate and urgent need for giving scientific and technical education to our people, in order to build up our future economic life and to see that our people take to science, commerce, trade and particularly, well-planned industries. We should not forget that we have to compete with the world which is moving very fast in this direction. At the same time, we have to build up the character of our future generation. We should try, by sound education, to instil into them the highest sense of honour, integrity, responsibility and selfless service to the nation. We have to see that they are fully qualified and equipped to play their part in the various branches of national life in a manner which will do honour to Pakistan' (quoted in Curle, 1966, pp. 49–50).

Jinnah recognised that Pakistan—a developing, Muslim country which had inherited an infrastructure from Britain—had to fashion its own educational system. Inevitably, there were many challenges, some of which remain over half a century later. For example:

- In 1947, the majority of the population (80 per cent) did not have access to modern sector schools. Today, there is a great demand for primary schooling which has not been met by the public sector.
- Literacy rates were very low. The present literacy rate in Pakistan is approximately 30–40 per cent.
- There were inequities in access to education between males and females, urban and rural dwellers. Today, only four per cent of rural girls remain in education after the age of 12 and less than one per cent at aged 14.

Added to this desperate scenario is the contemporary reality that the education sector has received consistently low priority in Pakistan's national budget. Indeed, the social sector as a whole, including health, education, and rural development, receives less than five per cent of GDP, compared to Defence and the Military, which together receive in excess of 50 per cent. A third of Pakistan's GDP is devoted to re-servicing the national debt.

In recent years, there has been a rapid proliferation of private schools catering to all income levels. Across the country, a variety of bodies have established schools: market-oriented business, religious organisations, community groups and philanthropists. This expansion has happened for a number of reasons, including the difficulty of making improvements on a significant scale in the public sector; limited financial resources; and the creation of a parallel educational system through the 'madrassahs' (education establishments which have played an important role in the promotion of religious and formal education since the earliest period of Islam). The madrassahs have not been co-opted into the modernising process, remaining separated from new fields of knowledge and contemporary approaches to learning. Given this scenario, the process and practice of educational reform in Pakistan has been difficult.

to transmit knowledge was through workshops and given the pressure on resources, the cascade model of knowledge had become over-stretched.

However, these caveats do not diminish the major successes of the project. The ILP has had a significant impact on teachers' thinking and practice, and created a common set of terms for teachers to discuss, share and frame their own professional practices.

Analysing the impact of innovations in the late 1980s and early 1990s, Warwick and Reimer (1995) focused on the following:

(1) The Teaching Kit—a box with some 100 instructional aids;

(2) Mosque schools—designed to increase primary-school enrolment at low cost;

(3) The building of female residences—to resolve shortage of adequate housing in rural areas;

(4) The development of the Nai Roshni (New Light) Programme—drop-in school centres for students who had never attended school, or who had dropped out; and

(5) Learning coordinators—the development of a cadre of people to provide professional support to school teachers.

Warwick and Reimer analysed the factors which had contributed to the relative success or failure of each of the innovations, concluding that designers of innovation needed to focus not only on the innovation itself, but also on the field conditions needed for successful implementation. On the basis of their analysis of the five projects, the authors offered seven lessons for educational change in Pakistan which are also applicable to other developing contexts:

Lesson 1: The concept of the innovation must be clear

An innovation can only work if the organisation and individuals responsible for carrying it out share the same understanding of what the project aims to achieve.

Lesson 2: The innovation must be integrated into the larger organisation of which it is a part

Lesson 3: Innovations must be compatible with the prevailing culture

Lesson 4: An innovation must build user understanding and motivation

Those who are to be responsible for achieving success must understand the purpose of the innovation, the content of the programme, and its methods of operation.

Lesson 5: Politics has a mixed impact on innovations

Politics is a mixed blessing for innovations. When the political will favours an innovation, its chances of success increase. However, if the political intervention is perceived to be for dubious motives, then the innovation is seen as corrupt. Properly applied, however, politics can give public legitimacy to an innovation, help raise the money for implementation, and encourage field staff to carry it out.

Lesson 6: Effective implementation requires sensitivity to pivotal field conditions

Innovations need to be sensitive to local circumstances and culture. The female residence scheme failed, for example, because conditions dictated by the culture were not met, such as a high perimeter wall to detract onlookers. Similarly, the learning coordinators project faced resentment when staff were given higher allowances than colleagues in more senior positions.

Lesson 7: There are no teacher proof innovations

Attempts covertly to entice, spur, or press teachers to change their practice through technical devices are unlikely to succeed. For example, the Teaching Kit purportedly provided teachers with resources but its core aim was to entice teachers towards activity-based learning—an aim neither known nor understood by teachers.

More recent innovations in Pakistan have attempted to learn from these early lessons; develop public-private partnerships; and encourage practical school-based improvement approaches. One example of such an approach has been the development of an initiative designed to bring teacher education and professional development together in ways that will have an impact on classroom practice.

In 1993, the Government of Pakistan in partnership with the United Nations Development Programme (UNDP) supported the establishment of the first private sector teacher education institution in Pakistan: the Aga Khan University Institute for Educational Development (AKU-IED) based in Karachi in the south of Pakistan and the Ali Institute of Education based in Lahore in the north. The AKU-IED set out to train 'Professional Development Teachers' (PDTs) who would become:

- exemplary pedagogues;
- skilled teacher educators with insight into actual classroom conditions; and
- inspired change agents.

This initiative, which included schools in the government and private sectors, was based on participation in a two-year field-based M.Ed. programme (Bacchus, 1996). At the outset in 1993, the AKU-IED worked with 22 schools (private and government) in Karachi. By 2000 it had trained in excess of 140 Professional Development Teachers in the M.Ed. programme and over 2,000 in the Visiting Teacher (INSET) programmes.

The programme had a strong conceptual framework designed to enable participants to become 'change agents' in the school improvement process. The 'Professional Development Teachers' were to be encouraged to reconceptualise their own teaching practices and beliefs; develop more effective classroom approaches; and reflect critically on their own learning and the conditions facing their peers, from the perspective of pupils' learning needs and development (Greenland, 2002).

A longitudinal research and documentation study (Khamis, 1997; 2000) concluded that the AKU-IED approach had been effective in the majority of the participating schools, both government and private. This was as the result of an overall approach which attempted to reduce the barriers between teacher educators and school practitioners and

Key steps to success

Step one—Develop teacher collaboration
Structure planning to enable teachers to work together;
Reward teacher collaboration and highlight the ways in which professionalism and peer review can benefit children's learning;
Develop a culture of collegiality which encourages teachers to learn new things rather than rely on external 'experts'.

Step two—Concentrate on improvement at the classroom level
Introduce new strategies (subject-specific; classroom procedures and teaching strategies which are not imposed);
Develop mentoring relationships;
Conduct demonstration lessons;
Offer workshops based on the identification of teachers' professional development needs; and
Create a conducive informal learning environment for all teachers by encouraging informal discussions in the staff room, stronger personal relationships and shared outside school activities

(Khamis, 1997; 2000).

Figure 7.3 School improvement and teacher development

to focus on the centrality of the role of the teacher in the classroom. The PDTs were the vehicle for achieving this.

Within schools, the PDTs were seen as 'changed persons' who took on greater responsibility and who demonstrated that teacher education, as a first step, could lead to school improvement—when supported by other measures. One such measure was ensuring that school principals were aware of the ideas and practices advocated in the teacher education programme. This allowed them to understand and facilitate the work of teachers involved in in-service programmes. Equally important were the provision of in-service professional

Reflection 4

What can be done to encourage teacher collaboration?

support to teachers through teachers' associations; peer mentoring; and opportunities for teachers to gain accreditation as teacher educators and to participate in a research culture which disseminated teachers' research findings to a wide audience.

Classroom observations undertaken as part of the review of the programme indicate that pedagogical practice improved. Figure 7.3 provides information about how this was achieved.

Table 7.1 Levers for Change and Reform: A Framework for Analysis and Review Applied

	England—Woolwich Reach and Plumstead Pathfinder Action Zones (WRaPP)	Interactive Learning Project The Former Yugoslavia Republic of Macedonia (FYRoM)	Pakistan—The Aga Khan Institute for Educational Development: The 'Professional Development Teachers' Initiative
The system drivers **The reform imperatives which motivate reform**	*National context:* • All children to achieve, at least, targets set at key stages of schooling • Widening participation in learning, in post school education (Life Long Learning) • Some increases in expenditure *Local WRaPP context:* • High levels of socio-economic disadvantage • Demotivated teachers • Need to create new learning opportunities for children	• A traditional top-down educational system from the Federal Republic • An over-detailed curriculum for primary and secondary • A range of difficulties associated with transition economies • Diminishing resources • High unemployment, particularly amongst young people • View that more child-centred approaches need to be introduced in schools • Involvement of international and bilateral agencies	• Outdated and inappropriate curriculum, teacher training, pedagogy and examination system • Low spending on education • Growth of private sector shools as a result of disenchantment or lack of public school provision • Lack of tertiary research-based institutions of standing or quality to impact on educational policy or practice • Policy changes and involvement of international and bilateral agencies

The levers for change	**Major national lever: Accountability and Standards agenda** • National curriculum and programmes of study • National tests (7, 11, 14), public exams (16, 18) • Evaluation of teaching and institutions through inspection and public reporting • National strategy for literacy and numeracy • Promotion of a range of new initiatives e.g. Education Action Zones *Major levers: WRaPP* • Focus on capacity building by encouraging teacher creativity and professional development and supporting school leadership • Encouragement of innovations in teaching and learning • Setting framework of self-evaluation, collaboration and networking	• Use of extensive training programme to introduce new teaching methods and encourage teachers to improve the learning environment • Use of problem-solving approaches and the introduction of investigative procedures • Development of an approach which focuses on the needs of individual pupils and aims to increase their motivation • Development and strengthening of teacher and school director networks	• Improving the status, professionalism, and education of teachers in order to initiate and sustain fundamental educational change • Focusing on classroom processes: teaching, learning, assessment and peer review • Reconceptualising teaching-learning by linking them to notions of impact, quality and relevance, based on child development and particiapation
Partnership for change	*WRaPP:* • Strong locally based partnership with teachers, headteachers, pupils • Newly emerging partnership with parents • Partnerships with Higher Education to support teachers as researchers	• New partnerships with schools and municipalities • Attempts to bring parents into the partnership	• School-University partnership • Bridging theory and practice to create a field-based teacher development programme • International collaboration to develop an in-country post-graduate qualification for school teachers

Table 7.1 (Continued)

	England—Woolwich Reach and Plumstead Pathfinder Action Zones (WRaPP)	The Former Yugoslavia Republic of Macedonia (FYRoM)—Interactive Learning Project	Pakistan—The Aga Khan Institute for Educational Development: The 'Professional Development Teachers' Initiative
Achievements	• Established professional development programme and linked networks • Development of school leadership • Enthusiasm for change has raised morale and improved teacher recruitment • Major changes in teachers' attitudes and practices which are having an impact in classrooms • Development of teachers as researchers • Access for teachers to a new Masters Programme in Teaching • Creation of an enthusiastic core of change agents('lead learners', 'change leaders')	• Much enthusiasm for the changes from teachers and little cynicism • Strong indications of changes in classroom environments and in teaching and learning activities • Overwhelming enthusiasm from pupils about the changes in classroom practice • The development of a cadre of 'Trainers of Trainers' who support dissemination of training on a larger scale in a cost-effective manner • Project likely to become a national initiative for all schools	• Training programmes for all cadres of school personnel developed and taught by local faculty • Faculty development and training (many to doctoral level) • Subject-based in-service programmes leading to post-graduate diploma • Certificate in management programmes for headteachers and aspiring heads • Involvement in school and teacher education curriculum development • Creation of local research capacity • Establishment of teacher associations • Replication of 'professional development centres' by private sector and collaboration with public sector to upgrade the work of the Institutes of Teacher Education
The challenges: Current and future	• Maintaining momentum • Maintaining learning, given relatively high teacher turnover in inner-city schools • Including all teachers and schools • Widening knowledge about the Project to other schools in the locality • Maintaining strengths of national and local initiatives	• Developing strategies which focus on the school as the unit of change (which support the current focus on individual teachers) by, for example, introducing a framework for School Development Planning • Developing capacity building for greater depth and reach for Bureau Advisers, School Leadership Teams, Pedagogues, Mentors and Teachers • Tackling system-wide issues such as: limited training for school leaders; lack of systems to measure teacher quality or to introduce school-based management	• Retaining qualified and trained teachers in the school-system • An examination system that does not facilitate pedagogical innovation • Reaching out to remote, rural and ultra-poor communities • Maintaining a focus on the needs of female educators, including training women for leadership roles • Maintaining a focus on the importance and priority of research in response to local needs • Building an indigenous knowledge and culture to make education both effective and relevant

LESSONS FROM THE THREE CASE STUDIES

Using the framework to map the analysis

In Table 7.1 we have summarized the key elements of each of the three case studies in the chapter against the framework, Levers for Change and Reform: A Framework for Analysis. This mapping illustrates how the framework can be used as a tool for review and reflection and as a way of highlighting both differences and similarities across contexts.

Lessons learned

What do these three illustrations tell us about educational reform and change and school improvement? In looking at Table 7.1 there are clearly differences in relation to context and levels of resources. Nevertheless, a number of common issues emerge:

- *Levers for change:* there is a strong common focus on capacity building, networks and collaboration.
- *Partnerships:* the successes have been achieved through strong and mutually supportive partnerships.
- *Achievements:* the achievements commonly include the development of a cadre of enthusiastic 'change agents' who are personally motivated by the goals of the reform, but who also enjoy collaborating with their peers. What appears to motivate all of them is the focus on the gains for pupils, not just those for teachers.
- *The challenges:* while the contexts for the challenges differ significantly, not least in terms of levels of resources and political and economic pressures, there are also common issues about how to maintain momentum and enthusiasm. Schools are constantly shifting and changing which means that there are always new groups to bring in, and new ideas to develop based on the experience of those groups.

On a broader level, we conclude that each of the three initiatives described in this chapter has been successful in changing teachers' thinking and practices. While the specific details and the day-to-day elements of the change process differ, the core issues about teaching and about learning remain the same. These are to do with changing teachers' perceptions about the many and varied ways in which students learn; encouraging them to see themselves as learners; and enabling them to recognise the ways in which their own behaviour has an impact on the learning environment.

A cross-national study of change and improvement in England and Singapore reinforces this observation. While the authors found no one recipe for improving schools, they did find that successful efforts to achieve improvement in very different contexts had a number of common elements: motivating staff; focusing improvements on teaching and learning; enhancing the physical environment; and changing the culture of the school. On the basis of their findings, they offered three key messages to policy-makers which can be applied to many contexts:

- improvement techniques must fit with the grain of the society, rather than go against it: indiscriminate borrowing from other cultures may not achieve the desired results;
- in themselves, resources do not guarantee improvement—but they help convince staff, parents and students that their society believes in the school and is prepared to invest in it; and
- change has to be carried out by the school itself (Mortimore et al, 2000, p.143).

As has already been argued in this chapter, substantive change in what teachers actually do in the classroom has been one of the most elusive goals of school reform. The first stage in achieving that goal is to change teachers' beliefs. Both the English WRaPP project and the Former Yugoslavia Republic of Macedonia's Interactive Learning Project have undoubtedly changed teachers' beliefs about what is possible and enhanced their confidence in their own ability to improve the classroom learning environment. Pakistan's Aga Khan University's Institute for Educational Development, Professional Development Teachers' Initiative has served to create new expectations about what can be achieved in schools and set a framework for mutually beneficial partnerships between schools and higher education.

We would like to conclude this chapter with some final reflections. The three illustrations reflect some of the ongoing debates in the school improvement and school effectiveness research community, especially relating to the cultural dimension of improvement and reform strategies (see Chapter 7 and Gray and Wilcox, 1995; Slee et al, 1998; Mortimore, 1998; Sammons, 1999; and Teddlie and Reynolds, 2000). There are some obvious lessons which are not new to those who are involved in looking at education reform and change. These include the following:

- reforms initiatives need to be grounded in the day-to-day realities of their cultural context;
- initiatives take time to embed, particularly when they are based on public/private partnerships;
- coercion doesn't work but clear partnerships and shared goals do.

However, the more fundamental message from this chapter is that the business of education change and improvement is a slow and messy one. Teachers and schools embrace changes in different ways, at different speeds and with varying levels of commitment. The reform 'trick', if there is one, is to understand what it is that will catch teachers' imagination: What that key element is may be culturally specific.

Case study 1 In the English WRaPP example, in a national context which is relatively prescriptive, teachers' imagination was fired by opportunities to experience learning in new and different ways, and to transform that knowledge and understanding to their classroom practice. The school improvement process generated professional growth and encouraged risk taking, openness and collaboration.

Case Study 2 The FYRoM's Interactive Learning Project operates in a climate of economic uncertainty and diminishing resources. What has caught teachers' imagination is a way of transforming relations in the classroom: creating a more open and discursive environment which fits with the fledgling country's aspirations for democracy. The ILP has built on the strong pedagogical legacy and traditions of earlier years—rather than eroding these—and provided teachers with new avenues and approaches more readily open to their peers in Europe and North America.

Case Study 3   Our final illustration, 'Professional Development Teachers' in Pakistan was built on a recognition of the limitations of public investment in education in Pakistan and the need to develop new public/private partnerships. Creating a bridge between teacher educators and school teachers opened new avenues to each; helped develop capacity within the system; and inspired a cadre of change agents.

So much of all of that we have had to say in this chapter is about trust, mutual respect and learning. But it is also about recognising the ways in which our schools will need to change to meet the needs of our children and young people—the citizens of tomorrow.

SUMMARY

This chapter has reviewed how reforms that are initiated at system level can successfully transform learning in classrooms.

Three contrasting examples of reform have been explored and analysed using a framework of Levers for Change and Reform. The conclusions indicate that improvement initiatives must be tailored to the culture of the society, that initiatives take time to work and that teachers must be partners in the initiative.

ACKNOWLEDGEMENTS

We would like to thank all the teachers and other educators in Greenwich, London; the Former Yugoslavia Republic of Macedonia; and Pakistan who have contributed to our understanding of the issues discussed in the chapter. Particular thanks to Jill Jordan, Greenwich Initiatives and Elena Misik and her Unicef team in the FYRoM.

ENDNOTES

The WRaPP and the FYRoM evaluations were both carried out by a team led by Kathryn Riley. The FYRoM evaluation included a questionnaire distributed to over 1000 staff in 93 schools (translated into Macedonian and Albanian), with a response rate of 63 per cent; school-based discussions with 77 teachers in 11 project schools throughout the country; classroom observations of 34 lessons in those 11 project schools; and discussions with key personnel involved in supporting the project.

The research in Pakistan was based on in nine schools and involved some 45 teachers, 18 of whom had been trained through the AKU-IED programme.

RECOMMENDED FURTHER READING

Further examples of improvement projects in developing countries can be found in Anderson, S. (ed.), (2002): *Improving Schools through Teacher Development: Case studies of the Aga Khan Foundation Projects in East Africa*, Lisse: Swets and Zeitlinger.

Mortimore, P., Gopinathan, S., Leo, E., Myers, K., Sharpe, L., Stoll, L. and Mortimore, J. (2000) *The Culture of Change: Case Studies of Improving Schools in Singapore and London*, London: Institute of Education, Bedford Papers gives a comparative dimension to the management of change.

For management of change you might like to read Morrison, K. (1998) *Management Theories for Educational Change*, London: Paul Chapman, and Riley, K.A. (2000) 'Leadership, learning and systemic reform', *Journal of Educational Change*, 1(1), 29–55, Netherlands: Kluwer Academic Publishers.

OTHER USEFUL READINGS

Harber, C. and Davies, L. (1997) *School Management and Effectiveness in Developing Countries: The Post-Bureaucratic School*, London: Cassell.

White, J. and Barber, M. (eds), (1997) *Perspectives on School Effectiveness and School Improvement*, London: University of London, Institute of Education.

8

Educational Effectiveness

Pam Sammons, Anil Khamis and Marianne Coleman

INTRODUCTION AND LEARNING OUTCOMES

This chapter focuses on the effectiveness of educational institutions, particularly schools, in achieving their core purpose; the education of students. It will consider what is meant by the term 'effectiveness' in relation to education in the Western and in the developing world. In using these terms we are following Harber and Davies (1997, p.4) whose use of the term 'developing countries' relates to countries where there are stringent economic and political problems and who use 'Western' as shorthand for the industrialised countries of the world, rather than meaning a geographical area. The chapter then goes on to focus on the importance of the concept of 'value added' in relation to institutional effectiveness and the need to consider effectiveness at different levels, i.e. the institution as a whole, the department within the school or college, and the individual classroom. In addition, the criticisms of educational or school effectiveness will be reviewed, particularly in relation to the application of the concept cross-culturally.

By the end of this chapter you should be able to:

- engage with the meaning of the term 'effectiveness' in the context of education;
- comment on the importance of 'value added' in educational effectiveness;
- give examples of the fact that effectiveness research is multi-level: whole school, department and classroom, and that the three levels are inter-related;
- note cultural differences in the understanding of effectiveness;
- evaluate the applicability of effectiveness research to the developing world;
- know which of the major criticisms of school effectiveness research is most relevant to your context.

WHAT DO WE MEAN BY EFFECTIVENESS?

Although the concept of effectiveness in educational research can be applied to all educational institutions, it is usually linked with schools. The research on effectiveness has shown that:

> schools matter, that schools do have major effects upon children's development and that, to put it simply, schools do make a difference. (Reynolds and Creemers, 1990, p.1)

This focus is clearer if you consider the origins of school effectiveness research which arose in reaction to the publication of influential studies during the 1960s and 1970s (Coleman et al, 1966; Jencks et al, 1972) which claimed that the particular school attended by a student had little influence on their educational outcomes in comparison with factors such as IQ, 'race' and socio-economic status (SES). The emphasis was on structural inequalities rather than on the influence of schools. The first major studies of school effectiveness in the UK were those of Rutter et al (1979) and Mortimore et al (1988). Studies undertaken in a variety of contexts, on different age groups, and in different countries (the United States, Netherlands, Norway, Hong Kong, Taiwan, Singapore, Canada, Australia and New Zealand), have confirmed the existence of significant differences between schools in students' achievements even where their intakes were broadly similar.

A focus on effectiveness in schools, is sometimes criticised as being narrow (Slee et al, 1998; Thrupp, 1999). Although we are all aware that 'schools do make a difference' the concentration on institutions may be at the expense of considering the wider issues of the failures of social policy to address the injustices of socio-economic status, class, gender and ethnicity. A further criticism of effectiveness studies is that by concentrating on the difference that schools can make we may unintentionally give fuel to governments in the UK and elsewhere who have established a managerialist agenda of numerical targets for schools and teachers, thereby undermining some aspects of the professionalism of teachers (see Chapter 11). The importance of the wider social and economic context cannot be denied, but improving the effectiveness of educational institutions remains a focus for those who lead and manage in education.

This section is headed 'what do we mean by effectiveness?' and the answer to that question will vary according to what is considered to be the prime purpose of education. However, school effectiveness research does seek to increase our understanding of school and classroom processes and the way in which these can influence students' educational outcomes. This research therefore provides empirical evidence that can assist in the evaluation of classroom practice and educational policy. At its best it empowers teachers and leaders and managers in schools by increasing their understanding of the ways in which school and classroom organisation and teaching behaviour can influence both attainment and progress towards social and affective outcomes desired and valued by society. However, despite the widening of the concept, school effectiveness has been criticised as concentrating too much on narrow measures and on means/ends relationships neglecting processes and values. While some studies have only focused on outcomes the most influential have studied school and classroom processes in depth (for example, *15000 Hours* and the *School Matters* research involved in depth classroom observations over several years).

Reflection 1

What do you mean by an effective school? Is effectiveness just to do with academic outcomes or does it encompass other indicators? If so, what are they?

The normal measurement of effectiveness is usually to do with better than expected academic outcomes, but, particularly in developing countries, effective schools may be seen primarily as those that are preparing the citizens of the future. Harber and Davies (1997, p.4) point out that outcomes of schooling should be 'fit for purpose'. In effect very little literature related to developing countries has centred on student outcomes (Davies and Iqbal, 1997; Warwick et al, 1991; Qaisrani, 1990). The most prominent reason given for this is the lack of resources in such countries to undertake such research (Heyneman, 1984).

Our first task in school effectiveness research and thinking is the obvious one: that we should identify the most desired outcomes of a schooling programme and devise precisely matching evaluative measures. There is no point in stating that the aim of a school is to produce concerned citizens, but then measuring the school only on academic achievement, hoping somehow that significant clues about organisation policy will emerge which might be relevant to democracy or citizenship. Conversely, there is little point in thinking up an outcome measure and then engaging in statistical international research to compare schools and countries on its achievement. If schools are not geared into this measure, then the way they organise will have different meanings. One might identify, for example, 'education of parents' as an important measure, but a school educating parents about the importance of academic achievement for their children will be different from a school educating parents for their own literacy, and different again from a school educating parents about HIV/AIDS.

Remember that what you are considering is an 'effective' school, not a 'good' school. The concept of what is a 'good' school is highly problematic and does relate specifically to values in education. Rather than attempting to define 'good' and by implication 'bad' schools, effectiveness research focuses on a narrower concept of effectiveness which concerns the achievement of educational goals using specific measures of progress or outcomes. It is argued that effectiveness is a necessary but not a sufficient condition for a 'good' school (Sammons, 1999).

WHAT IS EFFECTIVENESS RESEARCH?

School effectiveness research attempts to disentangle the links between what the student brings to the school and the educational experiences that the student has at the school and to see how the two strands influence the student's attainment, progress and development.

The student brings to the school innate abilities; prior attainments; personal and family attributes.

At school, the student meets the impact of educational policy, the ethos, management and leadership of the school and a variety of classroom experiences.

The research will therefore seek to find out how and by how much the different aspects of schooling will impact on the potential the student brings to the school, with the aim of making the school more effective.

The main areas that are investigated in school effectiveness research are related to academic achievement, but latterly have also been concerned with social and affective outcomes such as attendance, attitudes, behaviour and self-esteem. For example, Gray, a leading writer in the school effectiveness field (1995, p.27), considers that school quality can be assessed by three basic performance indicators, two of which can only be measured through qualitative research involving the interviewing of pupils.

1. Academic progress—quantitative
   What proportion of pupils have made above average levels of progress over the relevant time-period?
2. Pupil satisfaction—qualitative
   What proportion of pupils in the school are satisfied with the education they are receiving?
3. Pupil-teacher relationships—qualitative
   What proportion of pupils in the school have a good or 'vital' relationship with one or more teachers?

Nevertheless, the key features of effectiveness methodology are that it:

- is mainly quantitative, although case studies may also be used;
- values reliability and replicability;
- seeks to make generalisations.

   But it also:

- works in partnership with practitioners;
- values views and perceptions of teachers, students and parents.

The fact that it is mainly quantitative has contributed to the criticisms of effectiveness research as it can be seen as over-deterministic, ignoring much that is important about the process of schooling. However, the main strength of school effectiveness research is that it recognises and works with the concept of 'value added' taking into account the important variable of the differences in the intake of schools. It therefore actually provides a powerful critique of the publication of league tables, or tables of school performance based on exam results (Sammons et al, 1997).

Value added

The key definition of an effective school is that it is one in which students progress further than might be expected from consideration of its intake. An effective school is therefore one which 'adds value' to its students' academic achievements and/or social and effective outcomes in comparison with schools serving similar intakes. The concept of value added by the school is key to the separation of the two strands mentioned earlier: what the student brings to the school and what the school contributes to the student. In measuring the value that the school has added it is therefore important that factors such as gender, socio-economic status, mobility and fluency in the majority language at school are all taken into account when progress is measured. In the following case example, taken from the Improving School Effectiveness Project (Macbeath and Mortimore, 2001), the results of students are analysed in a way that takes account of prior attainment, age, gender and other variables, so that it is possible to see which schools can be classified as 'outliers'—those which lie well outside what might be expected as 'normal'. The outliers may be schools which are particularly effective, or particularly ineffective.

Case Example 1 Value added in Scottish Schools

School effectiveness research can only distinguish between schools where students' progress (or other outcomes) is significantly better or poorer than predicted on the basis of their prior attainment and characteristics. Using confidence limits based on the number of students included in the analysis, it is possible to calculate whether differences between actual results and those predicted on the basis of prior attainment and intake factors are statistically significant ($p < 0.05$). Studies suggest that the proportion of schools identified as significant *outliers* (extremes in terms of effectiveness or ineffectiveness) can vary between 15 and 33 per cent. Table 8.1 shows results from the Improving School Effectiveness Project conducted in Scotland (Macbeath and Mortimore, 2001). This shows findings for 36 secondary schools and is based on a value added analysis of Standard Grade results. The results provide measures of progress over two school years (from age 14 to 16 years) taking account of prior attainment in English and mathematics and background (including age, gender, SES). Schools are divided into three groups:

- Positive Outlier,
- As Expected, and
- Negative Outlier.

The three outcome measures are: English, mathematics and an overall performance (7 best Standard Grades). More schools were identified as outliers (students' progress significantly better or worse than expected given their prior attainment and background) for mathematics.

While patterns in overall examination results may be fairly stable from one year to another, subject results can vary more from year to year. It is therefore important to monitor outcomes over several years (three is the minimum to identify trends) to establish whether schools or departments are improving, declining or fairly stable in terms of effectiveness. Only a small minority of schools are likely to be identified as significant outliers over several years.

Table 8.1 Example of value added feedback from *Improving School Effectiveness Project*: Secondary Schools' Standard Grade Results

Value added effectiveness category	Standard Grade Mathematics		Standard Grade English		Best 7 Standard Grade results	
	n	%	n	%	n	%
Positive outlier[*]	8	22.2	5	13.9	7	19.4
As expected	20	55.6	24	66.7	23	63.9
Negative outlier[*]	8	22.2	7	19.4	6	16.7

Number of secondary schools = 36, [*] $p < 0.05$

In this case you can see that what the pupil brings to the school (e.g. gender, SES and past achievement) are taken into account, so that the differences in outcomes are likely to be a result of differences in the schools. In this case, you cannot see any differences at levels within the school, but those schools which are generally achieving better or worse than might be expected are identifiable and, as a result, information can be fed back to them to help them either improve or sustain their achievement. The study does point to the existence of departmental (subject) differences between English and mathematics, and some schools had significantly better results in one area than another.

The size of effects

On average, reviews of studies in developed countries such as Australia, Netherlands, UK, USA show that schools account for around ten per cent of the achievement differences between students after controlling for initial differences. This is still larger than the impact of individual pupil characteristics such as gender or free school meals on attainment. However, with regard to developing countries, Harber and Davies (1997, p.37) point out that the effects of educational processes on student achievement are larger, sometimes indicating a variance of up to 28 per cent resulting from the differential effectiveness of individual schools, whilst Scheerens (2001) quotes the figure of 30 per cent.

A systematic review of effectiveness research (Scheerens and Bosker, 1997) showed that schools in the UK, USA and the Netherlands seem to matter more (i.e. have a greater effect) for the underprivileged and low achieving students. They report that:

- school effects for black students were almost twice as large as for white students in the USA;
- differences between public and private schools were almost twice as large for low SES (socio-economic status) students as for middle class ones, and the differences between schools for high SES students were small in the USA;
- school effects vary for students by 'race' and low prior attainment in England. School effects were larger for initially low attaining and for black Caribbean students;
- primary school effects vary for students with low, compared with high, initial attainment in England, being larger for low initial attainers;
- Dutch primary schools are highly stable in effectiveness across grades for low SES students, but less stable in effectiveness across grades for high SES students;
- secondary school effects are larger for low SES and initial low attaining students. There is some evidence of differential effects by 'race' and gender.

Further consideration of school effectiveness studies across cultures (Reynolds et al, 2002) reveals the complex interplay between the factors that relate to school effectiveness and cultural strengths. Before considering the relationship of effectiveness studies to culture any further, you need to know about the key factors associated with school effectiveness through research.

THE PROCESSES ASSOCIATED WITH SCHOOL EFFECTIVENESS

One of the main outcomes of research into school effectiveness has been the identification of processes and characteristics of schools seen to be effective. The lists that have been extracted tend to have a great deal in common. One of the most recent is that of Teddlie and Reynolds (2000) in the *International Handbook of School Effectiveness Research* (see Table 8.2).

Most of the lists that have been extracted from research are quite similar, across time and across cultures focusing on whole school issues like leadership, culture, professional development and relationships with parents, and more classroom-based issues relating to effective teaching and learning and high expectations of students.

The lists tend to be drawn mainly from Western cultures, but a list of characteristics which is a little different and which relates to schools in less developed countries as well as to those in the West has been identified by Davies (1997) who selected the factors that she considers are 'specifically controllable by management' (p.29):

1. a combination of firm leadership and decision-making processes where teachers feel their views are represented;
2. ample use of rewards, praise and appreciation for both students and staff;
3. opportunity for students to take responsibility in the running of the school;

Table 8.2 The processes of effective schools

1. The processes of effective leadership	Being firm and purposeful Involving others in the process Exhibiting instructional leadership Frequent personal monitoring Selecting and replacing staff
2. The processes of effective teaching	Unity of purpose Consistency of practice Collegiality and collaboration
3. Developing and maintaining a pervasive focus on learning	Focusing on academics Maximising school learning time
4. Producing a positive school culture	Creating a shared vision Creating an orderly environment Emphasizing positive reinforcement
5. Creating high and appropriate expectations for all	For students For staff
6. Emphasizing responsibilities and rights	Responsibilities Rights
7. Monitoring progress at all levels	At the school level At the classroom level
8. Developing staff skills at the school site	Site based Integrated with ongoing professional development
9. Involving parents in productive and appropriate ways	Buffering negative influences Encouraging productive interactions with parents

(Source: Teddlie and Reynolds, 2003)

4. low rates of punishment;

5. care of the school environment, buildings and working conditions;

6. clear goals (possibly written) and incorporation (not coercion) of students and parents into acceptance of these goals;

7. high expectations and feedback;

8. teachers as good role models (time-keeping, willingness to deal with pupil problems, lesson preparation and maximum communication with the pupils);

9. clearly delegated duties to teachers and students;

10. consistent record-keeping and monitoring (not necessarily testing);

11. vigorous selection and replacement of staff;

12. maverick orientation, ingenuity in acquiring resources and risk-taking by heads;

13. heads 'buffering' schools from negative external influences;

14. convincing teachers they *do* make a difference to children's lives;

15. good external relations to aid financial and moral support for the school;

16. avoidance of nepotism and favouritism.

(Davies, 1997, pp.29–30)

Reflection 2

Look at the two lists and compare them. Which factors are different?

Although the two lists have much in common, there are some items in the second list that relate to specific cultural values such as item 16 mentioning nepotism. However, school leaders in developing countries have to deal with poorer levels of resources and greater problems related to the recruitment, retention and attendance of students and teachers than will their colleagues in Western countries. The following cases give examples of these and other factors.

Case Example 2 Pakistan

Whilst the last three decades have witnessed dramatic increases in student enrolment as well as training opportunities for teachers throughout the developing world, the majority of children in Pakistan still do not start school despite primary school enrolment having risen by 350 per cent between 1955 and 1988. The benefits of the dramatic increase in school enrolment have been mitigated by two countervailing tendencies. The population growth has outstripped the increased educational provision, and public expenditure on education as a percentage of the total budget declined steadily from the mid-1960s.

The situation in Pakistan is particularly dire with only about half of the students who enter school leaving with a primary certificate and less than half of all children able to access education in the first instance. Gender is an important variable in academic performance with girls less likely to access education than boys. According to UNICEF figures in 1994, the Gross Enrolment Ratio of boys was 54 against 30 for girls.

In Pakistan where teachers often receive lower incomes than unskilled labourers, some 50 per cent of those teaching at the primary level have a poor education (school leaving certificate is Class X or 'O' level equivalent) followed by one year of teacher training. The other 50 per cent may not even have a primary school leaving certificate and little or no formal professional training (Qaisrani, 1990).

Many factors (*Verspoor*, 1990) are seen to contribute to the poor and declining quality of education in developing countries:

- reduction in the availability of instructional material;
- absence of appropriate textbooks;
- overcrowding in schools;
- limited 'time-on-task' spent by teachers and students on genuine educational activities;
- rigid examination systems;
- incessant poverty which affects the nutritional and general health status of children;
- the distance many children reside from their schools.

Case Example 3 South Africa

Harber and Muthukrishna (2000) report on curriculum reform in South Africa which has established 'essential' outcomes, including those valuing 'democracy, peace and racial equality' (p.426). Research is being carried out for the Centre for Education Policy and Development in South Africa to monitor the implementation of the reform. The research reports on a series of indicators of whether the school is operating effectively. First, they check whether the school has electricity, a telephone, tapped water supply and a nutrition or feeding scheme and then comment on the following:

- learners are actively involved in school governance;
- all staff are represented and involved in governance;
- school governance is promoting democracy within the school and beyond;
- the school is free from violence and conflict;
- conflict and violence among and between staff and learners has been reduced;
- learners and teachers feel safe within the school and its environs;
- the school is not open to acts of vandalism, theft and other crimes;
- school admission policies are non-discriminatory and non-exclusionary;
- there are programmes to address issues of equity, discrimination and racism;
- the school is involved in community development programmes;
- structures and procedures within the school are democratic;
- authoritarian practices have been reduced.

(Centre for Education Policy Development, 1998, quoted in Harber and Muthukrishna, 2000, p.427.)

The issues in Pakistan and in South Africa relating to effective schools indicate some very basic needs for effectiveness including access to schools for all children, particularly girls; the numbers of teachers; the level of teacher training and resources like water, feeding schemes and possession of a telephone. Harber and Muthukrishna (2000) report that in the South African province of KwaZulu-Natal, two-thirds of schools do not have a telephone, and less than one half have electricity.

In both Pakistan and South Africa, effectiveness is seen as less concerned with academic outcomes per se and more concerned with access to education and then establishing conditions that promote better learning. In the case of South Africa, the goals for the schools are articulated in terms of governance, democracy and equity. In Pakistan, educational quality is seen to depend on competent teachers and better teacher training facilities.

The goals for schools and educational systems may vary, but the expectation is that schools will provide good learning environments that will enable the potential of their students to be fulfilled. However, as was seen in the Scottish case study above, with negative 'outlier' schools, that is not necessarily the case. Some schools are significantly ineffective in enabling the learning of their students. Hofman et al (2001) state that in 'the Netherlands, a student from a highly ineffective school would need an additional period of two years to attain the same achievement certificate at the end of secondary school as an equally talented student from a highly effective school . . . Thus, even small school effects can have substantial implications for students' school career' (p.131).

KEY ISSUES RELATED TO INEFFECTIVENESS

Research on ineffective schools seems to indicate the importance of *leadership*. It also shows that ineffective schools are not the opposite of effective schools. Three aspects of ineffective schools have been identified by Stoll and Fink (1996), amalgamating the findings of four studies (Rosenholtz, 1989; Mortimore et al, 1988; Teddlie and Stringfield, 1993; and Reynolds, 1996):

- lack of vision where teachers have little attachment 'to anything or anybody' (*Rosenholtz*, 1989);
- unfocused leadership; and
- dysfunctional staff relationships.

In addition, there is a range of ineffective classroom practices, including:

- inconsistent approaches to teaching;
- lack of challenge;
- low levels of teacher-pupil interaction;
- high classroom noise levels;
- frequent use of criticism and negative feedback.

(Stoll and Fink, 1996, pp.34–35)

Effective schools on the other hand appear to have a supportive culture and an ethos which supports effectiveness in the individual classroom. It would appear that effectiveness in schools operates at three levels at least, the whole school, the department and the classroom.

MULTI-LEVEL EFFECTIVENESS

It was mentioned above that differences in effectiveness of schools may include a school effect of about ten per cent in the Western countries, and up to 30 per cent in developing countries. Although the more sophisticated effectiveness research does use a multi-level approach, it remains difficult to disentangle the impact of whole school, department and classroom. Gray (1998) has also indicated the need to consider the single student. Most research relates to the three areas of: whole school, department and classroom, with the individual pupil nested within classrooms or schools.

Within the whole school effect, the role of leadership and management comes to the fore and the question of the extent to which effective leadership affects student outcomes may be the key one in the whole area of educational management and leadership (see also Chapter 12). As you consider the level of the effectiveness of the whole school, focus now on how leadership influences educational effectiveness.

1. Whole school

At the whole school level, the impact of leadership and culture on effectiveness is stressed in the research on effective schools. There is likely to be a relationship between the style and type of leadership and whole school culture or ethos. A review of the literature on effectiveness and leadership by Hallinger and Heck (1999) supports the relationship between leadership and effective schools, but points out that this effect is likely to be *indirect* as the school leaders are affecting the culture of the school as a whole and specifically the processes in the classrooms which are the ones that directly impact on students:

> the findings reinforce the notion that leadership makes a difference in school effectiveness, they do not support the image of the heroic school leader. School leaders do not *make* effective schools. Rather the image we draw from this review is that of leaders who are able to work with and through the staff to shape a school culture that is focused yet adaptable (p.185).

A study in the UK of the way in which leadership can enhance effectiveness in a multi-ethnic context (*Blair*, 2002), showed the need for a particular style of leadership where the headteacher was transformational and collegial in involving the staff, but also firm and strong in terms of implementing their vision of a multi-racial school in order to ensure good outcomes for all pupils regardless of ethnicity:

> Strong might not necessarily imply a dictatorial or authoritarian approach, but the strength to hold on to 'the vision' and the courage to examine and implement this vision in practice, sometimes in the face of strong resistance or hostility (Blair, p.186).

In this case the apparent effectiveness of some schools actually masked the fact that a group of students from an ethnic minority were not achieving at the level of the school as a whole, and the way to improve this was to work mainly on raising teacher expectations. The picture of school effectiveness outcomes is not always clear:

> a good deal more of the variation in pupils' performance lies within schools than between them; most schools have pupils who are doing well with respect to national norms as well as pupils who are doing badly (Gray, 1998, p.6).

2. Departmental level

There can be much more difference between subject areas in a school in terms of effectiveness than there is between schools. Sammons et al (1997) have shown that in the UK the differences between departments can be an important explanation for the differences in effectiveness of schools. This study examined the roles of the headteacher and head of department.

A study of effective departments in secondary schools (Harris et al, 1995) identified the main features of their success as including many of the features identified with effective schools: a collegial management style; a strong vision; good organisation; good monitoring; clear structure to lessons; a strong focus on the pupils; and on teaching and learning.

Hofman et al (2001) in a large-scale study of secondary schools in the Netherlands identified schools which had both effective school leadership and effective departmental leadership as being particularly cohesive and coordinated. When tested, taking into account student level and school level variables, like primary school recommendation and socio-economic status, the schools with this cohesive leadership and management showed significantly better results in mathematics.

3. Classroom level

The whole school effects and the departmental effects also have to be balanced against effective teaching and learning at the level of the classroom, an area that has not been researched fully in developing countries (Scheerens, 2001). However, the *International School Effectiveness Research Project* (ISERP), in studies ranging across North America, the Pacific Rim and Europe found that:

> At the classroom level, the powerful elements of expectation, management, clarity and instructional quality transcend culture (Reynolds et al, 2002, p.279).

The authors felt able to claim that the basics of teacher effectiveness, such as their classroom management and high expectations, can be regarded as 'universals' in their impact on effectiveness.

In Pakistan and in other developing countries issues relating to classroom management and teaching style may be particularly relevant to effectiveness. Traditional patterns and instructional methods dominate teaching in Pakistan where the main practice is for the teacher to speak most of the time followed by oral recitation by students. In Nepal, Pfau (1980) found that science teachers in Class 5 were spending three-quarters of their time lecturing, whilst in Botswana 54 per cent of the teachers' time was devoted to lecturing and 43 per cent to oral recitation by the students (Fuller, 1991). Allsop (AKU, 1991) notes the following:

> The pedagogy was identical . . . [with] a predominance of teacher assertion, aided by reference to the textbook or by use of the blackboard. Questions originated by the

teacher and usually used as a simple reiteration of what she/he had just said. Chorus answers were frequently accepted and encouraged. . . . My overall impression [of what was happening in the classrooms] was one of inertia, of schools where there were very few incentives to change timeworn practices.

The contrasts between the conditions for education experienced in Western societies and in developing countries indicate the difficulties in applying effectiveness findings across cultures. However, school effectiveness research has attracted criticism when applied to Western as well as to developing countries.

CRITICISMS OF SCHOOL EFFECTIVENESS RESEARCH

Some of the main themes addressed in criticisms of school effectiveness research have already been referred to in the introduction and elsewhere. They centre round three areas:

1. the political/philosophical; in that the concept of school effectiveness is seen to support conservative and market forces ideology and managerialism and to marginalise equity issues;

2. methodological; as it is a predominantly quantitative approach it focuses on outcomes rather than processes;

3. theoretical; the input-process-output model on which it is based implies causality and is inappropriately technicist. Also the findings tell us nothing new that is not common sense.

1. The first of these criticisms may be particularly relevant to developing countries, as the focus on the school being effective can take the political pressure off the government and the focus on the levels of poverty and state funding that the school receives. Instead, the causes of and remedies for ineffectiveness are seen to lie in the school as an institution. In a review of school effectiveness in developing countries, Scheerens (2001) doubts whether all countries really do strive for the maximization of educational achievement for all students. There are stresses at system, school and classroom level to keep the status quo and 'there are enormous interests in preserving the notions of differential ability which is the code for permanent failure for some' (Harber and Davies, 1997, p.169). Such criticisms do indicate the difficulties of assuming that Western concepts of school effectiveness as an ideal can be applied everywhere.

In the West, and in the UK in particular, school effectiveness research has been seen to support new managerialist ideas of target setting and accountability. It has been identified with 'taxonomies, checklists, performance indicators, league tables and target setting exercises' at the expense of values (Morley and Rassool, 2000, p.174). However, as Teddlie and Reynolds (2001) point out, in the UK, school effectiveness researchers have been strong critics of market policies and have countered the 'raw' league table approach with the concept of value added, which has been welcomed by many practitioners.

There is also criticism that school effectiveness research for example ignores the effect of social class and overstates the importance of schools. However, school effectiveness studies generally do include the effect of socio-economic status (SES), and the research generally tries to take into account background as a factor. In addition some studies have specifically focused on the impact of SES context, most notably the 10-year Louisiana school effectiveness research by Teddlie and Stringfield (1993).

2. An example of the methodological criticism of focusing on outcomes rather than processes is the difficulty that Harbison and Hanushek (1992) found in identifying a quantitative factor that differentiated a good teacher from a less good teacher in their large study in Brazil. Whilst they agreed that good teachers made a difference, they could not find a suitable indicator of what made a good teacher. It did not tally with qualifications or years of experience. They were left with the conclusion that' the choice of quantitative differences between teachers such as their years of formal education ignores other far more important aspects of their "art" ' (Harber and Davies, 1997, p.36).

Methodologically, effectiveness has been criticised for blurring correlation and causation. Ouston (1999) who was involved in the original research of Rutter et al (1979) gives what she terms a 'trivial example' to illustrate this. The effective schools studied from which the original list of features of effective schools was drawn, were pleasant places that were clean and well cared for with house-plants in the classrooms. She poses the question: 'If the less effective schools were cleaned and given plants for the rooms, would they become more effective schools?' The business of disentangling causes from effects and correlations from causes is a difficult one.

3. In relation to the criticism that effectiveness research relies too heavily on the input-output model, a further illustration in relation to developing countries may again be useful. Harber and Davies (1997) point out that the cultural context is most important in looking for links. For example, class size may be important in the West when it relates to class sizes of 30 or 15, but have less impact on teaching and pupil outcomes in classes that vary between 60 and 75.

In relation to the accusation that school effectiveness research tells us nothing that is not common sense, Sammons (1994, p.46) responds that 'Because school effectiveness research by its very nature sets out to identify the components of good practice . . . it is inevitable that some of its findings are unsurprising to practitioners'. However, she also argues that the crucial difference is that such research indicates those measures of process (policy or practice at school or class level) that are significantly related to better student outcomes, as opposed to ones which might be regarded as important but for which little empirical evidence is found. For example, teachers' age and experience are often held to be important variables but few studies find these are related to greater effectiveness, whereas features of teacher practice (nature of interactions with students, organisation, use of homework, etc.) are more important in accounting for differences in student outcomes.

Despite its critics, there are a number of strong arguments to be made for the contribution of school effectiveness research. It has:

- moderated the over-deterministic sociological theories about home and background;
- qualified an over-reliance on psychological, individualistic theories of learning;
- focused attention on the potential of institutional influences;

- provided, as a result, a more optimistic view of teaching and renewed attention to learning concerns as well as school management;
- advanced the methodology of the study of complex social effects;
- stimulated many experiments in school improvement;
- contributed to a growing set of theoretical ideas about how pupils learn in particular school settings (*Mortimore*, 1995).

It has had a strong equity emphasis in promoting effective schools for the disadvantaged.

Reflection 3

Review the criticisms and counter-criticisms of school effectiveness research. Which seem most relevant to you?

There have been particular problems in the UK in that effectiveness research has been identified with league tables, inspection and target setting. It should be noted, however, that school effectiveness research actually provides a powerful critique of raw league tables and decontextualised comparisons of schools. Case studies of more and of less effective schools have also provided a stimulus to the development of school improvement initiatives at both local and national level, and can provide valuable information for policy-makers and practitioners concerned to raise standards and promote better educational outcomes for disadvantaged students in particular. There are problems in applying the 'raw' concept of effectiveness to developing countries where the concerns may be more about establishing basic access to schools and books, or developing a more democratic culture. However, the measurement of outcomes can relate to more than narrow quantitative measures and there are many ways in which effectiveness research does move us forward in terms of improving the school experience for students. The methodology has been successfully used to study a range of affective and social and behavioural outcomes. Even where there is a narrow focus on academic outcomes, by raising the issue of 'value added', effectiveness research actually counters the simplistic notions implicit in league tables.

SUMMARY

In this chapter we have considered the meaning(s) of the word 'effectiveness' in relation to schools and education; the nature of effectiveness research, particularly the importance of the concept of value added; the likely size of the effects and the different processes associated with school effectiveness. Case studies from Pakistan and South Africa illustrated the difficulties of applying Western concepts of effectiveness cross-culturally. The potential for different levels of study: whole school, department and classroom was outlined and, finally, we looked at the criticisms and counter-criticisms of school effectiveness research.

RECOMMENDED FURTHER READING

For a particular insight into the links between leadership effectiveness read:

Hallinger, P. and Heck, R. (1999) 'Can leadership enhance school effectiveness?' in Bush, T., Bell, L., Bolam, R., Glatter, R. and Ribbins, P. (eds) *Redefining Educational Management: Policy, Practice and Research*, London: Paul Chapman.

MacGilchrist, B., Myers, K. and Reed, J. (2004) *The Intelligent School* (2nd edn.), London: Paul Chapman, particularly Chapter 1, gives an overview of effectiveness and improvement.

Sammons, P. (1999) *School Effectiveness: coming of age in the 21st century*, Lisse: Swets and Zeitlinger, particularly Chapter 8, 'Key Characteristics of Effective Schools' gives a good summary of the field.

Slee, R. and Weiner, G. with Tomlinson, S. (eds) (1998) *School Effectiveness for Whom? Challenges to the School Effectiveness and School Improvement Movements*, London: Falmer Press, present a critical view.

9

Evaluation in Education

Marianne Coleman

INTRODUCTION AND LEARNING OUTCOMES

Evaluation in education has a vital role to play both in relation to improvement and effectiveness, the subjects of the last two chapters, and as a general tool of management planning and development. In this chapter we will be considering what is meant by evaluation, what tools might be used for evaluation and the importance and relevance of underlying values. In addition, we will look at the implications of internal versus external evaluation and the links with improvement and accountability and the likely outcomes of each.

By the end of this chapter you should be able to:

- define evaluation and the ways in which it is used in educational leadership and management;
- relate evaluation to improvement and effectiveness;
- reflect as an education leader or manager on the importance of evaluation in education;
- show how internal and external evaluation relate to improvement and accountability.

WHAT DO WE MEAN BY EVALUATION?

Evaluation is a process which involves looking back systematically at what has been accomplished and measuring the present position against the original aims. It usually involves some sort of judgement on success in meeting aims and/or feedback which can be used for improvement. Review is the action following the evaluation which usually involves making a decision about whether we wish to continue with an activity, reject it, or modify it in the light of it being evaluated. However, in everyday use evaluation and review are often used as alternative terms. For details on evaluation of professional development, see Chapter 13.

Sometimes the term 'evaluation' is used interchangeably with the term 'assessment'. However, we would tend to use the word 'assessment' in relation to the work of students and to use 'evaluation' to refer to an activity that is related to management and is an integral part of planning and decision-making. Evaluation is a vital part of planning to assess how a plan has been implemented and to point to the next cycle of planning.

Another word that is associated with evaluation is 'monitoring'. We take this to mean checking on an activity whilst it is going on. So monitoring could be complementary to evaluation and provide data for the evaluation leading to the review.

Evaluation is often undertaken to check on the success of an innovation, or at the end of an activity or at a recognised end point before a new 'round' of activity takes place, for example at the end of a school year, term or semester or the end of a project intended for school improvement.

This chapter on evaluation follows those on effectiveness and improvement for a good reason. Efforts to increase effectiveness and to improve a school, college or school system have to be evaluated if they are to be meaningful because evaluation ensures that progress towards an aim or target can be measured or estimated. In this context, externally imposed evaluation can be seen as a tool of new public management or managerialism where is it associated with the imposition of targets and inspection on schools. However, as a purely internal measure undertaken in a spirit of professional collaboration, evaluation is associated with development and improvement. The following comment sums up the importance of evaluation in this respect:

> That is why self-evaluation matters. Because if schools themselves don't know how good they are and whether or not they are getting better or worse they will be pretty helpless and then it is easy to blame all sorts of conditions—bad students, inadequate parents, poor resources, lack of funding from the government. But with the knowledge of where their strengths and weaknesses lie, and with the tools to evaluate themselves, even the worst schools can improve (MacBeath, 2000, p.70).

Evaluation as a management tool can serve a number of purposes. According to MacBeath (1999) in education, the purposes of evaluation may be:

- for organisational development as in development planning;
- to improve teaching;
- to improve learning;
- political;
- for accountability;
- for professional development.

Thus it can be seen that whilst evaluation as a concept may be neutral, in practice it can be used in many different ways.

Some examples of where evaluation could be applied in education are:

1. at the end of a course or workshop run by a consultant and intended for the professional development of teachers;
2. after the introduction of a new curriculum development for students;
3. to estimate the quality of the teaching of a particular course to undergraduates in a university;
4. the usefulness of parents' evenings in a school;
5. the efficient use of sports facilities in a community college;
6. external inspection with summative outcomes.

These examples include most of the purposes identified by MacBeath (1999) above, i.e. evaluation for professional development, improving learning and teaching, and to aid organisational development. Example 5 might also relate to accountability as it could involve decisions about who takes responsibility for the sports facilities. This example might also illustrate a political purpose if there were disputes about who had prior use of the facilities. Example 6 is mainly about accountability and could also be seen to have a political purpose . The Ofsted system of inspection in England and Wales is regarded as an important aspect of Government policy in relation to what is generally considered a New Public Management agenda (see the example at the end of this chapter).

You will see further examples of micro-political purpose in evaluation a little later. Thinking about the first five of the examples raises a number of issues and questions about internally motivated evaluation including the *focus* of the evaluation and the *intentions or motivation* that lie behind it.

1. The course for the teachers will have been intended to inform them, and/or change their practice in some way—the evaluation will check on that, but will the only check be at the end of the course, or will a further evaluation be carried out in six months' time to see whether the course is having a long-term effect on their practice in the classroom? The longer-term effect is the one that matters, but longer-term evaluation is often neglected.

2. The new curriculum development will be intended to achieve certain learning outcomes for the students—the evaluation will check on this, but will the evaluators ask the students only, or check the teachers' perceptions or both? Much will depend on how student-centred the school is.

3. At the end of a semester, students may be asked to evaluate the teaching of a course, but what is the motivation for the evaluation and what is the intended outcome? Are motivation and outcomes related to the idea of improving future teaching or are they related to accountability on the part of the lecturer to do a good job for the student, 'the customer'? Does the use of the same evaluation instrument time and time again mean that it is de-valued and not taken seriously by the students?

4. An evaluation of parents' evenings may focus on how to improve them, but for whom? The parents, the staff, the students or all three? What will happen to the outcomes of the evaluation? To whom will they be reported? Will they be looked at once

and then filed away, or will the evaluation lead to recommendations for change that are then implemented?

5. The use of a gymnasium in a community college may be related to costs and benefits; who is benefiting and who is paying? There may be some difficult political issues raised about who has the responsibility for payment of upkeep. There are a number of stakeholders involved, students, staff, parents, governors and other community members. How are priorities decided?

Reflection 1

In these apparently simple examples, there are a number of quite difficult issues raised for managers and leaders. If you were the manager in charge of undertaking any or all of these evaluations how would you set about planning the evaluation?

Some of the basic questions that would face a manager involved in conducting an internal evaluation would be:

- When should the evaluation take place to be most meaningful?
- Who should do it?
- What methods should they use?
- What exactly is the evaluation meant to achieve?
- Who 'owns' the outcomes of the evaluation?
- What happens to the outcomes? Will they be public or kept private?

Case Example 1 Evaluation of School Improvement Programmes carried out by the Aga Khan Foundation in East Africa

In the brief case example that follows the bulleted questions above have been included, where they are appropriate, in square brackets.

Independent evaluations of projects were commissioned at the end of one or more phases of project funding, for example at the end of initial three- to five-year cycles of project implementation. [When should the evaluation take place?] The questions to be asked were 'guided by the terms of reference of the evaluation contracts. The evaluation sponsors have been open and receptive to the evaluation findings, including those that are critical of the projects. The Foundation has publicly disseminated the evaluation reports in their entirety. [Who 'owns' the outcomes and what happens to the outcomes?]

The Foundation has insisted that evaluations of all its school improvement projects be designed and conducted by evaluation teams that include host-country as well as international education researcher-consultants. [Who should do it?] This has helped ensure that the evaluations are sensitive to local education contexts in their design, in their interpretation of findings and in the recommendations arising from those findings.

Data gathering in each study typically included a two- or three-week period of on-site interviews with project stakeholders (teachers, headteachers, parents project personnel, etc.) observation of classroom practices and project activities and review of past project evaluations . . . [How should they do it?]

The evaluators were asked to include not only their evaluation findings and judgements, but also to highlight key recommendations. [What happens to the outcomes?]

(From Anderson, S. (ed.), 2002, pp.8–9)

These questions raise potentially sensitive and political issues. In the next two sections you will be looking first at the practicalities of carrying out an evaluation and then at some of the ways in which evaluation may be political (in the institutional as well as the national sense) and value driven.

THE TOOLS OF EVALUATION

Evaluation is a process and is a type of applied research:

Applied research in general is seen as being concerned with defining real world problems, or exploring alternative approaches, policies or programmes that might be implemented in order to seek solutions to such problems. Evaluation is primarily concerned with describing and finding the effects of a particular approach, policy or programme (Robson, 1993, p.171).

The fact that evaluation is being equated with research does not mean that it can only be done by professional researchers. Evaluation is at the heart of management activity and can inform all types of decisions. It is therefore often done by or for managers.

On a practical level all the tools that researchers might use for data collection are available to evaluators. The most common tool is probably some type of questionnaire, but for some evaluation purposes interviews or observation or other tools may be more appropriate. In advising on the choice of research methods for evaluation, Robson (1993) stresses the importance of the evaluator's sensitivity in choosing the appropriate research strategy:

A thorough knowledge of the programme being evaluated is an essential precursor to your selection and subsequent sensitive use of the methods. What is advocated is an open-minded exploration of the most suitable strategy and best methods for the task in hand. Rigour and systematic data collection are important. But what is particularly important is the usefulness of the data for the purposes of the evaluation, and not the method by which it is obtained (Robson, 1993, pp.185–186).

Similarly, Patton (1987) refers to the need for the evaluator to work with the stakeholders:

The evaluator works with stakeholders to design an evaluation that includes any and all data that will help shed light on important evaluation questions, given constraints of resources and time (Patton, 1987, p.21).

So it is important to match the methods to the circumstances of the evaluation. In a discussion of school self-evaluation, MacBeath et al (2000) categorise most evaluation methods as 'asking'. This can be done orally by interviews or in written form as a questionnaire. 'Asking' also includes asking people to complete a 'log' or diary of activity or getting people to undertake a force field analysis, analysing and discussing the factors that inhibit or facilitate a change. Observation, including the shadowing of an individual, can also be a tool of evaluation.

Reflection 2

As you read this section of the chapter, think about an evaluation which you could undertake within your own area of responsibility and consider which of the methods outlined here you might use.

In addition to these methods, it may be useful to evaluate your performance against existing data about other institutions. For example, the latest information on national pupil achievement will help to contextualise the achievement in the school, and international data such as the OECD Programme for International Student Assessment (PISA) published in 2002 gives an idea of how the schools of one country are achieving in relation to those of other countries. However, it is unwise to make simplistic assumptions on the basis of such comparisons because of the differences in the way that data are collected and interpreted in different places (Goldstein, 2001). It is possible to misrepresent the work of teachers and students through misplaced cross-national comparisons where like is not compared with like.

EVALUATION AND VALUES

Evaluation is not value-free, and may be carried out for a number of reasons, many of which have political and ethical aspects. It was stated earlier that evaluation may take place for political reasons:

> Contrary to common belief, evaluation is not the ultimate arbiter, delivered from our objectivity and accepted as the final judgement. Evaluation is always derived from biased origins. When someone wants to defend something or to attack something, he [sic] often evaluates it. Evaluation is a motivated behaviour. Likewise, the way in which the results of an evaluation are accepted depends on whether they help or hinder the person receiving them. Evaluation is an integral part of the political processes of our society (House, 1973, cited in MacBeath, 1999, p.5).

Robson (1993) drawing on the work of Patton (1981) and Suchman (1967) points out that evaluations may lack integrity. He quotes the following humorous examples:

'quick and dirty evaluation'—as fast as possible at the lowest cost,

'weighty evaluation'—a thick report,

'guesstimate evaluation'—what we think is happening without collecting proper data,

'eyewash'—emphasis on surface appearances,

'whitewash'—attempts to cover up programme limitations or failures,

'submarine'—the political use of evaluation to destroy a programme,

'posture'—the ritualistic use of evaluation without any intention to use it,

'postponement'—using the evaluation to postpone or avoid action.

You have probably experienced some or all of these in your working life and, although the terms used here are deliberately humorous they do indicate that ideally evaluations should be carried out rigorously and with integrity. They also indicate that the outcomes of an evaluation should be read critically and treated with some caution. Who has decided to carry out the evaluation? What are their values?

In the following case example it is clear that a differing underlying stance towards learning on the part of the teacher evaluators leads to different choices about the actual questions being asked and, as a result, very different information and responses will be produced. Both sets of questions are evaluating the same course.

Case Example 2 'Hidden assumptions about teaching and learning'

One of the most common forms of evaluation undertaken in higher education is the end of module or semester rating by students of the teaching on a course. Kolitch and Dean (1999) have shown how a particular view of 'good teaching' is implicit in the typical instrument used in most US universities, even though teachers may operate in different ways.

They identify two modes of teaching:

1. the knowledge transmission model (the traditional model)
2. the engaged-critical model (learner centred)

The typical evaluation form used in the American system is the Student Evaluation of Instruction (SEI). In this evaluation form, an example of which follows, the items seem typical of the traditional transmission model and the evaluators are operating within the confines of this model. The students are asked to rate the course on the following issues which focus on the *teacher*:

Organisation of Curriculum

- Made the objectives of the course clear
- Achieved the stated objectives of the course outline
- Adjusted his/her teaching to reflect the students' level of comprehension

Instructor's Teaching Behaviours

- Was well prepared for class
- Made effective use of examples and/or illustrations
- Was confident and competent with the subject matter
- Raised challenging and interesting questions/problems
- Stimulated students' interest in the subject matter
- Showed enthusiasm both for teaching and for the subject matter

Evaluation of Student Learning

- Clearly informed students how they would be evaluated
- Gave examinations that were appropriately related to the course material
- Gave helpful, instructive feedback (beyond a grade) on graded materials
- Returned students' work/examinations within a reasonable time frame
- Gave assignments that were appropriately related to the course

Relationships

- Treated students with fairness and concern
- Was actively helpful and concerned about students' progress
- Was easy to approach for help outside the class
- Was available for meeting with students during office hours

Overall Rating

- Overall was an effective teacher

Kolitch and Dean (1999, p.39) offer an alternative set of survey items that could capture the spirit of the engaged-critical paradigm of teaching and which relate much more to the *learner*. Here the students are asked to evaluate the extent to which:

1. the instructor encouraged students to express their own ideas;

2. students were invited to co-create the curriculum;

3. the instructor promoted classroom dialogue;

4. the curriculum reflected the identities of diverse groups;

5. the instructor modelled caring behaviour;

6. the instructor responded genuinely to students' needs;

7. the course incorporated students' personal knowledge;

8. the instructor presented knowledge as constructed within a historical context;

9. the instructor employed cooperative learning strategies effectively;

10. the instructor fostered intellectual rigour;

11. the students were encouraged to develop responsibilities for their own learning;

12. the instructor related the curriculum to issues of social justice.

The two sets of statements are both valid, but will produce very different information in responses. The first set takes it for granted that the teacher is central to the business of education and that knowledge is to be transmitted from teacher to student. The second set is focused much more on the student and the assumption is that learning is central rather than teaching. An assumption of the second set of questions is that the student is expected to take responsibility for their own learning and it is expected that learning will occur in different ways for different students as they bring different experiences to the learning situation (see Chapter 12 for more detailed discussion of learning).

> **Reflection 3**
>
> If you have been involved in evaluating a course recently what were the values that were implicit in the evaluation?

In an evaluation those who set the questions have a great deal of power, as the questions that are asked and the ways in which they are asked will frame and focus the information that is received. In a study of student views on their first year experience at City University Hong Kong (Geall, 2000), the evaluators were aware of their power and the potential for bias arising from this. They therefore involved the students during the development of the project, as well as in answering the final questionnaire which was the main tool of the evaluation. For example, students took part in focus group discussions to raise issues they felt were important and then these issues were fed into the questionnaire design.

INTERNAL AND EXTERNAL EVALUATION

Throughout the chapter a distinction has been made between an external evaluation with its implications of external accountability and an internal evaluation which is more likely to be for purposes of professional accountability (for a discussion of accountability see Chapter 4) and improvement.

An evaluation can take place at the level of an individual, a classroom, a department, a school or college or a system. A very important factor in the way that the evaluation is viewed is whether it is internally or externally initiated. An internally initiated evaluation is more likely to be 'owned' by an institution and one that is externally initiated may be experienced as an imposition. This is not always the case. For example, it is possible that an internal evaluation that is imposed by the senior management team may be resented by the teachers in the school and perceived as an imposition in the same way as an externally imposed evaluation. What is important is how stakeholders view the ownership of the evaluation and the perceived purpose.

You have already seen that (Chapter 7) collegiality and ownership are important in improvement initiatives and the same applies to evaluations. Is the purpose of the evaluation seen as part of on-going improvement or to check up on progress? These contrasting views of evaluation were clearly explained in an early but influential model of school self-review:

> A school self-review may focus on the whole staff or on individual teachers, and on the management and organisation of the school or on classroom practice, though none of these categories is mutually exclusive. Whatever the focus, two main purposes can be distinguished—internal development and external accountability. A review initiated by the head and staff and conducted for the purpose of school development and improvement can be regarded as an internal matter. No reports have to be submitted to external

agencies and the staff rather than the employers are in control. In contrast, if a whole school staff have been required to conduct a review by their employing authorities then we can say that the purpose of the exercise is to meet a demand for formal, external accountability (McMahon et al, 1984, pp.5–6).

At the end of this chapter you will focus on the evaluation of a whole school and look at two contrasting examples: one of schools undertaking self-evaluation according to a self-defined agenda and primarily for the purpose of improvement, the other of school inspections where the agenda is set by an external body, but first we will consider the two opposing models of evaluation more closely.

Internal self-evaluation

One of the earliest models of school self-evaluation in England, the Guidelines for Review and Internal Development (GRIDS) (McMahon et al, 1984), has already been referred to above. Key features of this system were that it was intended:

- for development and improvement not for the production of a report for external accountability;
- to extend beyond review to development for improvement;
- to involve all the staff in the school;
- that any decisions about the outcomes should be made by the teachers and others concerned within the school.

A more recent self-evaluation model developed as a result of the commission of the National Union of Teachers in England (MacBeath, 1999) illustrates a participatory process in its development. In the development of the model, the project team initially worked with a range of ten schools and interviewed six sets of stakeholders—teachers, management staff, support staff, pupils, parents and governors—asking them what they thought were the key characteristics of a good school. They also got them to rank a set of 23 criteria derived from Ofsted (the school inspection agency) in terms of their perception of importance. The distillation of these data led to the development of ten indicators that schools could use in their self-evaluation. These were:

1. school climate;
2. relationships;
3. organisation and communication;
4. time and resources;
5. recognition of achievement;
6. equity;
7. home-school links;
8. support for teaching;
9. classroom climate;
10. support for learning.

Obviously these are the main headings for the evaluation, and if you wish to know more about these indicators and their use read further in MacBeath (1999) *Schools must speak for themselves*.

Internal/external models

Some models of self-evaluation combine elements of external input or external validation, so that although the basic model is internal and aimed for improvement, there may also be a later independent evaluation validating the internal judgement. This is the model of school evaluation used by ECIS, the European Council for Independent Schools.

Meuret and Morlaix (2003, p.55) identify a slightly different model where in some self-evaluations: 'the judgement is delivered by the school on itself, but partly on the basis of criteria advised . . . by authorities'. They believe that this has led to the development of two quite distinct forms of self evaluation, which they call the 'Technical Model' which relies on quantitative indicators, imposed or provided by external authorities and the 'Participating Model' which relies on the judgements of the schools' stakeholders. Their view is that even where the Technical Model is applied, it is still operating within a participatory framework which differentiates it from a basically external and imposed model of evaluation.

There are other ways in which internal review and external review can be combined. In Singapore, the School Excellence Model, first developed in the UK is now being used for yearly internal school self-review with periodic external evaluation. Moving into a more purely external model the English inspection system (Ofsted) now includes a self-evaluation document and trains schools to carry out self-evaluation. However, the self-evaluation focus is based on the Ofsted framework, endorsing the statement of Ferguson et al (2000) that:

> Over the last decade the Office for Standards in Education has had such a potent influence in schools in England that some commentators have become concerned about its power to dominate teachers' thinking and take charge of the education agenda. But it is not simply the mechanisms of inspection that cause concern but the fact that the discussion of education that takes place in schools and elsewhere, increasingly employs a vocabulary and transmits values that are dominated by the Ofsted discourse (2000, p.5)

External evaluation: inspection

Inspection of schools and colleges by agents of central or regional government is part of most educational systems. However, in the last years of the twentieth century, in many countries inspection has taken on a sharper focus and become a more central and powerful aspect of the educational system. For example, in England the establishment of the Office for Standards in Education (Ofsted) in 1992 and the introduction of a Framework for Inspection (www.ofsted.gov.uk) has replaced the previous system of Her Majesty's Inspectors, and a system of relatively ad hoc inspections has given way to systematic inspections, first every four, and now every three years. The inspection reports on schools are publicly available and give an analysis of the school's strengths and weaknesses and a list of key issues for action. As a result of the inspection some schools can be 'named and shamed' if they are judged to be failing or in need of special measures or as having serious weaknesses. The inspectors must report on:

the educational standards achieved in the school;

the quality of the education provided by the school;

the quality of the leadership and management of the school;

the spiritual, moral, social and cultural development of pupils in the school. (Ofsted, 2003)

In order to do this, the inspectors amass pre-inspection evidence relating to the achievement of pupils in the school, the curricular provision and the Performance and Assessment report (PANDA). The PANDA report gives background information about the area of the school and enables schools to compare themselves with others of a similar type. The inspectors issue questionnaires, interview, and observe lessons and the life of the school during the course of the inspection, which normally takes one week in a secondary school.

The development of a comprehensive inspection system has had wide-ranging effects. Ferguson et al (2000) identify four main types of effect in England:

inspection has been a 'mechanism for delivering changes, ensuring that heads, governors and school districts or local education authorities (LEAs) comply with new statutory requirements . . . Although school inspection is said to be "independent"'; and it has an important accountability function, it is perhaps more appropriate on occasions to note its role as an arm of the State created to ensure compliance.

a critical inspection report can empower the consumer and 'the prospect of an impending inspection is sufficient to make teachers and heads feel apprehensive'.

surveys have shown that most headteachers are satisfied with their school's inspection and view the experience positively.

a great deal of information has been generated about schools, their performance, teaching and learning and their leadership and management. This has meant that the database for government, schools and researchers has greatly increased.

The Ofsted model has been emulated elsewhere, for example in Hong Kong where the Education Department implemented quality assurance inspection for the first time in the academic year 1997/98. The Education Review Office (ERO) of New Zealand is seen to parallel Ofsted in many ways (www.aare.edu.au). A report on OECD countries (CERI, 1995) showed that there was a variety of practice with regard to inspection amongst the seven countries studied, but that there was a common concern with quality procedures and a strengthening of accountability with a new stress on the performance of the school as a whole rather than a focus on teachers or subjects. The new levels of accountability were seen to be related to another development, the increased autonomy of the schools.

Scheerens et al (1999, p.87) go so far as to say that there may be a 'hypothetical relationship between centralization/decentralization and school evaluation . . . where external, output oriented evaluation could be seen as a counterbalance for decentralization'. In other words, the more that power is devolved to the schools, particularly in relation to finance, the more that there is likely to be an enforcement of accountability to the State and consumers through an external evaluation system. This type of accountability is certainly exemplified in England and Wales, where financial devolution is extensive but the inspection system is one of the most demanding. You might like to refer back to the concepts of decentralization and accountability discussed in Chapter 4.

Case Example 3 External inspection and self-evaluation in English schools

1. The Ofsted inspection (Lonsdale and Parsons, 1998, p.125)

Five schools (three secondary, one primary and one infant) following an Ofsted inspection. Their reports were largely satisfactory. Interviews were carried out with the headteacher, governors and heads of department in the secondary schools. There was also a longer-term follow up.

Some of the conclusions on the process follow.

'In schools with little systematic planning, poor evaluation and monitoring, Ofsted provided valuable impetus. In some "failing" schools it has finally highlighted deficiencies and put huge pressure on LEAs to rectify the situation'.

'In the vast majority of schools which are successful, Ofsted has caused considerable disruption to the normal life of the school. . . . It has disrupted the day-to-day routines of the school, the long-term planning process and the process of assessment and evaluation'.

In these schools the report seemed superficial and mainly highlighted things that the schools knew already. The authors conclude that the effects are generally unhelpful for teachers and governors who are already on the road to self-evaluation and have a culture to carry out real changes through long-term processes owned by teachers, senior managers and governors.

2. The self-evaluation

In a small primary school a headteacher reflected on school self-evaluation in the light of her experience of different types of evaluation and inspection over a period of years. 'My involvement . . . was one of the most powerful professional development experiences of my career to date. Not only did the report provide me, as a headteacher, with qualitative and quantitative strategies for analysing and planning school improvement, it also provided me with a resource bank of materials in my new role as an LEA adviser. My experience in schools, culminating with feeling a total victim of the Ofsted process in comparison with the positive nature of school self-evaluation, have convinced me that my early convictions about ownership and involvement were right. However, I do believe that the role of a critical friend is crucial. Unlike the current Ofsted hit and run model, external accountability and school improvement need to work hand in hand with schools being offered support to ensure that effective teaching and learning improves the quality of classroom experiences for every child.' (MacBeath, 1999, pp.86–87)

Reflection 4

What do you see as the implications of the evaluation processes for improvement and for accountability that arise from the two case studies? How do the cases compare to your own experience of evaluation?

The results from the schools in the first example appear to indicate that external inspection is likely to confirm what people already know, and may on occasions actually have negative effects rather than helping improvement. These are only five schools and therefore should not be taken as representative of how all inspections are experienced. It must be recognised that headteachers on the whole tend to welcome the outcomes of inspection and find them helpful. Ouston et al (1996) found that the vast majority of heads considered the Ofsted report valuable, and only six per cent of headteachers 'not valuable'. Similarly, Maychell and Pathak (1997) found that 90 per cent of heads thought the written and oral feedback helpful. Despite that, there is a feeling that teachers in particular may experience the process of external inspection as stressful and that inspection is something that is done *to* schools and teachers rather than *with* them. In contrast, the second case study stresses the ownership and involvement of those concerned, whilst acknowledging the contribution of Ofsted and other external inspections.

Although both external and internal evaluation may lead to school improvement, an internal evaluation where the process involves all staff who identify their own priorities and plans of action is more likely to lead to improvement and development. An external evaluation may lead to improvement by virtue of being a 'wake up call' or by endorsing existing knowledge about the school, but it may also undermine the morale of staff, possibly leading to decline rather than improvement and almost always to a post-inspection 'dip' in morale (Ferguson et al, 2000). From the point of view of accountability to both the government and the community, an external inspection with published outcomes does ensure that the progress and difficulties of schools are reported back rather than being kept confidential. The outcomes of the evaluation are freely available, and the inspection cannot be avoided. An internal evaluation is a matter of choice and there is no compulsion for a school to undertake one, unless it is part of an external framework. In addition, the outcomes belong to the school and need not be publicised and made available to parents and the wider community. Although internal evaluation is likely to be more successful in terms of bringing about improvement, it does not necessarily promote public accountability.

SUMMARY

This chapter has followed on from earlier chapters on effectiveness and improvement since measuring and evaluating progress against aims, objectives and targets is an essential part of the improvement process.

During this chapter you have been introduced to some of the methods used in evaluations and to the need for managers to consider the purposes, implications, sensitivities and values that are part of the evaluation process.

You have looked at internal (self-review) and external (inspection) evaluation of schools and considered how both types of evaluation relate to the concepts of improvement and public accountability, concluding with the view that whilst external inspection is linked primarily to accountability, an internally originated evaluation which is owned by the staff and other stakeholders in the school is more likely to result in lasting and real improvement.

RECOMMENDED FURTHER READING

For further information about methods of evaluation you might like to read relevant chapters in Coleman, M. and Briggs, A. (eds) (2002) *Research Methods for Educational Leadership and Management* (London: Paul Chapman Publishing) and in Robson, C. (1993) *Real World Research* (Oxford: Blackwell).

For further reading on self-evaluation, you could explore further two books mentioned in this chapter: MacBeath, J. (1999) *Schools Must Speak for Themselves: The case for school self-evaluation* (London: Routledge) and MacBeath, M. with Schratz, M., Meuret, D. and Jakobsen, L. (2000) *Self-Evaluation in European Schools: A story of change* (London: Routledge). The latter also includes practical detail on methods of evaluation.

For a comparative view of evaluation of schools, see CERI (1995) *Schools Under Scrutiny: Strategies for the Evaluation of School Performance* (Paris: OECD) and for more detail on the Ofsted experience see Earley, P. (ed.) (1998) *School Improvement after Inspection? School and LEA Responses* (London: Paul Chapman Publishing).

You may also want to visit websites to look at examples of external inspection, e.g. www.ofsted.gov.uk; www.aare.edu.au; www.emb.gov.hk, www.ero.govt.nz.

Financial and Material Resources for Learning

Derek Glover and Rosalind Levačić

INTRODUCTION AND LEARNING OUTCOMES

As this is a book for educational leaders and managers, we focus in this chapter on the management of resources within educational organisations, and deal only briefly with resourcing decisions at government level, vital though these are.

By the end of this chapter you should be able to:

- appreciate the central role of resource management in promoting educational effectiveness and improvement;

- understand key terms and concepts, such as efficiency and equity;

- appreciate that financial systems both at governmental and institutional level need to be designed to give appropriate incentives to teachers, managers and learners if resources are to be used efficiently and with the desired degree of equity;

- understand the basics of budget resource planning and financial control in educational organisations.

All of us are faced with limited resources but this is particularly so for educational institutions and especially those in developing countries, where public sources of funding are very limited and even poor parents are often required to pay school fees. Therefore, it is imperative that educational organisations manage their finances and resources efficiently so as to secure the maximum learning benefit for students. While teachers and parents generally have no doubts that extra spending, more resources and smaller classes produce better results, the academic research on this issue has not unequivocally confirmed these beliefs (Levačić and Vignoles, 2002). Researchers disagree about the effects of resources on learning. Apart from problems of data and methods, one important reason for this controversy is that educational organisations vary in their efficiency. So an increase in spending does not necessarily mean an increase in student learning, if resources are not managed efficiently.

CRITERIA FOR EVALUATING RESOURCE MANAGEMENT IN EDUCATION

The essential relationship is that between resources or inputs and the consequent learning achieved by students. It is important to distinguish between real resources and financial resources. 'Real' resources are either human such as teachers, or physical resources such as buildings, furniture, materials of instruction, computers, textbooks and utilities (water, electricity, etc.) as against financial resources: the money, which is used to purchase human and physical resources. In some systems schools, and less often universities, are allocated real resources (buildings, teachers) in kind, but elsewhere educational organisations receive a global budget, expressed in money terms, from which they must purchase real resources. The latter system is becoming more widespread. When a school or college has a delegated budget a major management responsibility is how to spend the budget to best effect to achieve the organisation's educational aims. Much of this chapter is devoted to resource and financial management for schools and colleges which have delegated budgets and hence a major degree of financial autonomy.

There are four key criteria used to assess resource management. These are efficiency, effectiveness, value for money and equity.

- *Efficiency* relates to the relationship between an institution's inputs and its outputs. Efficiency entails securing minimum inputs for a given quality and quantity of education provided. This is achieved when a given quantity of output is achieved at minimum cost.

  Defining and measuring the outputs of schools and colleges is problematic. For one thing they are multiproduct enterprises—students learn a great variety of social skills and attitudes as well as specific cognitive knowledge and skills. Cognitive attainment, as measured in tests, exams and qualifications, is the most frequently used measure of output. The term 'output' is usually restricted to the immediate effects of school or university in terms of exam results, for example. 'Outcomes' of schooling are longer term and include employability, earning capacity and non-monetary benefits of education such as better health, better informed decision-making and enjoyment of cultural activities.

  Efficiency as the relationship between inputs and outputs can be illustrated by a simple example where two schools have 70 per cent of their leavers achieving a certain level of basic literacy but where school A spends less per pupil than school B. Provided that the students in the two schools have the same distribution of prior attainment scores when entering the school, then we can conclude that A is more efficient. This concept is further refined as *technical efficiency*—the relationship between the inputs used and the resulting quantity of output, and *cost efficiency*—that combination of teachers and equipment, given prevailing prices that produce a technically efficient output most cheaply.

The definition of efficiency we have given above is the internal efficiency of educational organisations. It takes the social value of output as given (e.g. basic literacy) and is only concerned with minimizing the cost of this output. The issue of whether the output of schools or universities is of value to society is a separate one. Colleges could be very efficient at producing pastry cooks for example, when society does not value these skills because nobody wants to eat cakes. Firms in the private sector have a direct signal of whether society values what they produce—this is the level of profits. Public sector institutions do not have such signals and so we need other criteria than profitability to judge the value of their outputs.

- *Effectiveness* refers just to the extent to which an organisation is judged to meet its objectives regardless of cost. It is a concept that endeavours to bring together both the measurable and the more subjective elements of education hinted at in the previous section. It is the relationship between the school's objectives and its outputs but both of these are difficult to quantify—and yet the 'hunch' about whether the school is effective or not may be an important reflection of the way in which it is using its resources. It is a concept which embraces an implicit, if not always, explicit, assumption about the social value of the output—and moves nearer towards an assessment of the outputs of an organisation.

- *Value for money*. If an organisation is both efficient *and* effective it is said to be providing value for money. This concept attempts to bring the measurable and the immeasurable, the objective and the subjective together. Value for money is used in two ways. One is as already defined—in terms of outputs compared to the inputs as judged in terms of effectiveness and efficiency. The second is more limited, being restricted to the requirement that the resource managers attain the best value purchases (e.g. by having several competitive price quotations) and that they subsequently evaluate what they have purchased against the needs of the organisation.

- *Equity* is an entirely different principle as it is about whether the allocation of resources to different students, subjects, institutions or other units is fair. What distribution is judged fair is a highly subjective matter. Most equity judgements involve a great deal of thought about the social ends of education as interpreted within the context of a school or college. Equity is a complex concept and has several distinct interpretations. One distinction is between equality of opportunity—people are able to make the same choices—and equality—people have the same amount of an item, such as income or education. Another important distinction is between horizontal and vertical equity. Applied to education horizontal equity is the criterion that students with similar needs should receive the same amount of resources. Vertical equity is the criterion that students with greater learning needs should receive more resources—though how much more is a difficult issue to resolve.

> **Reflection 1**
>
> In what ways are the concepts outlined above used to evaluate resource use within your organisation? What , if any, tensions arise as a result?

These criteria can all be applied to judgements of the work of schools and colleges but there is a further fundamental requirement—that of *adequacy* of funding. Put simply this is the extent to which the funding has been matched to the objectives for the school. In many developing areas educational progress is inhibited because the costing of stated objectives has been incompletely thought out and funding is inadequate. In the developed world where these data do exist, as in many deprived areas of the USA, local and national taxation as sources of income are inadequate for schools' needs. Whilst resource allocation may be managed in order to secure efficient and effective practice within the schools they cannot attain their objectives unless the funding is adequate and equitably used.

A FRAMEWORK FOR UNDERSTANDING RESOURCE MANAGEMENT IN EDUCATION

The relationship between resource inputs and learning outputs and outcomes is both complex and varied as it is mediated by many other factors. Education is essentially a close relationship between teacher and taught and between the school or college and its local environment. This relationship is sometimes called an open system because it is subject to influences from the context within which it functions (see Chapter 3). Various inputs are 'processed' within the school or college and then various educational outputs emerge. This framework is referred to as the context-input-process-output model. Three main elements in this model are:

- the external environment from which the school or college derives its 'raw material of students', acquires its other resources and to which it supplies the outputs;
- the processes that take place within the organisation—known as the production technology; and
- the human relations system, which forms a bridge between the external environment and the organisation and affects the ways in which educational production is undertaken.

Human resources are variable in quality and there has been a considerable move to enhance the consistency of teachers and support staff. Emphasis is now placed on training so that human resources can be developed to meet changing needs. Professional development thus becomes an essential part of the resource needs of an educational organisation (see Chapter 13).

PUBLIC AND PRIVATE SECTOR ROLES IN THE FINANCING AND PROVISION OF EDUCATION

The central issue for educational finance is what should be the respective roles of the public and private sectors in education. The relative importance of the two sectors varies between countries for political and historical reasons. There are two main reasons for the state needing to contribute to the financing of education. The first is equity so as to ensure that children's educational opportunities are not determined by the income and preferences of their parents or guardians. The other is for efficiency reasons, which arise from the fact that education has external benefits for society as a whole, as well as private benefits to the individual. Examples of the external benefits of education are a more productive work force which enhances the rate of economic growth, social cohesion, better health and parenting and better informed public decision-making through democratic political processes. As external benefits are available to everyone regardless of whether they pay for them, there is no incentive for private individuals to finance public benefits and a market will not produce as much of the good in question as society would wish to have in relation to the costs of producing the good. Therefore a collective decision must be made to raise taxes and purchase the good through the state.

However, the state can ensure that more education is produced by financing it, for example by paying for children to go to school: it does not need to enter production and be a provider as well. The distinction between the state financing education and actually providing it (i.e. producing it) is an important one. An important and controversial issue is whether state educational organisations are as internally efficient as private sector ones. One aspect of recent educational policies in many countries has been 'privatisation' or a greater reliance on private sector profit and non-profit making organisations for providing education, which is still funded by the state. The decision by parents to purchase private or 'independent' education may be because they believe that public provision is inadequate and so they purchase educational services in the hope of ensuring a higher future quality of life for their children. Within the developed world it may also be because of the wish to buy into networks based upon the private sector with implied future benefits, for example in securing university admission or employment advantages.

In many developing countries the state cannot raise sufficient tax revenues to provide universal free basic education. An example is Kenya where some public funding is put into the establishment of schools through community enterprise, but where parents are expected to pay fees for the running costs of the establishment. A very small proportion of local taxation is thus used for education, but in reality parents meet a considerable proportion of student costs. The World Bank has advocated parents paying fees to both state and private schools in developing countries in order to increase the supply of places. While such policies probably increase efficiency by expanding educational provision, the downside is increased inequity as poor parents are less likely to send their children to school. By contrast most educational provision in Eastern Europe is funded through disbursement at local level from a direct grant to the area from central government and few parents would expect to pay for their children's basic education.

The finance for publicly funded education may come from central government revenues or from local taxation—usually related to property values but also through local direct and indirect taxation. The balance in the proportion of funding from central and local government varies from country to country and changes over time. Higher education public funding is usually by direct payments to universities from central government, whereas most basic primary education is funded from local authorities that have varying amounts of central government grant to support their activities.

An important equity issue arises when some areas in a country are wealthier and can raise more tax to fund education than poorer areas. By contrast poorer areas often have greater need to spend on education because of lack of parental support. This problem is tackled by a redistribution of tax revenues from richer and less needy areas to the poorer and more needy. This is known as fiscal equalisation. It is practised in almost all European countries. However in many developing countries, such as China, central government does not have sufficient tax raising powers to undertake fiscal equalisation. In China basic education is funded at provincial, county and community level and is so very much affected by local income levels. This leads to a degree of locally based entre-preneurial activities such as farm enterprises to supplement available public funding.

Fiscal equalisation measures do not ensure equal education provision in different localities as often the actual decision on how much to spend on local services is left to local political decision-making, which may determine the levying of additional local tax to support education. National uniformity in educational provision and local democratic decision-making are not mutually consistent. Furthermore, increasing decentralisation of control of school administration has resulted in schools being free to enhance their basic funding through the use of locally raised support, which varies between areas.

In brief, the advantage of central government funding is that of equity and also in ensuring greater national uniformity in standards when education is regarded as a national and not a local public good. As governments have been increasingly concerned with the importance of the education sector in producing a highly skilled labour force, so tolerance of differential standards has diminished.

To secure some of the advantages of market responsiveness as a control mechanism in the public sector some argue that much is to be gained from the re-marketisation of public services. There has been an increasing and worldwide movement towards some degree of self-government for schools in the past 30 years. Within nationally prescribed frameworks and the retention of some central control through setting and monitoring standards, individual schools or colleges have been allowed to function without detailed central control, particularly over inputs. This has led to the development of quasi-markets, for example by allowing parents freedom of choice in selecting schools, an increasing degree of competition between schools in attracting students and funding schools largely in terms of the number of pupils they enrol. The extent to which such developments are politically acceptable appears to vary according to the socio-economic context of the schools and colleges concerned, as explored by Whitaker (1993). Allied to this are concerns that the decentralised management of resources may have intensified the bureaucratisation of educational organisations.

THE ALLOCATION OF FUNDS TO EDUCATIONAL ORGANISATIONS

Grants from central government take varied forms. This is because they are aimed at satisfying different objectives and can be used to secure particular policy implementation.

- Lump sum payments—these are made to a local authority as an agent or directly to a school or college. Lump sum payments allow freedom at local government or unit level and may promote a particular response to the needs of the community, e.g. by allowing a rural school to concentrate on agricultural education whilst permitting a school in an urban area to develop specialisations meeting local industrial needs. The disadvantage of lump sum grants is that they discourage local tax-raising.

- Under 'matched funding', the grant giver releases funds on the basis of the recipient matching the grant to a certain proportion (say 50 per cent) by revenue raised locally.

- Categorical grants are paid only to the recipient if it fulfils the condition of the grant which can be lump sum or matching. Governments favour categorical or earmarked funds in order to persuade schools to pursue government objectives. However, they are complex to administer and deny the principle that local decision-makers can assess their own needs better than more distant authorities.

- Grants may be allocated by formula or through bidding processes. Formulae may be weighted according to age, educational need to promote equity, and type of curriculum provision, e.g. by paying differential rates for students on medical and science courses compared with those on social science courses at university. Bidding tries to promote efficiency by ensuring the recipient is keen to use the money and meets certain criteria but bidding is also time consuming.

Reflection 2

Just *how* does an organisation known to you get all its income? How, if at all, are the principles of transparency and accountability applied to the allocation process?

As the above discussion indicates, the criteria by which resources are allocated to individual schools or universities are important for the efficiency incentives they signal to educational managers and for their equity implications see the vignette in the box below. The use of formulae for allocating a 'global' budget to schools based mainly on the number and ages of its pupils has become more widespread. As Ross and Levačić (1999) argue, a properly constructed formula can encourage both efficiency in resource use and horizontal equity (the same amount per similar student) and vertical equity—differential amounts per student depending on indicators of social and educational need.

Case Example 1 Bosnia and Herzegovina

After the war of 1992–95, which halved national income per head and from which the newly independent country is only slowly recovering, schools face great difficulties in operating efficiently and with adequate resources. The inevitable shortage of funding is exacerbated by the system of resource allocation. There is a rigid formula for allocating both teaching and support staff according to the number of classes the school has. Staff are paid directly by the local authority. Schools receive very small and irregular amounts for non-staff expenses. As a consequence schools are poorly maintained and have few books and equipment. Heating bills are paid directly by the local authority so there is no incentive for schools to use energy efficiently. Schools tend to be overstaffed especially with non-teaching staff. Headteachers and school councils cannot choose a more efficient pattern of resource use because they cannot switch funding between staff and non-staff expenditures. Small expensive schools cannot be closed because there is no provision in the budget for switching the money saved on staff to pay for transporting pupils to school. International consultants have recommended a switch to per pupil funding so that schools would receive a global budget, which could be flexibly allocated between the different resource needs as judged by headteachers and school councils.

ALLOCATING RESOURCES WITHIN AN ORGANISATION

Cost analysis

Simkins (2000) argues that effective resource allocation is only possible if those taking decisions know just how much the various elements of staffing, buildings and teaching materials actually cost. When devolution of funds, known as local management of schools, was introduced there was considerable professional concern that time taken to obtain such data was a loss to the core purposes of education. This is an illustration of the idea that most decision-making within scarce resources should be based on an assessment of *opportunity cost*. This can be defined as the value of resources measured in terms of the next best alternative use of the resources that are given up in order to spend them in a particular way. The opportunity cost of a teacher is therefore the benefits that would otherwise have accrued from spending the money on support staff and more computers, for example. Once a teacher is employed, the opportunity cost of their time becomes relevant. Is their day better spent out of school on a course or in teaching the class for example? Managers often ignore opportunity costs and think only in terms of money cost. They can devise ways of saving money, such as renting a cheap but slow photocopier, and ignore the consequent opportunity costs in teacher time spent copying.

Costs that are relevant for a decision depend in part on the timeframe over which the resources will be used. Recurrent and capital costs are therefore distinguished.

- Recurrent (or current) cost are those that have to be met year on year.
- Capital costs are for resources that will last for a longer period.

Definitions of what length of period is the cut off between recurrent and capital costs vary. In some accounting systems expenditure on books and equipment that last more than a year are capital costs, whereas in other countries only large items of equipment and buildings would count as capital costs.

Another problem when working out the cost of delivering education is how to attribute costs between resources that are directly used to produce the activity in question and those that are indirect costs because the resources are used to keep the whole school going. For example, in costing science lessons the direct costs are those that can be attributed to science lessons including staff, teaching and equipment. Indirect costs are those shared with all other learning programmes such as advisory staff, administration, maintenance and heating. These have to be attributed by some arbitrary rule, such as the proportion of lesson hours that are science.

Another distinction is between variable and fixed costs. Variable costs (similar to current and direct costs) are those that increase or decrease as output (numbers of pupils) rises or falls. By contrast, fixed costs are those that have to be met irrespective of the number of students involved, e.g. buildings, advisory services and administration. Over time all costs become variable. Only variable costs are opportunity costs and fixed costs are not opportunity costs. If the school recruits one more pupil it does not have to pay more for maintenance or management. Costs can be aggregated to give the total cost of the institution and this, divided by the number of students gives the unit cost or, if divided by the number of classes, the unit cost per class.

Planners are often concerned about the impact of providing for one additional student. The increase in costs due to producing one more unit—in this case educating one more student—is the marginal cost. If a school is organised with classes of 40 and there are two spare places in a class the marginal cost will be much lower than if another child means that the 40 limit is breached and so another class has to be started and another teacher employed.

The following example shows the way in which opportunity cost analysis affects decision-making in school.

Case Example 2 Mulawaru School

'Mulawaru School' in a growing suburban area in East Africa has 120 students aged 11–14 organised in three classes with the headteacher and three staff. The funding is by a central government grant for basic building provision and a modest fee income from parents to meet most other expenses. The headteacher has attempted to maintain a staffing ratio of 1:40 and is available as a 'floater' to support class teachers, teach smaller groups in basic subjects and to cope with administration—defined as 'fund raising and working with the local community'.

Because of these efforts and recruitment to the stated maximum for the school, he has been able to enhance the termly income so that another half-time member of staff can be employed or the money used in different ways. The alternatives are many and varied for a school with so many needs. The headteacher feels that an additional half-time member of staff would be beneficial because the part-timer could ensure that small group work was undertaken on a regular basis to support both those pupils seeking admission to a high school and those with special learning needs. The teachers favour continuing as they are but purchasing new furnishing to give every child a desk, up-to-date textbooks and some basic computer equipment to offer a chance to all pupils to understand new technology. The parents would like the money to be used to service a loan so that toilet facilities could be extended and the members of the local community council also favour this but feel that additional catering facilities would enable the school to do so much more for the adult community and those pupils with long daily journeys to and from school.

The district inspectors have reported that the school was not using existing resources wisely with the head and teachers spending so much of their time on administration and maintenance of the buildings. They recommended that any additional staffing should be used to ensure a greater degree of non-teaching support. Pressures are also growing from local parents who want to get their children into the school and the government agreed to fund the building of another classroom if satisfactory staffing arrangements could be made to ensure improved educational outcomes.

Reflection 3

How, and for what reasons, would you allocate additional funds? What would be your response to those who argue that there has to be flexibility in the system so that contingencies can be met?

Budget planning

The problem for resource managers is how to allocate the available resources so as to achieve efficiency and value for money. It is difficult to do this for educational organisations which lack good measures of outputs relative to inputs and do not have blueprints about how to use resources to maximum effect. Efficiency is likely to be promoted by a rational approach to decision-making in which professional judgement is used to evaluate alternative uses of resources in terms of their likely contribution to achieving educational objectives of the school or college. A rational approach requires some form of planning in which objectives are set out and ways of achieving them indicated. But management may also be political, with limited use of forward planning and with pressure groups exerting their influence upon the decision-making process.

The traditional approach has been for schools to use 'subjective' budgeting—this concentrates on the subjects of expenditure—the cost of all the teachers' salaries, all the building maintenance and so on. Most school budget statements are subjective and expressed in terms of expenditure on different inputs. The advantage of this is that all indirect costs are included, the disadvantage that it is difficult to relate planned or actual expenditure to the resourcing of teaching and learning programmes. It is also likely that planning will be incremental. This involves making annual adjustments to established patterns of expenditure by reconsidering this year's budget as the basis of planning for next. Changes are made if there is a change in income or the development of a new programme but by and large the organisation continues as it has before.

For those looking to develop schools in a responsive and flexible way such an approach minimises creativity and two other approaches are being used.

- Programme budgeting where the focus is on the programme—this might be a subject e.g. science, or a year group, or a cross-curricular programme such as health education. Levačić (1995) calls this objective budgeting because it results in allocation according to the objects of expenditure and is designed to ensure that expenditure meets the school's objectives. The advantage of such a system is that the work of the school or college is re-thought each year so that adequate plans are reviewed, prioritised, costed and implemented. The disadvantage is that it is time consuming and attributing indirect costs to programmes can be very difficult.

- Zero-based budgeting—this 'starts from scratch' every year and, whilst not specifically programme-based, it requires those responsible for teaching activities to justify their intentions before spending is allowed. One reaction to this is that sub-unit leaders inflate their requirements in the hope of securing a percentage of their request each year by playing the system. A further problem is that item-by-item costing is a time consuming process.

Preparation of the budget according to a rational perspective is increasingly driven by leadership vision. Strategic management is concerned with the achievement of that vision and resource management plays a fundamental part in this. Mintzberg and Quinn (1991) provide a working definition of strategy. 'A strategy is the pattern or plan that integrates an organisation's major goals, policies, and action sequences into a cohesive whole'. Caldwell and Spinks (1992) see strategy at a local and more domestic level although they recognise that the national context affects planning. The process of strategic management usually involves:

a. assessing the current position of the school or college related to its environment;

b. assessing the current strengths and weaknesses in the use of human and financial resources in the organisation;

c. reviewing the aims of the organisation and whether these should be changed in the light of this strategic audit process;

d. considering and costing the alternative ways in which the organisation could develop to meet its objectives;

e. reaching decisions on the priorities for future planning;

f. developing longer term, medium-term and short-term action plans for the use of resources to meet aims.

Weindling (1997) outlines the differences between strategic planning, long-term planning and development planning. The way in which all these are undertaken varies because each school or college is a unique establishment. There are diverse views on the desirability of rational planning which is driven by the attainment of aims, with some arguing that the tighter the organisation the less responsive it can be to changing need

(*Gunter*, 1997). There may be long-term stability with inherent tendencies to historic rather than creative development. The leadership style may vary along a continuum from the collegial to the bureaucratic and sometimes has no recognisable pattern at all. The way in which people work together, known as the culture of the unit, may be collaborative or individualistic and this may affect the structure of decision-making which again varies from the autocratic to the consensual. Scheerens (1997) brings these factors together and classifies the planning process as either *synoptic* planning, characterised by high predictability and sequencing of actions, and *retroactive* planning, characterised by reaction to events and incremental development.

In general the practice of rational planning is a cyclic process of:

- audit—to establish the present situation;
- determining and defining aims and objectives;
- identifying and costing alternative actions to achieve the objectives;
- prioritising—establishing which alternatives are logistically and financially possible and best achieve the objectives at least cost;
- linking—matching component parts to the development plan;
- implementing—putting the selected plans into operation;
- evaluating—measuring progress towards aims as a result of implemented plans; and then back to:
- audit, and so on in cyclic fashion.

If the rational approach is being followed an integrated, whole-school approach will emerge with development planning to ensure that all units within the school put forward their proposals within the framework of the strategic plan, and offer costed alternatives to achieve programme objectives. Effective development planning with the data it produces paves the way for budget preparation. However, the inter-relationship of plans and the eventual budget is not always as evident as it might appear in theory. The plans may not be the driving force that theorists envisage.

Reflection 4

What evidence is there for rational planning within your organisation? Can you classify it according to Scheerens' models—or is such a typology inappropriate? Why?

Budget preparation

Budget planning involves predicting income and planning expenditure within income constraints.

Income

One of the fundamental problems in planning is that forward forecasting is a very inexact science. Some form of government grant funds most public educational provision and is often subject to change according to local and national policies and financial well-being. Under formula funding income depends on student numbers. Private sector institutions rely upon fee paying students and there are questions about the extent to which fee increases will encourage or discourage applicants. The World Bank (Kremer et al, 1999) has provided considerable evidence of the extent to which fee paying in underdeveloped countries is achieved at enormous personal costs to families. Increasingly parents are being asked to supplement inadequate public funding. In China many agricultural and industrial schools supplement inadequate grant or fee income by selling goods and services to the community. An example of business enterprise is given in the box below. In the UK considerable local sponsorship matched by the government on a pound for pound basis has been used to foster educational development.

Case Example 3 Banja Luka Catering and Tourism Vocational School

This school in the Republika Srpksa part of Bosnia and Herzegovina has 1300 students between the ages of 15–19. It provides three and four year courses in catering, restaurant service work and tourism. It employs 68 teachers and 7 non-teaching staff. The staff are paid by the Ministry of Education and non-staff funding comes from the municipality. Non-staff funding from state sources is very tight. For many years the school has supplemented its income by running a restaurant which is open to the public. The students work and train in the restaurant, which also employs extra professional staff. It is an important source of additional income. Recently the restaurant was severely damaged by fire but is now accommodated in a brand new 520-seater building, suitable for wedding receptions. The bursar said: 'During the war people laughed at me for continuing to pay the insurance'. As this illustrates, making decisions with respect to risk is an important part of resource management.

Expenditure

In most schools there will be basic costs that have to be met year on year. These have to be entered into the budget at an early stage to allow for changes that may affect figures even at a standstill position. They include the provision of sufficient teaching spaces, of sufficient staff to ensure that all students can be taught in manageable groups, and the administration necessary for the organisation to function. A starting point could well be the financial report for the past year or the current year so that the costing of the existing total programme is known.

However, there are some costs that cannot always be other than a 'best guess'. Consider staffing costs. Unless all staff are paid the same salary there will be annual increases according to the initial salary on appointment; annual additions because of age, experience, or additional qualifications; responsibility payments, and increasingly some form of performance payment. Before the basic budget for staff can be worked out all these elements have to be added. Once the essential basic expenditure has been calculated any surplus between this and income can be allocated to development. If last year's full expenditure is merely rolled forward there will be no funds released for new developments.

Where schools first cost basic provision and then supplement this with partial programme planning they are much more likely to approach value for money than if practising incremental budgeting. If income is less than the cost of all the planned programmes opportunity cost reasoning has to be employed—something will have to be surrendered from the total programme if change is to be accomplished within limited resources.

Decision-making

Although a school may consider that it is rational in its decision-making and that it will be guided by agreed plans, many people will have a view on the priorities in the strategic plans. These are the stakeholders—those who have an interest in the school as parents, pupils, staff and community. The way in which these can attempt to influence the budget is shown in our example from an English school with a high degree of financial autonomy. Opportunity cost reasoning, adherence to the stated vision for the school, and personal and political pressures all come into play but ultimately the governors, a body of local people appointed to oversee the school, have to guide the headteacher according to their own view of the best use of resources.

Case Example 4 St. Michael's Primary School

St. Michael's Primary School is a small village school in a rural community with 120 pupils aged 4–11 years of age organised in five classes. The headteacher is allocated three days per week for administration, monitoring and evaluation throughout the school and so the total staffing is 5.6 teachers. The first look at the budget figures for the financial year April 2003–4 was presented to the Governors of the school in November 2002. In summary these were:

Teachers and supply teachers	£208,525
Support and administrative staff	£42,800
Maintenance	£16,828
Learning resources	£16,000
Administration and insurance	£12,700
Total planned expenditure	**£296,853**
Formula allocation	£257,035
Other grants	£27,773
Brought forward from 2002	£6,000
Total planned income	**£290,808**
Budgetary deficit	**£6,045**

The anticipated roll is dropping by 8 pupils (£12,000+) in 2004–5 and Governors have to plan for this from September 2004.

The Governors decided that the deficit, whilst not large, required structural change for future numbers and proposed that the staffing should be reduced to 4.6 teachers. This would anticipate the fall in numbers and allow for additional salary payments for existing staff, which, although allocated under a government performance management system, had not been paid (£8,000). It would also allow for the employment of additional support staff for all four classes instead of the two classes supported at present. However, they decided to seek the views of all involved. The following list of alternative suggestions emerged from the discussions.

Parents—opposed to any increase in class sizes and suggested local efforts to raise funds and to increase recruitment of students. They feel that the Governors have acted too precipitately and that additional recruits will emerge as the school's reputation for small groups is more widely known.

Teaching staff—opposed to so much administration time for the headteacher and felt that reorganisation would be unnecessarily drastic and educationally unsound but they also feared redundancy.

Support staff—felt that too much money was being spent on supply staff when teachers were away on training courses and that greater willingness to take students with special learning needs would increase local support for the school.

Community members—felt that more use could be made of the school hall for community activities and suggested that there could be more effective use of sports facilities at an economic price. They also pointed out that parents were fickle and may well withdraw their children if they thought that class sizes were going to rise.

In the event the Governors listened to all suggestions and proceeded to cost the alternatives. They decided to reduce supplies and services and to accept the parents' offer of fund raising for the coming year but then to plan for a reduction in staff in the following year unless recruitment could be increased by ten students. To this end they are investigating earlier admission of pupils (at age 3.5) for a nursery group and a range of 'marketing strategies' including local publicity, change of school name and improved relationships with the surrounding playgroup organisers.

Reflection 5

Given this evidence, outline a critical evaluation of the decision made.

Weindling (1997) makes use of the ideas of *gap analysis*—where we are and where we want to be, and he considers the importance of the stakeholders—all those concerned with a school or college, in contributing to the long-term planning process to enhance their 'ownership' of policy and practice. This presupposes that the budgetary evaluation enables the 'gap' to be identified. The case study shows, however, that whilst the gap may be identified at one stage in the process it is subject to so many internal and external influences that tight planning is inhibited. In the event, in June 2003, a temporary change in government guidance allowed the school to divert funds from its long-term capital fund to meet current needs and a further £17,000 became available. Plans were put on hold three months into the financial year and a revised budget has allowed the status quo with 5.6 staff but this has only delayed essential structural changes.

MONITORING, EVALUATION AND FINANCIAL CONTROL

Achieving ends

When used for planning the budget is forward looking and is a statement of intent. Once the financial year starts the budget is used as a record of the income and expenditure flows that have occurred or are committed up to the present time. This backward looking form of the budget is an essential tool in implementation and is used for monitoring and evaluation. Some stakeholders within schools and colleges do resent the time taken on such activities which they see as being in the past and therefore not relevant (Glover, 2000).

Although the phrase 'monitoring and evaluation' is used fairly readily it is important to distinguish between the two (see also Chapter 9).

- Monitoring. This is undertaken through regular checks between the intended expenditure at a stage in the year under any subjective heading and the actual expenditure at that time. Where discrepancies occur they may, for example, be due to incorrect 'posting' of payments by wrongly entering data or a mismatch between order and payment so that the payment is posted to a later period. They may also be due to unforeseen changes in expenditure and income. Monitoring the budget is part of financial control—discussed below.

- Evaluation. This considers how resource use meets the overall objectives for the organisation. It is much more strategic in its viewpoint concerned not so much with detail but with the impact of the plans that the resource use has fulfilled. It also prompts thinking about the quality of the outcomes arising from resource use.

Whatever the objective evidence final decisions about the effectiveness of a school and the attainment of value for money are subjective and dependent to some extent on the professional judgement of those undertaking monitoring and evaluation. Much more objective is the way in which the accountants view the use of resources, although some practitioners urge that we should not lose sight of the turbulence of educational life and plead for the recognition of core concerns rather than accountancy practice.

Financial control: ensuring probity

Operational financial management is concerned with ensuring that money allocated in the budget is properly spent for authorised purposes and that budget plans are adhered to or if not, changes are properly authorised. Although the teaching profession is custodian of the highest values there have been examples of what at best is called mismanagement, and at worst is blatant criminality. A recent example of embezzlement of funds on a major scale (estimated at over £500,000) by a head teacher in England clearly deprived the school of funding for a long period and resulted in a five year prison sentence—effective financial control was missing!

Financial control is shown in the following areas of administration:

- purchasing of goods and contracting of services;
- banking of funds paid into and out of the school or college;
- the management of the payroll for all employees;
- the security of assets;
- the maintenance of petty cash accounts;
- the maintenance of voluntary funds;
- insurance matters and, increasingly;
- data security to prevent the misuse of information.

Although it is assumed that all involved in education are of the highest moral character there are times when financial mismanagement occurs in schools and colleges. This may not be a deliberate act but could be the result of a failure to check details, carelessness in putting money into the office or a bank, or the use of 'short-cuts' that appear to be cheaper than the recommended procedure. Problems may also arise because of the complexity of the organisation. In order to avoid possibly fraudulent practices auditors suggest five essential practices.

1. That there should be a separation of powers within the system. The same person should not place the order for goods, check their arrival and then arrange for payment.

2. That contracts with suppliers of goods and services should include full and rigorous specifications, require that tenders are submitted following open advertisement and be subject to monitoring and final approval before payment.

3. That payments should only be made by authorised signatories (often requiring two signatures for payments over a stated amount) and only on the presentation of authenticated delivery notes for the goods or services provided.

4. That all sections of the school or college should maintain inventories of all stock completed when goods arrive in the department and available for independent checking at all times.

5. That there should be firm guidelines for financial practice within the school or college including responsibilities, procedures, and the necessary record keeping for both official and unofficial funds.

Internal audit occurs when a specialist member of the organisation, usually looking at the detail of operational management, undertakes this financial checking. External auditing is undertaken by persons unconnected with the organisation. It may go beyond financial checks and report on how the organisation is achieving its stated aims and making use of its resources. Often external auditing informs and then prompts policy development. The greater the degree of devolution of responsibility for resource management to the schools, the more important is financial probity and the achievement of value for money for both current expenditure and asset management.

> **Reflection 6**
>
> Is evaluation as important as planning in resource management? How would you convince a colleague that looking back is as important as looking forward?

ASSET MANAGEMENT

In order to secure value for money an organisation must manage its assets well. Managing the assets involves a number of processes.

- Maintaining security. With so much public property in the hands of the school it is possible for misuse, misappropriation and fraud to occur. Asset stocks are best maintained by ensuring good records, clear staff responsibility and regular checks to ensure that misuse does not occur. The cost of lockable storage may well be recouped by the additional security for easily portable items of equipment.

- Maintaining existing assets. By this is meant that there should be regular inspections of the property, preferably with the help of a buildings expert, and equipment. Since experts could have a pecuniary interest in recommending maintenance, the inspections should be independent of maintenance contracts. Maintenance needs to be included in budget plans.

- Disposal of assets. There are times when the school or college will have assets that have reached the end of their life-span or are no longer needed. Decision-making about disposal needs to be undertaken by more than one person so that there can be no accusation of fraudulent activity.

- Replacement of assets. There is always pressure on resources and the need to purchase for new developments may inhibit the planned replacement of equipment, or routine repair to property or regular grounds maintenance. When these are postponed the likelihood of increased expenditure in the future has to be offset against postponement at this stage. Asset management is most effective if those items likely to need replacement are charted in an asset management plan.

- New assets. In most schools and colleges there is along list of the new assets that teachers would like to have available if resource funding allowed. Adequate asset management requires that these items are identified and then incorporated into strategic planning.

The development of asset plans at every level within a school, college or district allows educational resource use to be maximised. Whatever the means of funding three elements are used in analysis of assets.

- Condition—with a focus on the physical state of premises to ensure safe and continuous operation within local and national building regulations.

- Sufficiency—with a focus on the quantity and organisation of places for students in an area.

- Suitability—with a focus on the way in which the provision meets curriculum needs, e.g. science accommodation, ICT facilities.

Schools and colleges are dynamic in nature and face changing requirements. Over time assets become obsolete and worn and depreciate in value, needing eventually to be replaced. Within the private sector this is usually achieved by setting aside funds so that at the end of the depreciation period adequate replacement funds will be available. In the public sector this has not generally been the pattern and assets have been run down in the anticipation that funds will be available from public sources at a necessary time in the future. This is beginning to change, as part of the general efficiency drive, and will involve school leaders in the process of capital evaluation which is beyond the scope of this chapter.

CONCLUSION

Managing finance and resources for educational organisations is a challenging task. The outputs and outcomes of educational organisations are multiple and have both private and public benefits. There are many different stakeholders with different interests in how resources are used. Ambiguities in relating inputs to consequent educational outputs and outcomes make it difficult to measure efficiency in education. This chapter has shown how equity and efficiency, though difficult to make operational, are used as the main criteria for assessing how education is funded and how its provision is divided between public and private sector organisations.

Because of critiques of public sector inefficiency, government policy in many countries has been increasingly concerned not just with how much is spent on education but on establishing funding systems that promote equity and that contain appropriate incentives for educational organisations to manage their resources efficiently. A marked trend has been toward formula funding based in large part on student numbers so that funding is demand led and gives incentives to providers to perform well. Decentralised budgeting has also been encouraged on the principle that local managers are better informed about local needs and costs than those at the centre. In both developing and even developed countries mixed public and private funding is more prevalent as educational institutions are encouraged to raise some of their own resources both to ease the tax burden on the state and to ensure that students and parents have incentives to demand good quality education from providers.

However, a number of potential tensions remain. Efficiency incentives may harm equity. For example, schools have an incentive to recruit students who are less costly to educate and private sources of funding inevitably lead to differential quality linked to income. Because of the increasing political importance of education, governments still wish to intervene to achieve specific policy outcomes despite promoting decentralised budget management as a means to enhanced efficiency. There are tensions between the desire for national cohesion via uniform public education and private demands for differentiated education. In a world where public sector educational organisations are experiencing greater degrees of financial autonomy with its increased uncertainties and opportunities, educational managers need to cope both strategically with the impact of these policy tensions on their organisation as well as attend to the careful details of day-to-day budget management.

SUMMARY

This chapter first focused on the criteria of efficiency, effectiveness, value for money and equity in their use in resource management. It then went on to examine the context-input process-output model of an educational organisation, the role of the public and private sector in financing education and the different ways in which funds can be allocated to educational organisations. Consideration was then given to the allocation of resources within an organisation, to costing and to budgeting. Finally the importance of monitoring, evaluating and of financial control and probity were examined.

RECOMMENDED FURTHER READING

For fuller discussion of allocation methods in varied settings Ross and Levačić, listed in the references, offers a valuable critique of systems in action, and the practicalities of resource management are dealt with in greater detail in Coleman and Anderson, also listed below. The complexity of resource allocation and management is such that few texts are universally applicable.

Publications by UNESCO (www.unesco.org/publications), OECD (www.oecd.org/publications) and the World Bank (www.worldbank.org/publs) pertinent to national and regional educational resource management are worth perusal because much of their material is both contextual and practical in content . More advanced articles on educational resource generation and evaluation are available, amongst others, in the *Economics of Education Review* and the US Government publication *Selected Papers in School Finance* published annually.

11

Human Resources for Learning

David Oldroyd

INTRODUCTION AND LEARNING OUTCOMES

This chapter explores a big topic, some would say the most important aspect of the work of education leaders and managers—managing people to promote learning for all in schools and other educational organisations. The core task of all education systems is to promote desirable student learning, but in order to do this in an ever-changing world educators themselves have to continue learning in order to fulfil their tasks with a sense of efficacy. Educational staff make up the major part of all educational expenditure. It is obvious that we need to manage and value this human resource for learning to the best possible extent.

By the end of this chapter you should be able to:

- understand 'hard' and 'soft' human resource management (HRM) approaches to managing people in educational organisations;

- compare contrasting 'rational' and 'efficacy' models of HRM that offer a synthesis of the tasks and processes involved;

- grasp the elements of staffing, performance management and development processes;

- reflect on what motivates staff to perform and why they sometimes under-perform;

- deepen your understanding of the social and psychological side of helping people to be resourceful and to learn in educational organisations.

TWO DIMENSIONS OF HRM

Human resource management (HRM) is a seductive phrase in the lexicon of modern management. It is especially appealing to advocates of new public management with its concerns for 'value for money', 'quality assurance', accountability and 'levering up standards'. The label HRM has its critics in the field of educational leadership and management who may object to the whole idea of people being seen as a resource since this dehumanizes them (Bottery, 1992). A similar criticism of school effectiveness in Chapter 8 was that it put the emphasis on targets and measurable achievement rather than the wider processes of education. Managing professional people in educational organisations is about achieving results with and through those people. But it is also about empowering and developing the same people as persons, individual and collaborative professionals. This is why some prefer the term 'managing resourceful humans' to HRM.

This chapter presents two models that attempt to summarise the 'hard and soft' sides of managing people.

HRM has its 'hard' and 'soft' dimensions. The hard aspects place emphasis on the idea of *resource*—something to be used dispassionately and in a calculative, formally rational

'HARD' HRM (instrumental)	'SOFT' HRM (developmental/expressive)
Scope—institutional structures, policies and processes	**Scope**—individual and team relationships and organisational culture
Focus on the RESOURCE side—how to staff the organisation, manage the deployment and performance of this human resource to achieve organisational goals and results; develop and exploit them as fully as possible	**Focus** on the HUMAN side—nurturing the people who are the key to creating value from other resources (e.g. pupils, facilities and learning resources) and competitive advantage (e.g. exam results); managing resourceful humans
Leadership—'transactional', promoting efficiency and high standards	**Leadership**—'transformational', value-driven attention to feelings and beliefs
Outcome—efficient achievement of tasks and strategic goals of the organisation	**Outcome**—personal and professional efficacy and development of personnel
Key words—professional accountability, strategic planning; quality; standards; competition, efficiency	**Key words**—professional autonomy, motivation; commitment; empowerment, learning; teamwork, morale, efficacy
Examples—Management By Objectives(MBO); production targets and bonuses; performance-related pay (PRP); performance appraisal; line management	**Examples**—reflective practice; job enrichment/sharing; participative skills; collaborative teams; delegated responsibilities, collegial culture
Related disciplines—economic and systems theory	**Related disciplines**—occupational, cognitive and social psychology
Perspective—managerialist, results-oriented; 'humans as resources'—as means to an end	**Perspective**—humanistic, person-oriented; 'resourceful humans'—as ends in themselves

Figure 11.1 Two dimensions of HRM

manner. The soft usage lays emphasis on the term *human . . .*, on employee development, group relations and constructive supervision (Storey and Sissons, 1987).

The two dimensions mirror the dual purposes of leadership and management:

- *instrumental*—getting tasks done; achieving desired results;
- *expressive*—motivating and nurturing those who perform the tasks.

Figure 11.1 invites you to explore the contrasting 'hard' and 'soft' dimensions. Like the models that follow, it is an aid to understanding a wide range of ideas rather than a precise 'scientific' definition of the distinctions. Educational management is too personal and complex to be regarded as a precise 'science'.

The hard/soft distinction is to some extent arbitrary but useful for analytical purposes. In your role as a manager, a balanced and integrated approach that employs the best of both aspects of HRM is desirable and the skills of both sides should be part of your leadership repertoire.

Reflection 1

Figure 11.1 is packed with the 'buzzwords' of HRM both hard and soft. Are they all clear to you? Many of them appear elsewhere in the book. Check the glossary and index if necessary.

HRM IN THE BROADER CONTEXT

Many governments are promoting *managerialist* policies in the public sector and education. Managerialism is a complex concept, that you will have come across elsewhere in the book, e.g. Chapter 1. One simple definition is:

> The assumption that management is the solution to many organisational problems; often a pejorative term directed at those who see management as an end rather than means, particularly in the publicly funded services (Oldroyd et al, 1996).

This trend has increased the control of managers over professionals in several professions, especially in health, social services and education. This new approach is known as *new public management* (NPM). NPM is described as 'the drive led by politicians for higher, measurable, visible standards of effectiveness, efficiency and equity to meet the challenges of global competition in a rapidly changing world' (Oldroyd, 2002). It emphasizes accountability and performance management—setting targets, measuring and 'levering up' of standards. One mechanism for doing this is to introduce competition between educational institutions just as businesses have to compete for customers in the commercial sector. Business terminology is now widely used in the education sector. Some commentators see NPM's *accountability* approach (requiring professionals to account for or justify their performance) to be in conflict with the progressive humanist educational values and the traditional autonomy of education professionals in some countries.

Paralleling the rise of NPM, there has been growing interest in the 'soft' social and psychological aspects of leading and managing. Emotional intelligence (Goleman, 1998) has emerged as a concept that is increasingly applied to leading and managing organisations (see Chapter 1). Educators have long been aware of the crucial role that emotions and teacher-pupil relationships play in learning. Managing with the 'heart' as well as with the 'head' is now a major focus in the field of education.

A RATIONAL APPROACH TO HRM

The worldwide trend towards decentralising the management of schools has moved many responsibilities for managing people from system to institutional levels in recent years. Figure 11.2 sets out a rational sequence of key tasks of 'hard' HRM. These tasks may be divided between managers at system and institutional levels or be conducted as a joint responsibility. Practice varies considerably between countries depending on the degree of decentralisation already introduced.

'Hard' HRM is mainly to do with the structures, policies and processes for implementing a sequence of tasks designed to:

- get the right people in place to do the job (staffing the organisation);
- make sure that the job is done well (performance management);
- supporting their ability to achieve organisational goals and promotion (development and succession).

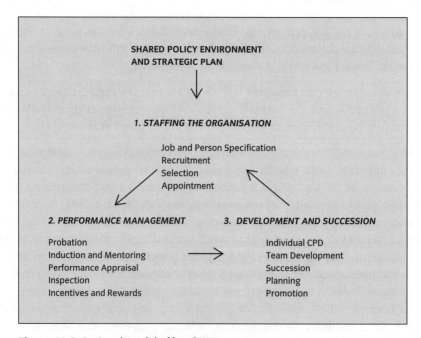

Figure 11.2 Rational model of hard HRM

Shared policies and a strategic plan of the organisation normally guide these HRM procedures. The processes follow a logical sequence for managing staffs' entry, performance and progress through the organisation whether it is a school, college, district education office or even a ministry. Upon promotion to a new role, the sequence starts again. Implementation of 'hard' HRM varies greatly between countries. You can now see how some of these steps are implemented in Poland, a central European country in transition. As you do so you can also relate what you read to practice in your own country.

STAFFING THE ORGANISATION

Case Example 1 Staffing Polish schools

SPECIFICATION

'Needed—a fully qualified Maths teacher' is about all you would see in an advertisement and job description in a Polish newspaper. Everyone understands that the teacher must have a Magister's degree (five years of post-secondary study including a pedagogical qualification). Person specifications that describe required personal qualities and experience are virtually unknown. Most commonly, new staff are recruited through word of mouth, social networks or the recommendations of inspectors, but the decision to appoint is made autonomously by the School Director who rarely involves colleagues in the selection process. More progressive School Directors sometimes require the candidate to teach a demonstration lesson or at least meet future potential colleagues. But the main emphasis in making the appointment is placed on the teachers' qualifications rather than performance. By 2006 anyone without the full qualifications will not be eligible to teach and will have to withdraw from teaching unless they are enrolled in a part-time upgrading course.

Selection, appointment and teacher supply

Applicants visit Regional Job Centres, the regional education authority or individual schools and leave their CV if they wish to apply for available posts. Sometimes advertisements are placed in public newspapers by individual schools. The School Director decides how many people to interview and whom to appoint, often guided by recommendations of an acquaintance. It is a highly personal and individual process, a vestige of the former system of autocratic leadership. The Director makes a formal contract on behalf of the regional and local educational authorities that have no say in the whole process.

National regulations authorised by Parliament almost guarantee teachers a permanent job. It is extremely hard to remove a teacher for incompetence. The Ministry of Education and Science attempted to liberalise the employment regulations to require teachers to work two extra hours a week but the teacher unions were strong enough to persuade the government otherwise. Fixed-term contracts that do not offer security of tenure are now allowed. This introduces more labour flexibility in all public service institutions including those in the education sector. There is an over-supply of qualified teachers at present, even in Foreign Languages and Maths where until recently teachers were in short supply. This means that there are many applications for each vacancy.

Did you see a *job description* before you were appointed that clearly specified the tasks and responsibilities you would have to undertake? Did those who appointed you make a *person specification* that set out the abilities needed for the job and the criteria by which you would be selected? Both job and person specifications that describe the work tasks and the personal qualities, skills and qualifications required, are the starting point for the rational management of staff. In Poland increased autonomy for and competition between individual schools have been introduced since the early 1990s. More responsibility for managing the staff is one of the many additional tasks passed down to school level along with managing budgets, facilities resource, curriculum, staff development and public relations. A 'hard' performance management approach is promoted, but a gap remains between intention and implementation in many areas. It is important to remember that:

> even in countries where educators are highly trained, their ability to take on the HRM role is problematic . . . it may be unrealistic to expect beleaguered, overworked and underpaid staff to take on an enlarged staff management role over and above their teaching responsibilities (Foskett and Lumby, 2002, p.68).

PERFORMANCE MANAGEMENT

Performance management is about agreeing goals or targets for individuals, teams, organisation and even countries, using monitoring and review processes, incentives and development activities to achieve and measure progress towards these targets. The degree to which performance can be managed by the means indicated in Figure 11.2 is contentious. Intuition, creativity and flair are qualities of good teachers and leaders that defy a tightly managed approach designed to 'increase productivity' or 'add value'.

- *Probation* is the process of assessing that newly trained and qualified teachers and other staff are competent in practice.
- *Induction* is the support offered to ease their adjustment to the demands of the particular job and organisation and to the profession in general. In many countries probation and induction hardly exist and new teachers are 'thrown in the deep end' to sink or swim.
- *Performance appraisal* has spread from the business world to the public services in recent years as an internal assurance of quality and is a key managerialist element of new public management. Like probation and induction it has two functions—*accountability* and *development*. Performance is judged through observing teaching and student outcomes or results. Recently in a growing number of countries a third function—*reward*—has been added. Controversy surrounds appraisal schemes in education systems. Often the schemes are heavily bureaucratic. They involve

considerable time and paperwork, but it is frequently hard to demonstrate improvements in performance that follow the setting of targets.

- *Performance-related pay* (PRP) is the payment of bonuses or salary increases based on formal appraisal. In general, teachers favour appraisal for development rather than for accountability. Many teachers appreciate the opportunity of receiving constructive feedback, support and additional income, but the process of appraisal is stressful, particularly when it is not done skilfully and sensitively. It places considerable demands on principals of schools and by rewarding teachers differentially it can lead to a sense of unfairness. The business ethic of rewarding success clashes with the principle of equity traditionally associated with the public service ethic.

- *Career paths or ladders* linked to pay are found in many countries to provide incentives for teachers to stay in the profession and to engage in development. Increasingly, PRP systems are linking salaries to assessments of performance (merit pay) rather than to years of service (experience or seniority).

- *Inspections* by external inspectors usually result in action plans that focus mainly on the school as a whole, but also involve specific targets for departments that the teachers must implement. Like appraisal, inspection is hard to do well, challenges teachers' professional autonomy and remains a controversial and stress-inducing aspect of new public management for managers and teachers alike.

Performance management has been adopted in education from the business sector. Whether a management strategy such as HRM designed to suit the business world is in fact appropriate for an educational establishment is much debated. Fidler (1988) lists a number of difficulties in borrowing this means of managing people's productivity:

- the higher level of professional autonomy in the teaching profession;
- qualitative objectives that are difficult to measure, or even to agree;
- a limited range of rewards available for teachers;
- unclear links between teaching and learning;
- several people to whom teachers are accountable;
- a lack of infrastructure and time to implement the processes.

Case Example 2 Managing performance in Polish schools

INDUCTION, APPRAISAL AND INSPECTION

In the first year of teaching it is normal that an experienced colleague (mentor) offers support and advice. Mentoring is not a formally developed programme required by law. It depends on the practice of the individual school. The School Director carries out periodical formal appraisal of teachers. Two negative reports in succession disqualify a teacher from teaching but this rarely happens because the appraisal is based on lesson observation and is announced in advance. Provincial inspectors make external inspections of schools every five years, using quality standards elaborated by each of the 16 provinces. Schools and colleges are also required to conduct self-evaluations on themes identified by the Provincial Education Department. The provincial standards will eventually be replaced by national standards.

REWARDS

Each year the district education authority provides each school with a sum of extra money to reward teachers of high merit. The School Director or a nominated committee decides who will get this award. Many schools give everybody the same amount ignoring the intention to reward high performance. Often the School Director is reluctant to take responsibility for this difficult and controversial process. Pressure placed on School Directors to use the rewards as intended varies between different regions.

CAREER LADDER

Salaries of teachers depend on:

- years of teaching (a salary increase of 1 per cent for each of 20 years starting after 3 years' experience);
- rank on the career ladder;
- a motivational bonus paid to selected teachers each year.

There is no pay for middle managers such as heads of departments and the system is criticised as 'money awarded simply for growing older'! Excellent teachers can be getting 5 per cent above their starting salary while an older, longer-serving incompetent teacher gets 20 per cent.

The rungs on the career ladders are as follows:

Probationary Teacher—newly employed teacher, fully qualified, whom the School Director must assess before progress can follow to the next level.

Contract Teacher—has job security after the first successful year of employment.

Nominated Teacher—whose personal development plan and development portfolio is assessed to give more salary and greater job security. Nominated teachers can mentor contract and probationary teachers.

Diplomate Teacher—further assessment leads to a greater salary increase and more mentoring.

Professor of School—a title linked to higher salary for a highly experienced and successful secondary school teacher who has been a Diplomate Teacher for ten years.

Education policy in Poland is strongly influenced by new public management approaches. Performance management has been passed into law but has not been sufficiently supported by staff training. Bureaucratic procedures that should be applied universally and fairly ('*universalism*'), for example in progressing up the career ladder, are often affected by the '*particularism*' of personal affiliation and obligations and occasionally nepotism, as is the case in many countries. The low level of salaries adds to the desire to progress up the career ladder and the pressure to favour one's acquaintances or relatives.

MANAGING DEVELOPMENT AND SUCCESSION

- *Continuing professional development* (CPD) for individuals and teams, is logically placed after appraisal in the rational HRM model because one purpose of appraisal is to identify development needs. School-focused and school-based CPD and team development have become responsibilities of all team leaders (middle management) as well as specialist members of senior management teams in schools and colleges in many countries.

- *Succession planning and promotion* are part of a strategic approach to planning. A school or district development plan can incorporate succession planning to service any planned restructuring of the curriculum or staffing. This might mean involving particular staff in professional development courses, for example in preparation for new managerial responsibilities.

Case Example 3 Development and succession in Polish schools

INDIVIDUAL AND TEAM DEVELOPMENT

Teachers are organised into departmental or subject teams in many schools but there is virtually no time for meetings within school hours. Low salaries for teachers mean that many have to take additional work and teachers are contracted and paid only according to how many classes they teach. Recent reforms and training at Provincial Education Centres have prepared staff for school-based staff development roles in schools but there is a lack of time and resources for in-house programmes. The more dedicated teachers themselves pay to go on professional development courses.

Succession planning and promotion

It is still very common to 'groom' teachers for promotion, for example, when a School Director will shortly retire, although officially all promotions are based on open competition. Progression up the career ladder depends heavily on the patronage of the headteacher. To become a School Director a CV and letter of application presenting a vision for the school's development are required. A nominated body comprising two teachers, two school inspectors, two parents, a representative of the teacher union and two education authority representatives makes the appointment. All applicants and practising School Directors are required to have completed an educational management programme of at least 200 hours.

Reflection 2

How developed is performance management in your system in comparison with Poland? Do you favour pay based on seniority or merit? Do business practices fit well into education? Is 'particularism' still a feature of your own educational management system?

You will be able to explore CPD in greater detail in Chapter 13.

AN EFFICACY MODEL OF SOFT HRM

The efficacy model of 'soft' HRM is more speculative than the rational model that it parallels. Soft HRM encourages the *efficacy* (competence, confidence and capacity for success) of *resourceful humans* as Figure 11.1 suggested. Hard and soft HRM are not opposites or 'either-or' choices. They are complementary aspects of managing people that you need to weave together in order to satisfy both the needs of the organisation and individual employees. Figure 11.3 relates to the psychological and social side of managing educational organisations and staff—the 'heart' as opposed to the 'head'. It sets out desirable personal, professional and organisational 'human' features of successful HRM. It is less about performance and standards, more about emotions, relationships, motivation and values—the 'expressive' side of leadership. It concerns the management and nurture of:

- *self*—awareness and management of one's inner thoughts and beliefs, motivation and associated behaviour;
- *others*—inter-personal relationships and communication;
- *teams*—development of collaborative synergy and creative problem-solving capacity;
- *organisational culture and learning*—making a satisfying and motivating place to work and learn.

It requires leadership that empowers staff. Such leadership is emotionally intelligent (demonstrating personal and inter-personal efficacy), growth-enhancing (encouraging efficacy in others) and distributed (shared with others) throughout the organisation. Leadership may be a better term than management to use in relation to 'soft' HRM

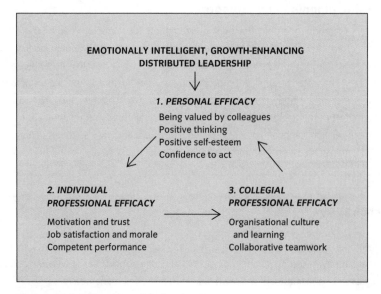

Figure 11.3 Efficacy model of soft HRM

because of the emphasis on values, motivation and emotions. Where individuals have *personal efficacy* and this is enhanced through soft HRM, then they are more likely to demonstrate *professional efficacy* as individuals and in collaboration with colleagues. Working and learning with efficacious colleagues in a growth-inducing environment inspired by leadership will tend to promote greater motivation, trust and personal efficacy. A self-reinforcing virtuous circle of high performance is the ideal consequence.

The content of the 'hard' and 'soft' HRM models differs mainly because the former emphasizes performance for the sake of the organisation, whereas the latter focuses on individuals and persons as well as in their role as productive workers. Rayman (2001) in a book on dignity at work argues that in addition to the purpose of earning a living, work should satisfy individual needs for self-respect and for exercising social responsibility. Both these purposes are aligned with the efficacy model.

PERSONAL EFFICACY

Personal efficacy is associated with high emotional intelligence (EI). Goleman (1998) elaborates the qualities of EI, all of which can be improved through appropriate learning:

* self-awareness—of thoughts and feelings, preferences, resources, intuitions, actions;

* self-regulation—states of mind, impulses, resources, openness to feedback, persistence;

* motivation—emotional tendencies, drive towards clear goals, deferred gratification, zeal;

* empathy—active listening, awareness of other people's feelings, needs and concerns;

* social skills—inducing desirable responses in others, negotiation, assertiveness, compromise, collaboration.

These personal qualities are the key to all three types of efficacy and are the basis for resourceful performance in personal and professional life. Selecting people of high emotional intelligence is the first step to building a learning organisation. But qualities of EI can be enhanced through conscious self-development, role modelling, socialisation, constructive feedback and creating an open and positive organisational culture. Educational leaders and managers can encourage personal reflection and learning through *metacognition* (thinking about one's thinking) and *metacommunication* (communication about communication). Personal efficacy arises from a combination of inner psychological processes and external environmental factors. Both are strongly influenced by ethnic and regional differences, gender and class factors between and within societies.

In 'hard' HRM performance management is based on target-setting, monitoring and appraising performance and offering incentives and extrinsic rewards, such as PRP and promotion for achieving desired results. Cognitive psychology links performance to people's inner processes of thinking and believing and particularly their view of self. The term 'self-talk' is used to describe the unending but controllable flow of words, pictures and feelings that comprise our consciousness. Figure 11.4 illustrates the cognitive and affective processes that underlie both personal and professional performance. A basic assumption of personal development is that we can exercise a high degree of control over our self-talk-cycle in any situation. Whether we think and act positively or

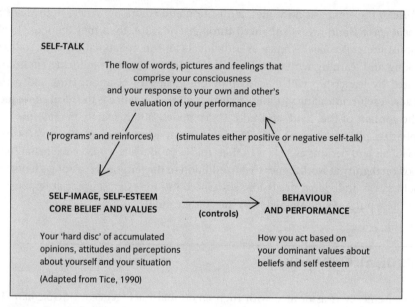

Figure 11.4 The self-talk cycle

negatively is a matter of choice. The higher your EI, the better your choices. But educational leaders and managers can help to create a work environment and relationship with staff that encourage positive rather than negative thinking, feeling and behaviour.

Feeding a positive self-talk cycle might be seen as the soft HRM equivalent to performance management. Of course in many organisations and individuals a negative version or 'vicious circle' of self-talk exists. Negative leaders, inter-personal relations and organisational culture can diminish people's self-esteem and discourage initiative and high performance. Personal efficacy is greater in people who are self-aware and choose to regulate negative self-talk even in difficult circumstances.

INDIVIDUAL PROFESSIONAL EFFICACY

Motivation is perhaps the most important factor in individual professional efficacy. It underlies job satisfaction, morale, initiative and consequently how you perform or fulfil your professional role. Based on Evans (2003), distinctions between these 'soft' HRM terms can be summarised as:

- *Motivation*—the complex individual drive to perform in order to achieve desired goals and to satisfy perceived needs. This depends on individual mentality, in particular self-image, self-esteem, goal-orientation and expectations, as well as on the work and broader environment.

- *Job satisfaction*—the state of mind resulting from present conditions and experiences in the workplace. It depends on how well the job fits the person as well as on each person's assessment of whether they are being respected, treated fairly, managed competently, offered adequate support.

- *Morale*—the degree to which an individual anticipates the possibility of achieving personal and professional goals. Group morale is the sum total of group members' individual sense of this possibility. For example, if teachers expect to be respected and well paid and are not, then their morale will suffer.

- *Initiative*—the personal efficacy, energy, enthusiasm and imagination to start something new without being ordered to do so. A major factor in countries that are in transition from central 'dependency cultures' to decentralised control is the need to encourage more initiative in both educational staff and students and pupils.

Clearly, educational leaders from ministry through district into colleges and schools would hope for positive values to characterise all these features of the workforce. Owens (2002) explores the complexity of motivation that arises from the interplay between personality and environmental factors. Drawing on decades of research mainly conducted in North America, he shows how important educational managers are in creating growth-enhancing environments that encourage extrinsic and intrinsic motivation of educational workers. He illustrates the need for *situational leadership* involving different approaches by educational managers in differing contexts and with different groups of staff. For example, inexperienced staff tend to need a lot of guidance and praise whereas those with much experience and professional efficacy value being trusted to take on challenges with minimal supervision.

Numerous theories try to capture the complexity of human motivation and are useful as a background for 'soft' HRM. Content theories include:

- *Maslow's 'hierarchy of needs'* that suggests that people are driven to meet the basic needs of security and affiliation and higher order needs for self-esteem, autonomy and self-actualisation, and that the former must be met before the latter can be achieved.

- *Herzberg's 'two-factor' theory* argues that motivation at work consists of two separate independent factors; *motivational factors* ('motivators') that can lead to job satisfaction and *maintenance factors* that if not sufficiently present can lead to dissatisfaction or apathy ('dissatisfiers'). For example, inadequate pay is a dissatisfier but well-paid staff are not necessarily highly motivated if they do not experience the 'motivators' of achievement, recognition, responsibility and challenge in their work.

- *McGregor's X and Y theory* contrasts two sets of assumptions that managers hold about their subordinates. Theory X assumes that staff are intrinsically lazy and need to be supervised continuously and coerced to perform well. Theory Y assumes that people yearn for responsibility and will be high achievers when trusted and encouraged.

Process theories include:

- *expectancy theory*—people's work effort relates to the outcomes that they expect to gain;

- *equity theory*—equal treatment or fairness is a key factor in determining motivation;

- *goal theory*—people are motivated by goals that are clear, specific, achievable and to which they are committed.

To be acquainted with these theories provides you with concepts for metacognition and metacommunication about your own motivation and that of others. They also offer guidance to managers wishing to design conditions and relationships in the workplace that facilitate motivation. But as was noted in Chapter 2, these predominantly 'Western' theories have to be tested against cultural values. In Scandinavian or Japanese cultures, affiliation needs are much stronger than in more individualistic societies. Many traditional and not fully democratic, high-coercion societies still exist where Theory Y strategies seem too radical for both managers and the managed!

In her research on managing motivation in English schools, Evans refers to the importance of factors specific to each institution in motivating teachers:

> [T]he most strikingly common factor to emerge as influential on teachers' morale, job satisfaction and motivation is school leadership . . . the leadership effected by their headteachers was clearly a key determinant of how teachers felt about their jobs (Evans, 1998, p.118).

There are, of course, many other influences. You may find aspects of your own work de-motivating and stressful due to a variety of institutional and personal factors that contribute to under-performance, for example when you:

- lack clarity about what you must do and to what standard (role ambiguity);
- lack the skills to perform well (skills deficit);
- are required to do things that clash with your beliefs and values (value conflict);
- are short of time (role overload);
- have other major obligations that take priority (role conflict);
- feel bored and not challenged by your work (under-stimulation);
- feel you are not learning and developing (excessive routine);
- feel undervalued and unappreciated (ineffective 'soft' HRM).

Teachers in virtually all countries complain of an overload of work and a growing bureaucratic burden of paperwork. Using research from Canada, Hargreaves (1994) describes two forms of teacher guilt:

- *persecutory guilt*—caused by external demands for accountability;
- *depressive guilt*—resulting from a failure to meet the high expectations one sets for oneself as a dedicated professional wishing to serve the students to the best of one's ability.

Personal efficacy, emotional intelligence and positive use of self-talk are the basis for developing the inner strength to deal with these pressures. Educational leaders have an important role to play in modelling and encouraging professional efficacy and diminishing the de-motivating organisational factors that produce stress, low morale and under-performance.

Under-performers are 'difficult people' for those who manage them. Defining the concept, let alone managing, 'difficult people' is not straightforward. In an autocratic environment such a person could be anyone who challenges the status quo or the exercise of authority. In dynamic, change-oriented situations, the passive colleague might be seen as the difficult one to manage. Common difficulties of under-performance include time wasting, absenteeism, inappropriate relations with colleagues and students, isolationism, 'empire building', and blocking or sabotaging change. These difficulties arise from failing to perform appropriately and to the standards expected. There may be many reasons for this that arise from the interaction between the person and the environment, both within and beyond the organisation. The sources of de-motivation and stress listed above will remind you of the complex factors that contribute to difficulties in job performance. Managers who try to minimise these sources of de-motivation will enhance both the efficacy and performance of their staff.

Coaching and *mentoring* relate to hard and soft HRM respectively and can be used to combat under-performance. Both provide constructive feedback and are key managerial skills in assisting under-performers and in providing professional support to all staff. Mentoring pays more attention to the social and psychological aspects of the beneficiary than coaching which focuses primarily on professional and technical skills.

Reflection 3

Consider your own work situation in the light of the characteristics of personal and individual professional efficacy outlined above. What motivate and de-motivates you in your work? Do you believe that you can 're-program' your own negative self-talk?

COLLEGIAL PROFESSIONAL EFFICACY

The third part of the efficacy model of 'soft' HRM involves the collegial side of organisational life (collegiality is discussed in Chapter 3). Building a positive organisational culture that favours collaborative teamwork is enhanced where staff exhibit high personal and individual professional efficacy. High performing teams and professional learning communities are characteristics of collegial professional efficacy (see also Chapter 12).

Traditionally teachers have worked largely as individuals within a 'culture of individualism'. In recent years team-based 'collegial cultures' have increasingly been advocated for schools and other educational organisations. This requires teachers to work in teams to plan, implement and assess the curriculum and to organise extra-curricular activities and pastoral care. The reasoning behind teamwork is that it creates *synergy* (the whole is greater than the sum of the parts) that leads to better overall performance and more creative solutions to problems. Collaboration is a key characteristic of an effective team. It requires a deeper form of inter-personal relationships than simply cooperation in groups. Figure 11.5 summarises some of the features of collaborative teams using the distinction between 'hard' (task-oriented) and 'soft' (person-oriented) aspects of teamwork. Coaching of teams would focus on the hard element and mentoring would address the softer characteristics of teamwork.

'Hard' collaboration (focused on tasks)	'Soft' collaboration (focused on relationships)
Involves shared:	**Involves shared:**
• goals	• commitment
• resources	• surrender of autonomy
• work tasks	• feelings
• problem-solving	• uncertainty
• pressure	• support
• outcomes	• trust

Figure 11.5 Collaboration and levels of organisational relationships

A second principle behind teamwork is its contribution to staff motivation. Peer pressure and peer support are features of collaborative teams. High performing teams combine features of hard and soft HRM and are a great asset in managing change. Blanchard (1990) lists the features of such teams using an appropriate acronym:

- **P**—urpose   common, clear goals and strategies
- **E**—mpower   collective sense of power, mutual support
- **R**—elationships   open, honest, warm, accepting, differences valued
- **F**—lexibility   shared leadership, adaptability
- **O**—ptimal product   high quality output, creative problem-solving
- **R**—ecognition   appreciation of individuals
- **M**—orale   confidence, pride, cohesion, team spirit.

Unfortunately, as Judith Little (1990) has pointed out, 'serious collaboration, by which teachers engage in the rigorous mutual examination of teaching and learning, turns out to be rare' (p.187). Staff collaboration is never straightforward. It is in tension with the desire for classroom autonomy. In general, teachers prefer to collaborate at the pedagogical level rather than in policy-making and school planning (Hoyle, 1996). To encourage collaboration a leader has to create both structures and cultures in the organisation. Hoyle concludes that:

> Whilst the effective head will establish appropriate structures for teacher participation in decision-making . . . it is clear from recent research that effective collaboration will perhaps more importantly be the function of the culture which the head generates which is marked by collaboration and consensus but can also encompass diversity and conflict.

Creative conflict is also a feature of collegial professional efficacy. It applies to high performing teams that contain people with a diversity of opinions and values. Where sufficient trust exists between team members, it is possible through open-minded dialogue and disagreements, to generate new meanings, policy and practice that contribute to collegial efficacy and the effective management of change. As Belbin (1993) and others have demonstrated, these processes are also enhanced when teams contain a blend of people of different types who can assume a variety of roles within the team. As schools and other educational organisations develop team approaches, the task of leadership is increasingly diffused throughout the staff. To be effective, team leaders need to be able to:

- diagnose the patterns and dynamics of the team (who talks to/influences who);
- stimulate creative conflict and resolve destructive conflicts;
- share decision-making and delegate responsibilities in order to empower and satisfy team members;
- adapt to changing circumstances shifting focus from task to persons when appropriate;
- solve problems creatively and collaboratively;
- create a climate of norms, expectations and opportunities for continuing professional development;
- maintain a focus on goals, high quality and performance through a process of continuing review of assumptions, processes and outcomes.

The efficacy model of 'soft' HRM culminates with organisational culture and organisational learning. Both *organisational culture*, which encompasses prevailing values, norms and ways of behaving in organisations, and *organisational learning*, the collective making of meaning for understanding and improving organisational life, are strongly influenced by resourceful leadership.

DEVELOPING RESOURCEFUL LEADERSHIP FOR LEARNING

Bhindi and Duignan (1997, p.119) eloquently suggest that:

> It is argued that no matter whether in educational, religious, public service or business organisations, authentic leaders encourage and support ways of thinking and doing that are ethical and people-centred. It is proposed that leaders in the new century will need to be more sensitive and caring in their attitudes and relationships and more adaptable and flexible in their practices, if they are to release the potential, and tap the diversity of talents, of those who work with them.

They signal the need for leaders to attend to the inner self and spirit of their staff or colleagues and to act as role models of personal integrity. A case study from Kazakhstan illustrates how resourceful leadership can combine 'hard' and 'soft' HRM to improve organisations that are in considerable difficulty.

Case Example 4 Transforming a Kazakh school

Three years ago Shymkent Basic School No. 39 had 600 pupils and was badly affected by conflicts between the director and deputies that led to a legal dispute. Along with the under-funding and dilapidated conditions that affect almost all schools in Kazakhstan, this situation added to the low morale of the staff and the low reputation of the school. It was a school in regression.

A new school director was appointed. He was a former deputy director of the city education department who had resigned when it was reorganised. His PhD, completed eight years previously, had looked at 'economic mechanisms for managing social structure' analysing the local education system of Shymkent, a southern city of 60,000 inhabitants and many social problems. After three months unemployment when he made a living buying and selling horse and camel milk, he took over the school with a determination to breathe life back into the staff and modernise its management structure and the quality of its education.

Kazakhstan is a country where most school personnel are reluctant to exercise the initiative that the Law on Education allows them. This school director had the experience, character and confidence to justify his new approach by finding the appropriate legal articles relating to extra-budget fundraising and restructuring schools, to legitimate the following changes:

- a policy of raising as many extra-budget funds as possible seeking sponsorship without overburdening the parents;
- cooperating with teacher unions as social partners in order to get their professional support for improvements in the school and for the socially deprived students;
- a management structure that grew from two to eight leadership roles, each with a clear job description in a senior management team that holds weekly planning and review meetings;
- appointing five former colleagues from the city education department to occupy these roles;
- delegating considerable responsibility to his colleagues with the incentive that all extra work be rewarded from the extra-budget income to supplement extremely low official salaries;
- making all documents available for inspection by the parents' committee and trade unions in the interest of transparency;
- adopting a leadership style that combined pressure and support with a view to creating a positive collegial culture in which staff are valued and rewarded with financial incentives ('economic mechanisms') including twice-yearly bonuses and supplies of food;
- building trust throughout the school and community by acting with openness and integrity ('I never lie to anybody, unlike many directors who say, think and act in contradictory ways'); and
- taking every opportunity to advertise the progress of the school through conference presentations, public meetings and publicity materials to enhance its reputation.

In the last two years the school has expanded its enrolment from 900 to 1,600. Although the director's dream to have decent salaries for his staff is a long way from being realised, his entrepreneurial spirit is compensating for the chronic under-funding of the education system in this transition country. Investment from the income generated locally is targeted on providing better conditions for study that includes providing lunches for 500 of the poorest students in a school where 84 per cent of the graduates formerly were classified as suffering from physical ailments arising from poor nutrition.

This 'transformational leader' combined hard and soft HRM with astute financial management to turn the school around. He is tackling head-on the problem of under-investment that results in low teacher morale, de-motivation and poor student outcomes in a socially impoverished community.

Leadership is the driving force behind both models of HRM presented in this chapter (see also Chapter 1 where you were introduced to theories of leadership). An issue facing educational leaders that reflects the distinction between 'hard' and 'soft' HRM is how to accommodate the possible tension between two images of leadership:

- *transactional leadership*—more readily associated with the strategic purposes of 'efficiency, effectiveness and performance';
- *transformational leadership*—focusing on the human dimension of 'values, learning communities and shared leadership' (Gold et al, 2003).

For Gold and her colleagues transformational leadership 'is dispersed or shared throughout the school' and 'focuses on the people involved—relationships between them, in particular—and requires an approach that seeks to transform staff feelings, attitudes and beliefs'. High personal and professional efficacy and the ability to encourage them in others are associated with transformational leadership.

In a more recent concept, Evans (2003, p.37) proposes *'teacher-centred leadership'* as a service provided by leaders to those who are being led. It takes its name from a child-centred approach to teaching and proposes that:

leaders and managers have as much responsibility towards the staff whom they lead and manage as they do towards the pupils and students within their institution, and that this responsibility extends as far as endeavouring to meet as many individual needs as possible, within the confines imposed by having to consider more corporate needs.

This is an interesting link, particular to the educational sector, between leading and teaching. It confirms the need to address personal as well as professional efficacy. But it may also be a particularly 'Western' concept of educational leadership. It is obviously less relevant in countries that still struggle with the problems of 'getting teachers into school for the required hours' (Foskett and Lumby, 2002) or ensuring compliance with a totalitarian ideology or coping with the disastrous erosion of school and college life due to the HIV-AIDS pandemic. It is obvious that economic, political and social conditions external to education systems can place great constraints on pursuing currently favoured prescriptions of good practice. This is also true in developed societies. A major debate in the UK continues about the limitations placed on values-driven leadership by NPM or the 'managerialist project' of politicians to lever-up standards in schools and colleges.

SUMMARY

Rational HRM derived from business practice is now widely advocated in increasingly decentralised education systems. This managerialist trend that conceives of humans as resources to be deployed and managed in the same way as other non-human resources remains controversial. Managing 'hard' HRM can be seen as a logical progression of tasks required for:

- staffing the organisation;
- managing staff performance in reaching targets and standards;
- managing their development and succession in pursuit of the organisation's strategic goals.

'Soft' HRM focuses on empowering resourceful humans; it is a developmental humanistic approach to leadership and management. It requires leaders to encourage three kinds of inter-related efficacy:

- personal efficacy;
- individual professional efficacy; and
- collegial professional efficacy.

It is hard to demonstrate empirically the effects of HRM policy and practice in education on productivity or achievement of organisational goals. It is also questionable whether performance management alone and the promotion of efficacy are appropriate strategies for countries whose educational systems are in an early process of development or transition. Undoubtedly the quality and motivation of staff is the key to effective education. People are the most important factor in developing professional learning communities (see also Chapters 5 and 13). Educational leaders need to strike a proper balance between performance management and creating the conditions for efficacy in the workplace. Inspiring the commitment of people at all levels of education to the core task of learning is a high moral purpose that distinguishes leadership and management in education from that in other fields.

RECOMMENDED FURTHER READING

'Managing people in education' in Foskett, N. and Lumby, J. (2002) *Leading and Managing Education: International Dimensions* (pp.64–69) offers you a sceptical examination of some 'conventional wisdom' about HRM as presented from a 'Western' point of view. In the first part 'Analysing environment' you are led to four myths that the authors identify about HRM and in the second part, its feasibility in many countries is questioned. In the same book 'People and performance' (pp.74–85) raises important questions about cultural differences that relate to people's motivation and performance in different education systems.

For a classic summary of motivational theories as they relate to education see Owens, R. (2002) *Organisational Behaviour in Education* (6th edn) London: Allyn and Bacon, pp.137–157. Cognitive and humanistic theories of motivation are synthesised and the complex interplay between personality and environment is dealt with from the perspective of educational leadership. Another useful overview of theories of motivation is offered by Colin Riches in the edited collection by Bush and West-Burnham (1994). *Principles of Educational Management*, Harlow: Longman.

You may find it interesting to read the trenchant criticism of HRM inThrupp, M. and Willmott, R. (2003) *Education Management in Managerialist Times: Beyond the Textual Apologists*, Maidenhead: Open University Press.

12

Leading for Effective Learning

Eileen Carnell and Caroline Lodge

INTRODUCTION AND LEARNING OUTCOMES

This chapter considers the key issue of effective learning for both young people and adults and its relationship with leadership. The chapter starts with a discussion of different conceptions of learning relating them to recent research and outlining different models of learning. The discussion then focuses on the meaning of effective learning and factors that promote and hinder effective learning in classrooms, before moving on to consider how the principles of effective learning connect with and support the principles of effective leadership. Finally, consideration is given to the implications of distributive leadership in organisational learning and the ways in which leaders demonstrate they are encouraging effective learning.

By the end of this chapter you should be able to:

- understand different conceptions of learning;
- reflect on the implications of different models of learning for leadership and the classroom.

In addition you should have greater insight into your own practice. You are invited to consider your individual learning intentions in relation to this chapter.

WHAT DO WE MEAN BY LEARNING?

Conceptions of learning

First we consider different conceptions of learning. We begin by noting that the word *learning* covers a range of different meanings for people. A group of researchers

(Marton et al, 1993) found that people had a range of different everyday conceptions of learning:

- acquiring more knowledge;
- memorising and reproducing;
- applying facts or procedures;
- understanding;
- seeing something in a different way;
- changing as a person.

These different conceptions may be held by different people or by the same person in different circumstances and for different purposes. This research was carried out with a group of university students learning at a distance. We note that the conceptions of learning are limited. They represent individual activity, the social dimension of learning, understandably, is not identified. We prefer to consider this list as progressing from poorer to richer conceptions of learning but some writers refer to deep and surface learning (Entwistle and Ramsden, 1983).

Different conceptions and purposes in learning may depend on a number of different aspects listed in Table 12.1.

This list indicates how complex learning is and how each occasion is different. Some learning may occur later. A young person at school may have less control over many of the aspects of learning listed in Table 12.1, but when they are learning out of school they may share the same aspects as adults (Resnick, 1987). We now turn to other people's images and descriptions of learning.

Conceptions of learning in schools

We now present four illustrations of learning in schools: three drawings by young people and a photograph. Images can tell us a great deal about how people understand learning.

Table 12.1 Aspects of learning specific to a learning occasion

degree of formality
presence or not of a teacher
presence or not of others
your own purposes
prior learning
purposes of others
physical context
importance of the learning
feelings
strategies

In Picture 1, the child has drawn the teacher as dominant. The children are seated in rows, separated from each other, all facing the teacher. The teacher is explaining a sum. Children are responding positively. Their responses may be in their heads, and they are not engaging in conversation.

This child has drawn a fairly traditionally view of learning—a transmission view (see below). Young people's conceptions of learning often match those identified by adults. Sums are more frequently represented than other images when young people are asked to draw learning (Harris, 2002). It may be that sums represent the abstract knowledge that children understand school provides.

In Picture 2 the photographer has shown the dominant view of classrooms that was typical of its time. Many of the features of the classroom drawn by a pupil in 2002

Picture 1: A ten-year-old's picture of learning: 1 (Harris, 2002)

Picture 2: Photograph of a classroom, UK, 1920s

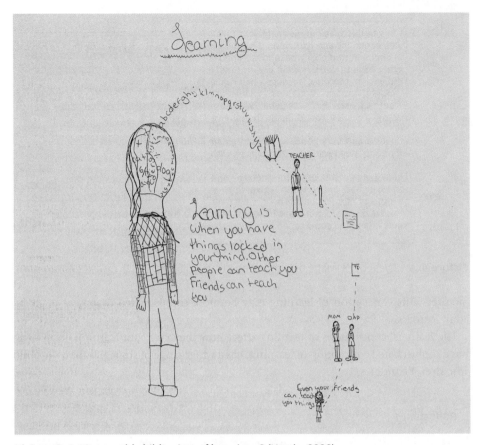

Picture 3: A 10-year-old child's view of learning: 2 (Harris, 2002)

appear again in this old photograph of an English classroom. This suggests that there are persistent visual classroom features. We note again the dominance of the teacher, the children sitting in rows (although sitting closer together in the photograph), and facing the front where the teacher's desk can just be seen.

The child is dominant in Picture 3. Although the young person is concerned with learning inside the head, she has also connected the learning to other people such as the teacher, her parents and friends. She has also connected to activities, such as rehearsing the alphabet and making connections between different learning activities. This suggests developing understandings. There is a social dimension illustrated here as she suggests parents and other young people contribute to her learning. The learner dominates, which might suggest that the learner is taking responsibility for her learning.

The young person who drew the tree and described his learning (Picture 4) has a rich view of learning and of himself as a learner. He is aware what helped him and where he struggles. The organic image appeals 'I had grown a lot over the week, not just in what I knew, but in how I thought I could tackle problems'. The tree has strong roots and appears to be blossoming. The Maths teacher does not feature. Other people have helped John with his learning indicating a stronger social dimension than in some other

I began this week in maths feeling that I was confident and had worked hard with my mum at home all weekend, so I had a great base to work from in lesson time. I did well on Monday, because I had really thought about fractions over the weekend and that was what we were doing. Tuesday was difficult though–we were set a problem-solving task and my tables aren't very good. I really struggled for about two lessons to get to grips with it. Mark really helped me understand the idea behind the problem though, and then it was like I could solve lots of problems like it–I had grown a lot over the week, not just in what I knew, but in how I thought I could tackle problems.

Picture 4: A 12-year-old's image of learning as a tree (Williams, 2002)

pictures. This conception of learning may be more sophisticated than that of many adult learners.

The learners' conceptions of learning affect how they go about learning. John, who has a sophisticated conception of learning, has a wider range of strategies than the child who drew Picture 1.

Reflection 1

How have the readings and pictures extended your understanding of learning and how people understand learning?

THREE MODELS OF LEARNING

This section considers three models of learning that can be found in educational organisations around the world. They help us understand how learning occurs.

- reception model;
- constructivist model;
- co-constructivist model.

Reception model

In this model the learner is a passive recipient of knowledge which is transmitted by the teacher. This model can be linked to the first two of the everyday meanings of learning discussed above. Basic or essential skills are emphasized while emotional and social aspects of learning are not addressed. Teaching in this model resembles transmission and stresses cognitive learning and logical, objective, abstract, sequential thinking.

Examples of this model are:

- The National Curriculum (UK) this defines for school children what they have to take in, regardless of their context, experience, interests or needs.
- Times tables.

This model could be described as quantitative, as learners are concerned with how much they can learn. The learner's role is seen as quite distinct from the teacher's. A problem with this model is that it encourages closed or fixed conceptions of the learner. Often these conceptions refer to ability or intelligence, which we know teachers assess early in their contact with classes, and construe as stable (Cooper and McIntyre, 1996). Many learners also come to define themselves in terms of ability and this can lead to beliefs about *inability* when faced with difficult learning tasks.

In the reception model the learner does not define the curriculum and it is not negotiable. The learner merely receives information which others have deemed significant. Assessment is largely related to the quantity of knowledge learned, and to mastery of basic skills. It is likely to encourage a dependence on others to decide what is important rather than develop the ability to learn throughout life. Young people are not encouraged to make connections, apply their knowledge in unforeseen circumstances or see things in different ways. In short, this model does not encourage the kind of learning young people need for their futures. The acquisition of knowledge, its memorisation and reproduction are important in learning, but are not enough for learners now or in their futures.

Constructivist model

The learners' construction of meaning is at the heart of this model. They actively construct knowledge through such activities as discussion, discovery learning, open-ended questioning, usually related to their everyday experiences, often with the help of those around them. The emphasis is less on *putting in* information and more on *drawing out* new knowledge and understanding. The emphasis is on the quality of the learning. The learner is helped to make connections and to gain new insights.

Examples of this model are:

- formative assessment—feedback comments that focus on helping the learner see and understand what can be done next, or differently;
- research activities—students identify what they need to know and find sources of information to extend their previous knowledge;
- investigative activities that invite students to find their own patterns and relationships.

The teacher is seen more as a facilitator. The responsibility for learning rests with the learner. The learner's ability is not seen as fixed, but capable of development through experience. The teacher is interested in finding out each learner's abilities, skills and interests. The relationship of the teacher to the student, however, remains one of expert to novice.

The curriculum, in this model, emphasizes relevance. Learning situations take account of social and emotional factors, but cognitive development is still the main purpose of learning.

Assessment in this model may rely partly on knowledge recall and interpretation, but can also include presentation of self-selected projects, portfolios, interviews and other less traditional forms of assessment.

This model of learning encourages aspects of effective learning. The learner is encouraged to develop judgement about what is important. It can encourage transfer of learning to different contexts, and may help the learner understand more about being a learner. While encouraging more aspects of effective learning, this model falls short of promoting the kind of learning young people need for their futures. They may remain dependent upon the teachers and not develop those dispositions required for future learners, for example as learners in a team.

Co-constructivist model

The co-constructivist model is an expanded version of the constructivist model. The essential features of this model are that it relies on dialogue and that the responsibility for learning shifts from individuals to emphasize collaboration in the construction of knowledge. Learning involves collaboration by learners in critical investigation, analysis, interpretation and reorganisation of knowledge and in reflective processes, in areas that have meaning in the learners' lives. This model of learning takes a holistic model of the learner. It takes into account the emotional aspects of learning, the dynamics of learning with others in groups, the significance of context, the purposes, effects and outcomes of their learning.

Examples of this model of learning in practice include:

- problem-solving dialogue between students;
- dialogues between learners and learners, and learners and teachers that focus on learning.

Dialogue prompts reflection, critical investigation, analysis, interpretation and reorganisation of knowledge. In this way feedback and reflection become part of the same process, enabling the learner to review his or her learning in its context and related to previous experiences and understandings.

The discipline of dialogue involves learning about group processes that support or undermine learning. The ability to communicate effectively about group relationships is essential for co-constructivism. The learning involved in peer dialogue gives learners greater control and responsibility rather than relying on the teacher. Dialogue is grounded in the assumption that learners are teachers and teachers are learners. Hierarchies are broken down and boundaries less evident. The role of the teacher is to instigate a dialogue between and with their students, based on their common experiences, but often the roles of teacher and learner are shared. In this approach learning is seen as complex, multi-dimensional and involving everyone.

The context, experience and concerns of the participants shape the curriculum. Learners engage in activities or solve problems that have meaning to them so that their learning is intrinsically significant, not just proof that they can do well in school.

In this model assessment and feedback are integrated into the process of learning. The model is not common in schools especially where there is an emphasis on performance rather than on learning, but it encourages the kind of learning which young people will need for their lives in the twenty-first century. It encourages confidence in dealing with complexity, flexibility, making connections. It encourages people to learn together, and above all it can help learners to become explicit about their learning. There is a need for more of this model in schools, but we do not underestimate the forces working against it.

Reflection 2

We suggest that the reception model (instruction or transmission) is the most dominant in classrooms across the world. It links with the dominant view of the teacher as more knowledgeable and in control and the learner as passive and dependant. To what extent are the three models reflected in learning in your organisation and your classroom?

EFFECTIVE LEARNING

This section examines the concept of effective learning. In many countries there has been an emphasis on effectiveness in education, and the word has been attached to learning too. It is important to consider what effective learning means, but it only makes sense when the context of learning and the goals are specified.

The contemporary context has some important features which mean that the goals of learning need to focus less on knowledge acquisition by individuals and more on knowledge generation with others. The reception model is a legacy of a time when it was important for people to learn a fairly static body of information. While these features vary in their impact in different parts of the world we note the significant effects of the following everywhere:

- more information is available—learners need know how to find and select relevant information, to process it, connect it, use it . . .

- learning and adapting needs to be lifelong because change is permanent

- employment requires being able to enhance and transfer knowledge and to operate collaboratively, and

- learning is increasingly taking place in different settings and with different relationships. Learning is a way of being. (Adapted from Watkins et al, 2002.)

All over the world effective learning increasingly means more knowledge generation with others (construction), less independent knowledge acquisition (coverage).

In every context the nature and the pace of change means that learners need to focus more on *how they learn*, with others, and to be strategic about their learning. Effective learners have gained understanding of the individual and social processes necessary to learn how to learn. They have acquired particular strategies and can monitor and review their learning to gauge the effectiveness of the strategies. Effective learning includes this vital ingredient of learning about learning or 'meta learning' (see Table 12.2).

An effective learner needs an appropriate context. The context needs to encourage activity, collaboration, learner responsibility and opportunities for opportunities for reflecting

Table 12.2 Effective learning and learners (adapted from Watkins et al, 2002)

Effective learning is . . .	An effective learner . . .
• an activity of construction	• is active and strategic
• handled with (or in the context of) others	• is skilled in collaboration
• driven by learner agency	• takes responsibility for their learning
• the monitoring and review of the effectiveness of approaches and strategies for the goals and context	• understands her/his learning and plans, monitors and reflects on their learning

Table 12.3 Classrooms for effective learning (adapted from Carnell and Lodge, 2002, p.39)

- the focus is on learning not on teaching; reciprocal teaching occurs—teachers are learners and pupils are teachers;
- participants identify joint goals, plan activities and group tasks that require inter-dependence;
- the pace is appropriate;
- language focuses on learning and meta-learning;
- learning is connected across all contexts;
- learners construct their own questions, help each other develop their ideas through investigation and research;
- learning is seen as dialogue;
- learning is holistic involving social, emotional and cognitive aspects;
- the learning community is fostered through goals, tasks, activities and social structures;
- many different sources challenge the learners' thinking and take their learning forward.

and monitoring their learning. The social dimension is important. Table 12.3 illustrates some features of classrooms that encourage co-constructivist learning.

A case example

We now present a case from Chieko Nakamura, a primary school teacher in Okazaki City in Aichi Prefecture in Japan describing her classroom. The purpose is first to analyse one account of a classroom related to effective learning, second to compare this with your experience of classrooms and third to consider how it may promote effective learning. Chieko writes:

Case Example 1

Each classroom has its own ethos which is made by teachers or sometimes teacher with the pupils. A description of the classroom ethos is put on the wall in front of the classroom. When I have a new class I spend two hours discussing what kind of class we want, for example, smile. And then, all pupils and I will do our best to maintain our 'smile ethos'.

At the beginning of the lesson we exchange greetings and we bow at the command of a class representatives'.

We use many styles of teaching. When students want to say something during class, they put up their hand. Some teachers use hand signs, to question and to indicate opinions both supporting and opposing what the students say. As teachers tend to talk a lot, we try to use student-to-student discussion. Students sit down facing the blackboard according to the teacher's plan. When they talk in groups, they move their desks.

Teachers always look around the classroom and walk by the desks and sometimes give students advice or information about the task.

If a teacher wants to know students' opinions, the teacher makes them write their opinion and checks and give them good advice. The classes are organised by a teacher, as the teacher knows student's opinion. It means every student can participate every class. The teacher gives students writing time and then they are able to participate in class discussion.

On the blackboard, teachers give students today's task so that what they study is clear to students. Students have their own textbook and notebook. They can study at home. As lessons are 45 minutes long, younger age classes sometimes divide the lesson in two because pupils cannot concentrate in class for a long time.

There is no chime [bell] because young people need to develop autonomy (but this is dependent on the school).

When students move classrooms such as music class, they usually line up.

There is usually one teacher for younger classes but upper grade classes are sometimes taught by other teachers. Sometimes team-teaching is also carried out.

All classes are taught by Japanese teachers in Japanese.

Chieko's description of her classroom has many familiar features. In relation to effective learning the arrangements encourage some activity, some collaboration and some responsibility for learning. Chieko does not mention any meta-learning. Another feature to note is the ethos of warmth and respect and somewhat formal greetings. Chieko has also described the routines that support young people's understanding about learning.

Reflection 3

In the first part of this chapter we have examined different conceptions of learning. We introduced research that identified different conceptions of learning and related these to dominant images of classrooms. We considered three models of learning: reception, constructivist and co-constructivist. We defined what it means to be an effective learner in the twenty-first century. Throughout we emphasized that effective learning involves activity, collaboration, responsibility and meta-learning. What has been most significant or striking so far in this chapter?

LEADING FOR EFFECTIVE LEARNING

We now consider how a leader can promote effective learning in their organisation. We draw on *Leadership for Organisational Learning and Improved Student Outcomes—What do we know?* by Mulford and Silins (2003), an article which explores how leaders can make a difference to students' learning. This connection has often been claimed but rarely with any evidence to support the claim. You might also like to refer back to Chapter 1, the introduction to theories of leadership.

Distributive leadership (from Mulford and Silins, 2003)

The first of four implication of the LOLSO (Leadership for Organisational Learning and Student Outcomes) research is that leadership that makes a difference in secondary schools is both position-based (head teacher) and distributive (administrative team and teacher) and that the effects of this leadership on student outcomes is indirect (through OL (Organisational Learning) and teacher work). The positional/headteacher leadership we are talking about is what we termed 'transformational'. What is important is the collective efficacy of the staff, their ability to engage in organisational learning. How the teachers are treated is reflected in how the students perceive the teacher's work which, in turn, is related to the outcomes of their schooling.

This first implication is consistent with the findings of a recent review of the research literature that identified three major and aligned elements in successful school reform (Silins and Mulford, 2004). The first element relates to how people are treated. Success is more likely where people act rather than always reacting, are empowered, involved in decision-making through a transparent, facilitative and supportive structure, and are trusted, respected and encouraged. The second element concerns a professional community. A professional community involves shared norms and values including valuing differences and diversity, a focus on continuous enhancement of learning for all students, de-privatisation of practice, collaboration, and critical reflective dialogue, especially that based on performance data. The final element relates to the presence of a capacity for learning. This capacity is most readily identified in an ongoing, optimistic, caring, nurturing professional development program.

The rejection in our findings of 'the great man or woman' theory of leadership should be noted. Faith in one person, 'the leader', as the instrument for successful implementation of the [UK] government's educational policy, let alone broader and longer term educational outcomes, might bring initial albeit temporary success but the dependency relationship that it establishes will eventually ensure mediocrity if not failure. There is a clear difference here between the LOLSO research and the Hay-McBer model of excellence for school leaders (Hay-McBer, no date). In contrast to the Hay-McBer 'model', the LOLSO 'model' has no emphasis on the leader showing initiative by acting decisively, having impact by persuasion, calculation and influencing, or creating the vision through, for example, strategic thinking. Nowhere is the difference clearer than in our different interpretations of the concept 'transformational leadership'. The Hay-McBer emphasis on the 'drive and the ability to take the role of leader, provide clear direction, and enthuse and motivate others' is a mile away from LOLSO's stress on support, care, trust, participation, facilitation and whole staff consensus.

The other three implications from the article briefly summarised are:

- second, successful school reform is all about development and learning;
- third, the context for leadership and school reform must be taken more into account;
- fourth, is the need to broaden what counts for effective education beyond academic achievement.

This article, and especially the section we have quoted above called 'Distributive Leadership', challenges some traditional ideas about leadership; especially the idea that leadership depends on one single person to be the instrument for successful improvements. The article suggests that while this might bring initial temporary success, the dependency relationship that it establishes will eventually ensure mediocrity if not failure. Secondly, qualities such as drive, provision of clear direction and the ability to enthuse others are not as significant for improving learning as support, care, trust, participation, facilitation and whole staff consensus. For a critical review of the literature linking leadership and management to school improvement and learning organisations see Hallinger and Heck (2003).

Factors in an organisation that affect the quality of learning

Many of the aspects of an educational institution that have to be lead or managed are external factors over which the leader or manager has little control. Others are more susceptible to the impact of organisational factors. Some have both external features—for example the quality of teaching may be affected by the availability of qualified teachers—as well as professional development promoted within the organisation.

Hofstede, a Dutch academic, researched 117,000 employees to discover the relationship between their core values and their practices in many different countries. As outlined in Chapter 2, he used these data to categorise cultures into five dimensions:

- individual-collectivism;
- power distance;
- uncertainty avoidance;
- status-relationships;
- long-short-term.

The degree to which each of these cultural dimensions affects ideas about learning, and about teaching, varies in different contexts, and it would be an oversimplification to assume that one culture pertains uniformly across a nation, or a region or indeed an organisation. Any leader or manager needs to be aware of these subtleties and think about how these cultural dimensions influence their activities. Table 12.4 uses Hofstede's cultural dimensions, mapping some implications for effective learning.

Table 12.4 Hofstede's cultural dimensions considered in relation to effective learning

Dimension	Implications for effective learning
Individualism—collectivism	The degree to which the organisation puts value on collaboration as significant in learning for organisations and individuals or on individual activity.
Power distance	How far an organisation encourages responsibility by learners for their learning or dependence on teachers.
	The degree to which deference to the teacher or engagement with the teacher is expected.
Uncertainty avoidance	The degree to which organisations encourage risk-taking, openness and vulnerability or encourage compliance in learning.
Status-relationships	How far organisations value performance in tests over effective learning practices.
Long-term—short-term orientation	The degree to which the institution values dispositions such as perseverance, persistence over protection of face and respect for established authorities.

Reflection 4

How would you describe your organisation in relation to each of these cultural dimensions, and what are the implications for learning that arise?

In order for the learning in an organisation to be effective, leaders need to attend to those dimension that promote effective learning, such as collaboration, lack of hierarchy in learning situations, encouraging openness and risk-taking. The following section addresses how leaders can promote supportive cultural norms.

NORMS IN AN ORGANISATION

The culture of an organisation (see Chapter 3) is the embodiment of common and accepted behaviours, beliefs and values which are referred to as norms. In the learning organisation norms that are learning-orientated dominate the culture. There are four norms that are particularly significant in learning organisations and we look at these in turn and suggest some ways in which these norms can be promoted by leaders:

a. collaborative climate among teachers;

b. problem seeking and solving;

c. acceptance of risk and experimentation;

d. feedback for learning.

Collaborative climate among teachers

We have already indicated the importance of a collaborative climate for effective learning and here we note its special significance in co-constructive learning for all members of the community. In organisations that promote effective learning, collaboration, rather than competition or individualism, imbues its practices. At the whole organisation level, active partnerships give attention to the voices of all stakeholders in working towards the goals of the organisation. Teachers, leaders and managers particularly contribute to the development of this norm through collaboration that integrates personal and professional learning. A particularly powerful way of doing this is through action research focusing on learning.

The combination of procedures, structures and collaborative enquiries into learning contribute to building the capacity of the organisation to develop as a learning community, and to sustain improvements in learning. Mitchell and Sackney have suggested that building capacity for a learning community requires the simultaneous building of personal, interpersonal and organisational capacities (Mitchell and Sackney, 2001). Leaders need to think about how to promote collaboration at these different levels, at the same time, in order to promote the norm of a collaborative climate.

Problem seeking and solving

A second norm is that the organisation constantly seeks and solves problems. Processes to do this are active, promote collaborative learning and encourage responsibility in learning and engagement in meta-learning. Referring to Table 12.4, a number of the cultural dimensions may be challenged by problem seeking, such as avoiding uncertainty, and some power relationships. One method of doing this is to use Appreciative Inquiry (Hammond, 1996) which starts by identifying what is already the best practice in an organisation and encourages participants to envisage more good practice.

Acceptance of risk and experimentation

A third norm is the acceptance of risk and valuing experimentation. Learning organisations encourage experimentation and provide a zone of security that allows for mistakes and wrong turnings (Clarke, 2000). In a climate that encourages compliance and certainty, risk and experimentation can be hard to encourage in organisations.

Although often very uncomfortable and difficult to manage, embracing risk is necessary in order that communities can learn. Managers and leaders will need to provide time for experimentation, trial and error and handling failure (Reed and Stoll, 2000).

Feedback for learning

A fourth important cultural norm is that feedback is regarded as significant for minimising the undesirable effects of risks taken. This engagement in feedback takes place at student and teacher levels as well as at the organisational level. It means team teaching, mentoring, action research, peer coaching, planning and mutual observation and feedback by teachers, and teamwork to develop whole organisation aspects. These activities imply support, mutual respect, openness, celebration and humour. This communication is important in setting the climate or culture. Feedback from the students, on all aspects of organisational life, is heard in the dialogue of the learning organisation as the Australian research (Mulford and Silins, 2003) demonstrates.

Leaders and managers therefore need to think about the organisation in a systemic way, that is, to look at the whole as well as the parts and their connections. Thinking systemically is the opposite of reductionism, which is the idea that something is simply the sum of its parts. Learning communities look beyond the immediate to find patterns over a wider spectrum or longer period of time and encourage feedback to identify problems and successes. This kind of thinking gives leaders some control over their future and their preparations for it (O'Connor and McDermott, 1997). To do this leaders will need to encourage dialogue between students and teachers, and teachers with teachers, and all of these people with the leaders (see chapters by Askew and Lodge, Carnell and Watkins in *Feedback for Learning* edited by Askew, 2000).

Bringing about a shift in culture is not easy, especially if all the dimensions in Table 12.4 are working against promoting the cultural norms we have emphasized.

The leader's view of learning

The cultural context of an organisation affects how far the organisation and its leaders promote effective learning. The views that the leader has of learning are just as important in promoting effective learning. Indeed the leader's views of learning will influence the ways in which he or she carries out his or her leadership role. We now link leadership activities to the three models of learning described earlier.

1. Reception

Leaders who see learning from this perspective are likely to:

- focus on teachers more than learners;
- talk about learning in ways that conflate learning with teaching and with performance;
- view the curriculum as a body of knowledge;
- value concrete products which are easily measurable;
- favour modes of assessment which are timed, summative performances;
- de-emphasize social dimensions of learning.

2. Constructivist

Leaders who see learning from this perspective are likely to:

- focus on the way people make sense of their experiences;
- view curriculum as addressing thought-demanding questions;
- value processes which make learning visible;

- favour modes of assessment which ask people to explain to one another;
- promote people known as learners;
- ask of every policy and every procedure: 'What do we learn from this?'
- encourage others to do the above.

3. Co-constructivist

Leaders who see learning from this perspective are likely to:

- focus on social and collaborative processes;
- view curriculum as a process of building knowledge;
- view learning as a process of action and dialogue;
- value processes which enhance collaborative outcomes;
- favour modes of assessment with a community product;
- seek to improve learning by enhancing collaboration enquiry;
- talk about learning as a collaboration of building knowledge and culture.

A second case example links the themes of this chapter to practice. Naheeda Maharasingam, a deputy head of a primary school in London, talks about leadership and effective learning.

Case Example 2

When I became a deputy head I wanted to put into practice in my leadership role the principles of effective learning that I had introduced in my classroom. I see the classroom as a microcosm of the school. Focusing on learning had been really helpful for the pupils' learning and I wanted to show that in my role of leader the same principles could apply.

First, I want to demonstrate that I have all the things that a learner needs: enthusiasm, passion, that I take responsibility, that I am an active listener and able to adapt to change. Also I want to show that I have emotional intelligence, that social relationships are key. The people in a school are the most important things. As a deputy head I am accountable. I try to carry out my role showing that I have energy, self-awareness and reliability.

Second, I want to use the principles of effective learning in the way I manage conflict. As a leader I want to have an impact on the culture of the school. What you say to people when dealing with conflict is what you want them to be thinking about and learning from. There needs to be trust, honesty and openness. You need to work hard to continue to express the concepts of learning in a concrete way. If you don't get the social relationships right then nothing will happen. You need perseverance and consistency.

Third, there are issues about change. Change is a massive undertaking; there is a lot of un-learning to do and you have to keep on learning. Being responsible can be scary and it can also be energising. I keep saying to myself 'I can make a difference' and 'I can support learning in my role'.

Fourth, you need awareness of the importance of the role. As a leader it is about all the things that support the smooth running of the school, including some tedious things.

Fifth, is about relationships with colleagues. Team teaching is really important as a leader. Learners get a better deal—both young people's and colleagues' learning. In this way you can support colleagues' professional development. You need to trust other people as well as yourself. You need to remove the competitiveness and performance orientation. Relationships need to be more about support. You have to be brave and you need to learn to be tactful. The most important thing is to develop a professional dialogue. Staff meetings need to be effective if people are to be learning; all meetings with staff need to be interactive.

I don't much care for the term leadership. I think the best leaders are those you don't hear much from. You want teachers to take on their own learning. Teachers need to identify for themselves what needs to change and what they need to learn, otherwise it does not lead to sustained learning. The problem is the government imposes change. But as an effective leader you don't impose on others. It is best to get the teachers to talk about their ideas. Teachers need to feel good about what they are doing.

Sixth, is about the external context which is all about achievement, performance, grades, results etc. In school I want to see a focus on learning. It is not idealistic. Those two contexts don't have to be contradictory. Taking on a sole role as a leader may be letting the teachers down. I need to stay in the classroom for some of the time because if you lose that contact with pupils you can't talk to teachers about young people's learning. I can't lead from above. I have to lead alongside teachers. You need to know the children; making them feel good is important.

Finally, it is good to have doubts and you need to communicate passion and share that. This is something that doesn't take an awful lot of energy. A question I sometimes ask is 'Where is the support for the leader? ' You need to manage your emotions. You can't expect to get happiness from the other members of staff. You are there to problem-solve but not to solve other people's problems.

Naheeda's account challenges the traditional ideas about leadership; especially the idea that leadership depends on one single person to be the instrument for successful improvements. Her case demonstrates that qualities such as drive, provision of clear direction and the ability to enthuse others are not as significant for improving learning as support, care, trust, participation, facilitation and whole staff consensus. Both these points were referred to in Mulford and Silins (2003). Naheeda demonstrates how this can be effective in practice.

Naheeda's account speaks strongly of her encouragement of trusting social relationships, responsibility and collaboration. She explicitly links these with her views of learning. She tells of her active encouragement of passion, trust, consistence and perseverance. Naheeda models behaviour to promote learning in classrooms and the school. This modelling is important. The research by Mulford and Silins suggests that the way teachers organise and approach young people in the classroom and their learning is influenced by leadership practices. Pupils' perceptions of teachers' work directly relates to their participation in school and their participation is related to academic achievement. They highlight four features of leadership as especially significant:

- establishing a trusting and collaborative climate;
- having a shared and monitored mission;
- taking initiatives and risks;
- ensuring ongoing and relevant professional development.

Reflection 5

We have drawn connections between effective learning and leading. Unless leaders think about and aim to improve the learning in their organisation there is little point in them being leaders. We invite you to consider how you would approach improving learning in your organisation.

SUMMARY

We have emphasized that leadership needs to be distributed. The learning of the teachers alongside the young people has also been emphasized. This implies that young people are listened to and their views taken into account. The teachers' and leaders' learning is affected by the learning of the young people. Learning is a reciprocal process.

We have emphasized that the culture and context of a school is crucial and there is not a universal prescription for effective leadership for learning. Leaders in an organisation need to consider carefully and continuously what they do. Leaders will only know if their leadership is effective by ascertaining the contribution of their activities on the teachers and students. They need to listen carefully to the teachers and students in the organisation to ensure that the leadership is promoting learning. Collaboration does not sit easily in a hierarchical organisation, but collaboration is essential to effective learning for the students, the teachers, the organisation as a whole as well as for the leaders. Leaders may therefore need to develop a less hierarchical organisational structure.

Leadership approaches based on learning principles encourage learning organisations, that is when learning is active and collaborative, where learners take responsibility for their learning, and they learn about learning. This will create organisations where people want to be together, to learn together, where tension and conflict are used for learning and where there is laughter and harmony.

RECOMMENDED FURTHER READING

For more about feedback in the different models of learning see Askew, S. (ed.) (2000) *Feedback for Learning*, London: Routledge Falmer.

For more detailed discussion about the different models of learning together with how schools (and different roles and teams in schools) can promote effective learning see Carnell, E. and C. Lodge (2002) *Supporting Effective Learning*, London: Paul Chapman.

A research review that considers recent research into effective learning is Watkins, C. et al (2002) *Effective Learning*, London: Institute of Education, National School Improvement Network, Research Matters Series No 17.

This next paper is one of the few studies that links leadership to pupil outcomes. It emphasizes distributive leadership and the affective aspects of leadership. Mulford, B. and Silins, H. (2003) 'Leadership for Organisational Learning and Improved Student Outcomes—What do we know?' *Cambridge Journal of Education* 33(2), 175–196.

The following article provides a critical review of the literature linking leadership and learning. Hallinger, P. and Heck, R. (2003) 'Understanding the contribution of leadership to school improvement', in Wallace, M. and Poulson, L. (eds) *Learning to Read Critically in Educational Leadership and Management*, London: Sage.

Continuing Professional Development: The Learning Community

Peter Earley

INTRODUCTION AND LEARNING OUTCOMES

This chapter builds on Chapters 11 and 12 to consider the professional and personal development of all adults as a key part of a professional learning community. Continuing professional development (CPD) is sustained within the culture of an organisation and relies on shared vision, team learning and the head or principal as lead learner. The chapter begins by claiming that human resource development (HRD) is crucially important at all times, but especially in times of recruitment and retention difficulties. This is followed by a discussion of the nature of professional development before turning our attention to leading and managing CPD. Finally, the notion of a learning community, including a networked community, for all who work or study within them is examined.

By the end of this chapter you should be able to:

- reflect on the importance of developing people;
- understand the concept of continuing professional development and the various forms it might take;
- comprehend the management and leadership of CPD, including the training and development cycle;
- be familiar with 'learning communities' and the styles of leadership, organisational culture, professional development and forms of learning underpinning them.

PEOPLE MATTER

The importance of professional development cannot be underestimated, especially during recent times when there have been increased demands throughout the world on teachers' expertise and growing expectations for their achievements within enhanced accountability frameworks. Policy makers, administrators and others increasingly see professional development as central to any change efforts. Learning should be at the centre of any educational institution, and not only for the pupils or students. This is particularly important as delegated budgets and devolved funding enable educational institutions to become self-managing and increasingly autonomous. Devolution to site-based managers means increased responsibility on the part of school leaders for the quality of staff, especially teaching staff and the education delivered to students. But who is responsible for this learning and how is it managed and led?

Reflection 1

Consider the following quote from Roland Barthes, a former US principal and well-known writer on school improvement:

'Probably nothing within a school has more impact on students in terms of skills development, self confidence, or classroom behaviour than the personal and professional development of their teachers' (1990, p.49).

Do you agree? This is a bold assertion. Can it be justified?

Continuous professional development has to be seen as a *collective* responsibility—the responsibility of both staff (teachers and support staff) and the organisations in which they work. Individuals and their places of employment should take joint responsibility for professional development and training, which should clearly be for the benefit of both. Institutional and individual needs have to be regarded in a *complementary* and *holistic* way. Organisations operating in this way are more likely to have a motivated and better performing workforce with high morale.

In recent writing and research, growing attention has been given to organisational 'cultures' and the emphasis given to the training and development of the workforce. Ongoing or continuing professional development is sustained within the culture of the organisation and relies on shared vision, team learning and the lead learners setting an example through their actions. The experience and expertise of staff—both teaching and support—is generally recognised to be the organisation's most important but also its most expensive resource. Leading and managing CPD has to be seen as a central part of the responsibility of managing the school's total resources (Craft, 1996). The quality of teaching largely depends on the quality of the teachers, which in turn depends to a considerable extent on the quality of their ongoing professional development.

People and their training and development—their continuing professional development—must be seen as an *investment* and it is therefore important that a CPD or HRD policy is successfully implemented. As funds and responsibilities are progressively transferred to educational organisations they are being deployed in varied and creative ways leading to more responsive and effective systems of CPD. Educational organisations must take the main responsibility for developing the quality, motivation and organisation of their people—for managing and developing their human resources.

There is increasing recognition that the development of people—human resource development—is more effective in enhancing the performance of organisations than any other single factor. There is a growing body of evidence showing that the careful management of people and investing in employees as the most valued company resource, achieved greater returns in terms of productivity, customer satisfaction, profitability and employee retention. In educational organisations a large proportion of total budget is devoted to 'staffing' but far less to HRD. The latter is likely to be determined by grants made available by central government but also by the attitude of the organisation and its leadership.

Educational leaders play a pivotal role—vital for both successful implementation of CPD and in ensuring that training and development programmes meet the needs of both staff and their organisations. Possible tensions exist between system needs and individual needs—educational leaders must try to ensure that there is little or no conflict between the needs of the system (as expressed in the school or institutional development or improvement plan—SDP/SIP) and the needs of the individual—the individual development plan (IDP). Performance management can play a key role here.

WHAT IS PROFESSIONAL DEVELOPMENT?

The first question we have to ask is 'what is professional development?' so this section offers a number of definitions and discusses the various forms it may take.

Reflection 2

Before reading this section what do you consider professional development to mean?

One of the hallmarks of being identified as a *professional* is to continue to learn throughout your career. The professions, broadly defined, range from the well-established and powerful to those which are still trying to establish their professional status. Continuing professional development has become the term widely used for ongoing education and training for the professions. If teaching is seen as a profession—and a case for this has long been argued—an important characteristic or hallmark of a member of a profession is the commitment shown towards self-improvement or development. This is not, however, for its own sake but to ensure that the beneficiaries or clients—pupils or students and their parents—are provided with the best possible service.

The prime responsibility for securing individual professional development of teachers is not, however, the exclusive concern of the employer—teachers themselves must expect to play a key role—and professional development opportunities must be available for individuals to help them become better practitioners.

Reflection 3

The General Teaching Council for England argues that its members should consider that it is their professional responsibility continually to improve their skills and abilities and to extend their knowledge (GTC, 1993).

Do you agree?

Are teachers considered as professionals and how strongly held is such a view in the educational system that you are familiar with?

But what is meant by the term CPD and is it different from *personal development* or *staff development* or *in-service education and training (INSET)*? Broadly speaking, continuing professional development encompasses all formal and informal learning that enables individuals to improve their own practice. Professional development is an aspect of personal development and wherever possible the two should interact and complement each other. The former is mainly about occupational role development whereas personal development is about the development of the person, often the 'whole' person, and it almost always involves changes in self-awareness. As Waters (1998) explains:

> It is the development that can occur when teachers are construed first and foremost as people, and is predicated on the premise that people are always much more than the roles they play (Waters, 1998, p.30).

A definition of CPD might refer to:

> any professional development activities engaged in by teachers which enhance their knowledge and skills and enable them to consider their attitudes and approaches to the education of children, with a view to improve the quality of the teaching and learning process (Bolam, 1993).

In this sense it is perhaps little different to how some have defined in-service training or staff development. For example, Oldroyd and Hall (1991) define INSET as:

> planned activities practised both within and outside schools primarily to develop the professional knowledge, skills, attitudes and performance of professional staff in schools.

In Britain the seminal James Report (DES, 1972) defined INSET as:

> the whole range of activities by which teachers can extend their personal education, develop their professional competence and improve their understanding of education principles and techniques.

An analysis of the literature does, however, reveal a number of nuances and slight differences for the different concepts used. A simple but most useful conceptual breakdown is offered by Bolam (1993). He makes use of a three-fold distinction between *professional education, professional training* and *professional support* and gives examples of each.

- *Professional training,* e.g. short courses, workshops, conferences emphasising practical information and skills.
- *Professional education,* e.g. long courses and secondments emphasising theory and research-based knowledge.
- *Professional support,* e.g. activities that aim to develop on-the-job experience and performance.

CPD is an *ongoing process* building upon initial teacher training (ITT) and induction, including development and training opportunities throughout a career and concluding with preparation for retirement. Some argue that it constitutes an entitlement (see Jones, 2003). At different times and at different stages, however, one or other may be given priority but the totality can be referred to as continuing professional development. Development is therefore about improvement—both individual and institutional improvement.

Continuing professional development embraces those education, training and support activities engaged in by teachers following their initial certification which aim to:

- add to their professional knowledge;
- improve their professional skills;
- help clarify their professional values;
- enable pupils to be educated more effectively (Bolam, 1993).

In their survey of continuing education for the professions, Madden and Mitchell (1993) state that CPD can fulfil three functions:

- updating and extending the professional's knowledge and skills on new developments and new areas of practice—to ensure continuing competence in the current job;
- training for new responsibilities and for a changing role (e.g. management, budgeting, teaching)—developing new areas of competence in preparation for a more senior post;
- developing personal and professional effectiveness and increasing job satisfaction— increasing competence in a wider context with benefits to both professional and personal roles (Madden and Mitchell, 1993).

Day (1999) has noted how most definitions of professional development stress its main purpose as being the acquisition of subject or content knowledge and teaching skills, whereas for him it must go beyond these:

Professional development consists of all natural learning experiences and those conscious and planned activities which are intended to be of direct or indirect benefit to the individual, group or school and which contribute, through these, to the quality of education in the classroom. It is the process by which, alone and with others, teachers review, renew and extend their commitment as change agents to the moral purposes of teaching; and by which they acquire and develop critically the knowledge, skills, and emotional intelligence essential to good professional thinking, planning and practice with children, young people and colleagues through each phase of their teaching lives (1999, p.4).

More recently, the English government in launching its strategy for professional development in 2001, offers a further, albeit succinct, definition when it states:

By 'professional development' we mean any activity that increases the skills, knowledge or understanding of teachers, and their effectiveness in schools (DfEE, 2001, p.3).

What is recognised as central to the success of the strategy is the need for staff to work in schools with collaborative cultures, where there is a commitment to improving teaching and learning and, in the words of the Department, where there is 'learning from and with other teachers' (p.6). Learning on the job and learning from the best are key characteristics of this CPD strategy, and we will return to these themes in a later section.

Reflection 4

Having considered other people's definitions of CPD, how would you now refine your own?

To summarise, CPD is an on-going process of education, training, learning and support activities, which is:

- taking place in either external or work-based settings;
- engaged in by qualified, educational professionals;
- aimed mainly at promoting learning and development of their professional knowledge, skills and values;
- to help decide and implement valued changes in their teaching and learning behaviour so that they can educate their students more effectively thus achieving an agreed balance between individual, school and national needs.

(Based on Bolam, 2002.)

Perhaps the single most important feature of CPD is to encourage and promote a commitment on the part of the individual to professional growth. Leading and managing human resource development—making CPD work—therefore means providing structures and processes to promote growth and help staff develop and improve their workplace performance.

MANAGING AND LEADING CPD

If the expertise and experience of staff is increasingly seen as the most precious resource then the management and leadership of CPD must be seen, not as an adjunct, but as an integral part of managing the organisation's total resources. Educational organisations often link CPD to objectives or targets as identified in both institutional development and personal development plans and these in turn are related to a system of staff appraisal or performance management. In this way it is likely that an appropriate balance will be retained between institution (and group) needs and the personal and professional needs of the individual. Teachers and other staff will always feel the need to be *valued* and this should not be forgotten when considering the balance between individual and institutional needs.

The effective management of CPD should ensure that support is available and conditions created which enable staff to work together and to develop and improve their workplace performance. Through headteachers and principals, CPD coordinators and other staff helping to create a climate or *culture* which is conducive to learning—of both staff and pupils—schools and colleges are well on the road to becoming *learning communities* where investment in people is given the priority it deserves. Student learning is a key goal of all educational organisations, whereas the ongoing learning of teachers and other paid employees is not always prioritised or adequately resourced.

Creating a culture of learning is crucial and this is going to be shaped by the attitude and approach of the leaders towards CPD. What messages are the organisational leaders giving about the importance of professional development? Are they participating in training themselves, particularly in school-based events, are they 'leading the learning'? As Senge has noted:

> effective leadership depends not merely on how you set up the circumstances for people to learn together, but on how you learn with them (2000, p.423).

If it is true that children learn more from adults' deeds than their words and that 'in order to develop a love of learning in students, teachers must first be learners themselves' (Jalongo, 1991, p.48), then this is equally true of teachers and others working in the organisation.

Managing CPD in any organisation, be it a small primary school or a large multi-purpose college, requires an understanding of the training and development cycle. This consists of six stages: identifying and analysing training needs, planning and designing programmes, their implementation or delivery, and monitoring and evaluation (see Figure 13.1). Each of these six stages can be seen as issues that require attention if training and development is to be managed effectively. Two of these stages—needs identification and evaluation of training and development—are considered.

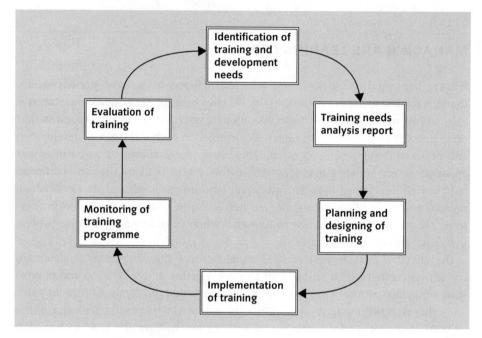

Figure 13.1 Training and development cycle

Training needs identification

Training needs identification, the measurable discrepancy between a present state of affairs and a desired state of affairs, is the first and pivotal issue of CPD or staff development management. It is the cornerstone of an effective staff development programme and no kinds of CPD should be undertaken without taking into account what teachers and other staff already know and can do. It is therefore important to identify individuals' needs along with those of the school or college and the education system in which the individual works.

So how are needs assessed? Appraisal or performance management reviews can be helpful. Effective performance management arrangements provide schools with a route to better reconciliation between the individual's and the school's needs and priorities for development. They allow individual, departmental or section and whole school developmental needs to be identified and they enable individuals to see how their own development fits into, benefits from, and contributes to the wider school or departmental developmental agenda.

Commonly used methods to elicit participants' views of their needs are interviews and questionnaires. But these methods are not always useful because it is often difficult for teachers 'to think about those areas of their own practice where they feel least knowledgeable, skilled and competent' (O'Sullivan, 2000). There are few examples of programmes where training providers assess needs, especially in the less developed world. O'Sullivan (2000) suggests this may be for a number of reasons, perhaps because of the lack of guidance on how to do it. O'Sullivan's work is a good example of how needs identification was undertaken in relation to unqualified primary school teachers in Namibia (see Case example 1).

> **Case Example 1**
>
> Adapted from: O'Sullivan, M. (2000) 'Needs assessment for INSET for unqualified primary teachers in Namibia: An effective model', *Compare*, Vol. 30, 211–234.
>
> O'Sullivan notes the critical role of needs assessment for effective in-service training (INSET) or CPD, and also the shortage of empirical research on the process. The few studies in this area have focused on the use of questionnaires and interviews as the prime means of gathering data about teachers' training needs.
>
> The article is based on a three-year (1995–97) action research study of an INSET programme in Namibia which 'sought to support 145 unqualified primary teachers' efforts to implement reforms related to English Language Teaching (ELT). The reforms were introduced in the early 1990s after Namibia gained independence from South Africa in 1990 . . . The study was concerned with the development of effective INSET strategies that would support teachers' reform implementation efforts' (p.212). The programme took place over four six-month periods and a comprehensive evaluation showed a considerable degree of success if implementation of the training in the classroom is used as an indicator. Effective needs assessment was seen as one of the factors contributing to the success of the programme.
>
> The author had difficulties with accurately assessing needs because the unqualified teachers in Namibia had limited education, were not sufficiently experienced or secure enough in their own professional development to participate fully in determining their own training needs. O'Sullivan had to use observation for corroboration purposes as well as assessing learners' work to get a realistic picture of the unqualified teachers' needs. The use of a multi-pronged approach to needs assessment facilitated corroboration and provided a broader picture of teachers' actual state. The time and effort put into identifying needs accurately enabled a training programme to be put in place that was helpful and effective. Without this the training would not have achieved the success it did.

The role of teachers in the identification of their needs has often been a minor one. Indeed where they do identify the professional development they undertake it can be in a random and ad hoc way. An example from Australia is given by Harris (2000), who notes:

> It involved them glancing through a list or booklet of advertised professional development courses prepared by their employing organisations or professional association. They selected a course to attend based on criteria such as their interest in the topic, when and where it was to be held, and/or its cost, and whether or not the school or employer will meet these costs. The linking of the course to their actual professional development needs appeared to be of minor significance (p.26).

Headteachers and other educational leaders have to ensure that training and development programmes meet the needs of both individual teachers (and other staff) and their schools, minimising any tensions that may exist between system needs and priorities (SDP) and those of individuals (the individual development plan).

The different approaches to HRM will make a difference: is the approach one of 'hard' economic utilitarianism or more of a 'soft' developmental humanism where staff are valued, morale is high and they are likely to be well motivated? It's important to remember that CPD can serve both individual *and* system needs—it's not always a case of serving one or the other and to make matters easier the two often go together— individuals' needs very often overlap with those of the institution. Also, it is important to remember that development can't be forced—it's the teacher who develops (active) and not the teacher who is developed (passive). Staff who are excited and motivated by the experience of their own learning are likely to communicate that excitement to their pupils.

Teachers therefore need a framework for CPD opportunities based on three priority areas (see Figure 13.2):

- *Individually focused*—these activities should focus on a teacher's own needs and be identified by the individual teacher as supporting their professional development and/or career objectives. Appropriate CPD activities might include attending courses, mentoring, developing a new teaching activity, exchanging ideas and good practice with colleagues and exchange visits.

- *School focused*—these activities should primarily be targeted at the requirements of the school that currently employs the teacher. The CPD requirements would be identified from the school development plan and relevant activities should largely be undertaken during non-pupil contact days, with any additional identified school focused activities financed from school budgets.

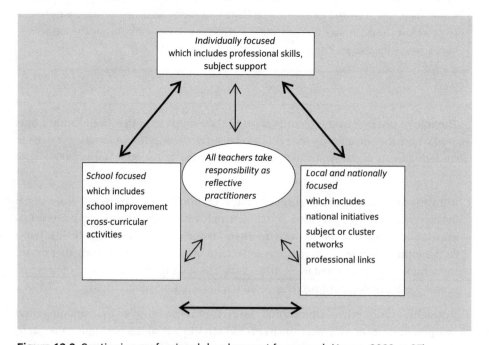

Figure 13.2 Continuing professional development framework (*Jones, 2003, p.37*)

- *National/LEA/District focused*—these CPD activities would meet the demands of national and local initiatives. They could involve activities organised on a cross-school basis such as cluster meetings or around a national priority.

What do we know about effective CPD?

As can be seen from the above framework, CPD may take a variety of forms—going on courses or training programmes is only one of a very wide variety of forms it may take. It might involve observing good practitioners, extending your professional experiences or working with pupils. A list of activities is shown in Figure 13.3:

---

i) Observing good practitioners

- Observing other teachers teaching
- Watching a colleague present an assembly
- Observing a visiting expert
- Shadowing a colleague
- Visiting and seeing other schools in action
- Taking part in developing a learning community
- Observing and working with an artist in residence

ii) Extending professional experience

- Leading school-based training
- Rotation of roles/jobs
- Developing own professional profile
- Coordinating/managing a subject
- Assuming the role of leader for a special initiative in school
- Carrying out action research in the classroom/school
- Contributing to a professional publication
- Gaining experience of interviewing
- Acting as a performance reviewer
- Being reviewed
- Serving as a governor
- Contributing to in-service courses
- Serving on professional committees/working parties etc
- Becoming a union representative
- Leading/supervising non-professionals who work in the classroom
- Working on extra-curricular activities

Figure 13.3 (*Continued*)

- Taking part in staff conferences on individual pupils
- Working with other professionals such as education psychologists
- Working with an exam board or marking exam papers
- Networking and sharing with a group of colleagues from another school
- Team teaching
- Learning through professional practice with others
- Developing pedagogy in the context of ICT
- Counselling parents
- Collaborating with peripatetic teachers
- Peer mentoring, i.e. mentoring a newly qualified teacher
- Organising a display in collaboration with colleagues

iii) Working with pupils

- Taking responsibility for a group of pupils on an off-site visit
- Developing teaching skills across a wide age and ability range
- Working with pupils on school councils
- Working with pupils to present an assembly, play, musical performance events etc
- Working with pupils preparing a school year book
- Integrating the use of pupil websites and on-line communities into teaching
- Using e-mail/video conferencing between pupils into teaching and learning
- Negotiating targets and evaluating work alongside pupils
- Mentoring individual pupils
- Counselling pupils.

Figure 13.3 Examples of CPD other than external courses (DfES, 2001)

Opportunities for professional development can take a wide variety of forms. Research suggests that 'on the job' experiences are seen as more significant than 'off the job' experiences, although there is a clear need for both. Earley et al (2002) show how important school-based experiences are for leadership development, whilst Bubb et al (2002) found that newly qualified teachers (NQTs) rated observing other teachers and being observed as the two most equally valuable activities. Going on courses was the least valuable.

We also know from research that there are a variety of factors making for effective professional development. Lee (2002) for example sees the key factors in the success of CPD as targeted objectives, a clear structure, planning, learner involvement, and high levels of expertise on the part of the deliverer. 'Drive by staff development', or the type of training that Senge (2000) refers to as 'read two chapters and call me in the morning', should be avoided. 'Workplace' rather than 'workshop' training is generally perceived to be more effective in bringing about change. A good example of the former would be mentoring and coaching (see Case example 2).

According to Joyce and Showers (1995) effective staff development consists of theory, demonstration, practice and feedback, and coaching. Coaching is where people (trainers) work alongside teachers, often demonstrating desired practices and approaches in the classroom or workplace rather than the training centre or workshop. Coaching allows the risk of innovation to be shared in a safe setting. Executive coaching has become common practice in business and commerce and is now becoming more popular with educational leaders in the UK and the USA.

Case Example 2

Harvey, S. (1999) 'The impact of coaching in South African primary science INSET', *International Journal of Educational Development*, 19(3), 191–205.

Stephen Harvey investigated the impact of classroom-based coaching on the teaching methods used by primary science teachers in South Africa. His work raises a number of issues about measuring the impact of CPD and is one of the few studies that has compared, using control groups, the effect of different types of CPD provision and to assess the 'value added' of coaching.

Peer coaching can be defined as 'a confidential relationship between professional colleagues working together to reflect on their teaching and share ideas in order to improve their professional skills' (Thijs and Van den Berg, 2002, p.55) or as 'a collegial approach to the analysis of teaching aimed at integrating new skills and strategies in classroom practice' (Joyce and Showers, 1982, cited in Thijs and Van den Berg, p.56). Joyce and Showers (1995) make a distinction between peer coaching that supports teachers with implementation of a specific innovation (see below) and that with a more general focus aimed at improving existing teaching practices.

The Primary Science Progamme (PSB) in South Africa is attempting to provide in the 46 schools involved a 'quality science education that is activity-based and that develops pupils' scientific knowledge, process skills and critical attitudes, in a balanced way' (p.192). The initial implementation strategy, which was not found to be effective, did not have a schools-based coaching component, relying on centre-based workshops and science materials or kits for teachers to use with the pupils. As a result 'classroom support' evolved which included any of the following: 'modeling demonstration lessons, co-operative planning, team-teaching, negotiated lesson observation, offering advice, mediating critical reflection, drafting school science teaching policies, supporting teacher collaboration, and supporting the management of learning resources' (p.192). As the programme developed Harvey increasingly worked on a one-to-one basis with teachers in timetabled science classes, spending two-hour long lessons with each of up to three teachers per school visit.

The coaching provided allowed opportunities for the teachers to acquire new skills and to put them into practice under the supervision and guidance of an expert. It also allowed 'the risk of innovation to be shared' (p.194). Following Vygotsky, and in particular utilising his concept of a Zone of Proximal Development (ZPD) (p.195), Harvey advocates a social constructivist view of adult learning (see also Chapter 12). Put simply, this underlines the importance of social setting and interaction in the learning process. The importance of collaboration between novices and more skilled individuals in the learning of complex skills is emphasised and the attention given during coaching allows the novice to focus on activities that are beyond their normal repertoire of skills but within their capabilities with assistance. It can take place in a safe or risk-free setting and feedback given by trusted and valued colleagues. Harvey notes that 'coaching during INSET can be viewed as an attempt to provide such a social context for learning that situates INSET within the ZPD' (p.195).

The article goes on to outline a research design and methodology for assessing the 'value added' of coaching in terms of observable changes in teachers' classroom practice. The methods used by teachers provided with both workshops and classroom-based coaching were compared with those used by teachers who received centre-based workshops only and a control group who received no INSET at all. The findings from the Primary Science Progamme, showed that teachers who received coaching made substantial changes, whereas most teachers who received workshops-only remained similar to the control group.

Coaching was shown to be an effective form of CPD but as Harvey notes it is expensive and labour intensive (p.202) and there is therefore a need to find cost-effective alternative ways of delivering support, taking into account that it cannot be provided by just anyone and that an open and trusting relationship was crucial. One way forward perhaps is to develop 'leader teachers' or 'advanced skills teachers' to provide classroom-based and pedagogical support within the school or a cluster of schools.

Thijs and Van den Berg (2002) undertook a similar study of peer coaching and science teaching in secondary schools in Botswana. The COAST study (Coaching to support Science and Mathematics) explored the levels of support that were needed to bring about effective peer coaching practices to support teachers implementing learner-centred teaching methods in secondary science and mathematics education in Botswana. Like Harvey's study, they found that peer coaching was beneficial in terms of developing teachers' professional skills, but it was organised as part of a wider professional development programme that included in-service training and the provision of exemplary curriculum materials. These were found to be important as well. The authors argue that teachers should receive training in coaching skills, such as classroom observation and discussion or feedback skills, and that collaboration should be made possible. Unsurprisingly perhaps, they suggest that for such conditions to be created 'strong leadership at school level is essential. This leadership is also important for motivational purposes and to stimulate the development of a collegial culture in schools' (p.58).

Evaluating the effects of CPD

Gauging the impact of CPD or evaluating its effectiveness—the final stage in the staff development cycle (see Figure 13.1)—is, as Harvey (1999) argues, difficult but not impossible. Bolam (2002, p.112) notes that few evaluation studies concerning CPD make any reference to its impact on teacher behaviour or student learning outcomes. However, evaluation is necessary to provide a sound basis for improving and upgrading programmes and processes but it needs to be relatively easy and inexpensive, otherwise it may be seen as diverting scarce resources away from other more important activities (see also Chapter 9).

Evaluation of training and development should be considered by educational leaders but it's often marginalised or fogotten about. A well-known framework for evaluating training is that developed by Kirkpatrick and first published in 1959 (see Bubb and Hoare, 2001). This has been adapted and developed over the years but Kirkpatrick's 'levels of evaluation', remains the model or framework for evaluating most training programmes in business and commerce.

Guskey (2000; 2002) has developed the model for education (see Table 13.1). He lists five levels of evaluation and, importantly, differentiates between different types of pupil outcomes.

In England Frost and Durrant (2003) have developed a framework to show how the process of development work culminates for the teacher in the transformation of professional knowledge. They argue that the outcomes of training or CPD can be seen not only in terms of professional development of individuals, but also in the extent to which there is an impact on pupils' learning, on colleagues' learning and on organisational learning. They suggest that teachers may also be able to make a contribution or impact at a fourth level—beyond their school.

- *Impact on pupils' learning*:
    a) attainment
    b) disposition
    c) meta-cognition
- *Impact on teachers*:
    a) classroom practice
    b) personal capacity
    c) interpersonal capacity
- *Impact on the school as an organisation*:
    a) structures and processes
    b) culture and capacity
- *Impact beyond the school*:
    a) critique and debate
    b) creation and transfer of professional knowledge
    c) improvements in social capital in the community.

                        (See Frost and Durrant, 2003 for the full framework.)

This framework enables teachers and schools to think beyond the effects of particular CPD provision and to focus more on its impact, in other words the authors concentrate on the actions of teachers instead of on the programme itself.

They note that causality is very difficult to establish, and the impact or effects of a particular programme or activity cannot be isolated. They have designed tools and activities to enable teachers themselves to plan, track and evaluate the impact of their activity and rather than retrospectively evaluating the impact that has already taken place, the

Table 13.1 Five levels of professional development evaluation (Guskey, 2002)

Evaluation level	What questions are addressed?	How will information be gathered?	What is measured or assessed?	How will information be used?
1. *Participants' reactions*	Did they like it? Was their time spent well? Did the material make sense? Will it be useful? Was the leader knowledgeable and helpful? Were the refreshments fresh and tasty? Was the room the right temperature? Were the chairs comfortable?	Questionnaires administered at the end of each session	Initial satisfaction with the experience	To improve programme design and delivery
2. *Participants' learning*	Did participants acquire the intended knowledge and skills?	Paper and pencil instruments Simulations Demonstrations Participant reflections (oral and/or written) Participant portfolios	New knowledge and skills of participants	To improve programme content, format, and organisation
3. *Organisation support and change*	Was implementation advocated, facilitated and supported? Was the support public and overt? Were the problems addressed quickly and efficiently?	District and schools records Minutes from follow up meetings Questionnaires Structured interviews with participants and district or school administrators	The organisation's advocacy, support, accommodation, facilitation, and recognition	To document and improve organisation support To inform future change efforts

Table 13.1 (*Continued*)

Evaluation level	What questions are addressed?	How will information be gathered?	What is measured or assessed?	How will information be used?
	Were sufficient resources made available? What was the impact on the organisation? Did it affect the organisation's climate and procedures?	Participant portfolios		
4. Participant's use of new knowledge and skills	Did participants effectively apply the new knowledge and skills?	Questionnaires. Structured interviews with participants and their supervisors. Participant reflections (oral and/or written). Participant portfolios. Direct observations. Video or audio tapes	Degree and quality of implementation	To document and improve implementation of programme content
5. Student learning outcomes	What was the impact on students? Did it affect student performance or achievement? Did it influence students' physical or emotional well-being? Are students more confident as learners? Is student attendance improving? Are dropouts decreasing?	Student records. School records. Questionnaires. Structured interviews with students, parents, teachers and/or administrators. Participant portfolios	Student learning outcomes. Cognitive (performance & achievement). Affective (attitudes & dispositions). Psychomotor (skills & behaviours)	To focus and improve all aspects of programme design, implementation, and follow up. To demonstrate the overall impact of professional development

intention is to encourage teachers to think more broadly about the influence they may have, thereby increasing impact as they adjust their planning accordingly. For example:

> they may be encouraged to introduce more collaborative working to draw colleagues into the inquiry process, they may talk to the headteacher to offer to run a staff development session in their school and they may agree to contribute to a conference or run a session for another Masters group on their specific area of expertise (Durrant, 2003, p.10).

LEARNING COMMUNITIES

The term 'learning community', first coined in America, is a relatively recent term having its origins in the better known concept of the 'learning organisation'. The latter first appeared in the business sector literature in the 1970s and 1980s (see Aspinwall, 1998) and became popularised by Senge's 'The Fifth Discipline' (1990), who later applied these same ideas to education (Senge et al, 2000). The use of the terms is sometimes restricted to business or education settings yet on other occasions they may be used interchangeably. The notion of a learning community is preferred here as the concern is not so much with structures and systems but rather with the people that operate them. Similarly, the term community—whether real or virtual—refers to the values, beliefs, feelings, motivation and aspirations of the people who make up an organisation.

Learning communities are also referred to as *professional* learning communities or communities of practice. The ideas of Wenger (1998) have been influential, stressing as they do the social nature of learning. He defines a community of practice as:

> a group of people who share a concern, a set of problems, or a passion about a topic, and who deepen their knowledge and expertise in this area by interacting on an ongoing basis.

Communities of practice are everywhere, and they are not new but as Wenger points out, not all communities are communities of practice, and not all practice gives rise to a community. The terms *community* and *practice* refer to a very specific type of social structure with a very specific purpose.

The term professional learning community is particularly appropriate to education. In a school, for instance, the question has to be asked, how can the idea of learning be central to it if its own staff are not engaged in that process themselves? There are two groups of learners within schools—young people and adults—and, as noted earlier, if teachers and other staff are not seen as continuous learners by the school itself how can adults engage youngsters in any meaningful pursuit of learning?

A succinct definition of a (professional) learning community is offered by Cibulka and Nakayama (2000) who see it as:

> a group of educators committed to working together collaboratively as learners to improve achievement for all students in a school. A learning community is one that

consciously manages learning processes through an inquiry-driven orientation among its members (2000, p.3).

As any teacher who has worked in more than one school will attest, the training and development culture may be quite different from one establishment to another. This is significant for as Judith Little (1990) has said:

> Imagine that you could become a better teacher just by virtue of being on the staff of a particular school—just that fact alone (p.514).

In some organisations the ongoing professional development of all staff is seen as integral, given great significance and is very closely linked to the institutional development plan. In such places there is an expectation that individuals and their managers will take a collective responsibility for both individual and organisational development.

An organisation wishing to become a learning community would therefore take its professional development responsibilities very seriously and strive to secure effective learning for both its pupils and staff. Leaders of such communities must engender an ethos that all in the organisation—pupils, teachers and support staff in a school, for example—are seen as learners in their own right. They must also seek everyone's views and involve all, in various ways, in decision-making processes, supporting, developing and empowering them to feel a sense of ownership in the future direction of *their* organisation. An active participation by all in a *collaborative* culture means that every-one takes responsibility for learning. Teachers and others working in such communities will discuss their work openly and seek to improve and develop their pedagogy through collaborative enquiry and the sharing of good practice. Can we ensure that what may be an effective learning environment in the classroom is mirrored in the staffroom or school as a whole?

Leadership for learning communities

Effective leaders more than anyone else help determine the culture of their organisation by their behaviour, for example, by constantly questioning the status quo to find better ways of achieving goals; creating environments where positive results and credits are widely dispersed; evaluating and affirming people; thinking positively and realising that every problem presents a learning opportunity; and seeking to integrate the best ideas in the task of building people and the organisation (Diggins, 1997, p.422). Learning com-munities are 'deeply committed to maintaining, developing and promoting the human capital they have' believing that they 'will become a reality when leaders become passionate about making the careers of other people happen' (Diggins, 1997, p.424).

Leaders in learning communities promote a strong sense of shared vision for the future; they lead the learning, by being seen to be learning with everyone else; they share and distribute leadership and empower others; and collaboration and continuous improvement is built into the fabric of the organisation. Collaboration and collegiality are seen as contributing significantly to both individual and organisational develop-ment. However, these terms are often ill-defined, their meaning not clear and open to different interpretations.

Collegiality can help to develop an emotionally supportive work environment and one that truly engenders significant professional development but, as Harris and Anthony (2001) argue, the presence of the former is not sufficient to ensure the latter. They found from their research in the US that it was only the more personal, collaborative and intensive relationships with colleagues (what Little calls 'strong ties') that showed potential to foster ongoing professional development. For colleagues truly to 'collaborate' and take ownership of the process of enquiry together, they need to have some shared values, goals and/or a common vision of teaching. They must have a relationship that is characterised by trust, care and mutual respect.

> They have to be comfortable sharing self-doubts without feeling like a failure, as well as celebrating successes without feeling arrogant. In a true collegial relationship, peers must be willing to give and receive both constructive feedback and reinforcement (Harris and Anthony, 2001, p.384).

The development of such relationships cannot be left to chance but neither can they be forced, mandated or prescribed.

Collaboration implies collegiality, cooperation, teaming and networking. According to Harris and Orlando (1992, cited in Bezzano, 2002) the major characteristics of collaboration include: mutual respect, tolerance, acceptance, commitment, courage, sharing of ideas and information, adherence to laws, regulations and rules, a philosophy of shared decision-making, teaming as the central mode of organisation for action, and a 'we' as opposed to an 'I' or 'you' paradigm.

Reflection 5

What do you think are the main factors preventing collegiality or collaboration from occurring? In terms of the above characteristics where would you place your own workplace or one that you know well?

　Is collaboration always a good thing?

The culture of a learning community is therefore likely to be one where there is a supportive and collaborative environment, featuring mutual trust and sharing of ideas and where:

- teachers are empowered to take a central role in their work;
- information is freely available and used to drive improvement;
- there is a commitment to working together as learners, where teachers and pupils alike are seen as learners; and where
- staff and pupils have a sense of community and work together cooperatively.

Groups of teachers who correspond outside of school, either electronically or in face-to-face meetings or networks show great potential as sites for focused, ongoing and self-directed inquiry. This is a long-standing form of staff training in Japan (see

Shimahara, 1998). These voluntary groups are now increasingly being seen in North America, Israel and the UK as a legitimate forum to promote teacher development. As Sachs (1997) writing about the Australian experience notes: 'establishing teacher networks and developing a culture of teacher enquiry holds some promise for reducing the randomness or serendipitous nature of professional development' (p.386).

Networked learning communities

Networks of learners, especially those connected electronically or 'virtually' are becoming very popular around the world, as they seem to provide:

- opportunities for teachers to both consume and generate knowledge;
- a variety of collaborative structures;
- flexibility and informality;
- discussion of problems that have no agreed-upon solutions;
- ideas that challenge teachers rather than merely prescribing generic solutions;
- an organisational structure that can be independent of, yet attached to, schools or universities;
- a chance to work across schools and district/local authority lines;
- a vision of reform that excites and encourages risk-taking in a supportive environment;
- a community that respects teachers' knowledge as well as knowledge from research and reform (Lieberman, 1999).

In England the *National College for School Leadership*, set up in November 2000, is encouraging the growth of networked learning communities to encourage change through learning at multiple levels of the education system. The 100 or so networks are made up of at least six schools and a higher education institution and the underpinning notion is that the learning is from each other, with each other and on behalf of each other (see Case example 3). (A useful account is given by Jackson, 2003. Also visit their website on www.ncsl.org.uk.)

There are six inter-connected 'levels of learning' which are the foundations for the collaborative planning and ongoing activity of each network:

- pupil learning—*pupils tell us about themselves as learners;*
- adult learning—*through joint work, adults teach each other the art and craft of teaching;*
- leadership for learning and leadership development—*leaders coach and facilitate others to lead;*
- school-wide learning—*adults become better every year at supporting pupil learning, just because they work in this school and network;*
- school-to-school learning—*our schools learn more because they are learning together;*
- network-to-network learning—*we feel part of a learning profession.*

Case Example 3

An example of a networked learning community is offered by Kellow (2003) who describes the origins of the *Primary Schools Learning Network* (PSLN) in Milton Keynes a town in central England. She explains that the network has developed as a partnership between 11 primary schools, an LEA (district) and a university department of education. At its heart is the notion of teachers as researchers and active learners. The PSLN has been founded upon ten professional learning precepts:

- successful schools are learning communities for adults as well as children;
- teachers learn best when they participate actively in decisions about the content, processes and outcomes of their learning;
- successful learning requires time for reflection;
- learning alone through one's own experience will ultimately limit learning;
- successful learning requires collaboration with others from inside and outside the workplace;
- teacher learning and development should contribute to school improvement;
- school leaders play a significant influencing role in teacher learning and development;
- at its best, learning will have personal and professional significance for teachers;
- supported, sustained learning over time is likely to be more beneficial to the individual and organisation than short term learning;
- if schools are to operate effectively in devolved systems, much reliance has to be placed on trust in professional judgement at school level (Day et al, 2003).

Based on these ten precepts the PSLN has five key objectives:

- to build and sustain capacity in schools for growth and improvement and for PSLN schools to develop into 'Learning Schools';
- to seek innovative practices in teaching and learning that result in improved pupil learning and raised standards;
- to develop leadership for learning, giving staff opportunities to lead and to develop their leadership potential;
- to work with other schools to share and develop knowledge and practice;
- through staff development increase staff motivation that will improve the retention of staff.

It is too early to know how successful the learning network has been or what impact it will have on pupil learning and attainment but the early signs are promising. Kellow (2003) reports the teachers involved in the network believe that it will have a positive effect and that belief in itself is significant as teachers are well rehearsed at pouring scorn on new ideas. The second year of the project will see it link with a group of primary schools in another English city and they plan to work together on joint projects. Interestingly, this initiative has not been led by headteachers and a deliberate decision was made that the leadership of the 'school improvement groups' should lie elsewhere. Nevertheless it is recognised that headteachers are the 'leaders of learning' in their schools and their influencing role is not to be underestimated. PSLN is one of the networks that has joined the earlier mentioned scheme run by NCSL. This has given participants further opportunities to link with colleagues in other parts of England. The project has created an excitement within the LEA—as one headteacher put it 'It's the most exciting thing to have happened here for years!'. Kellow concludes that through the work of the network 'teachers are beginning to regain some of their lost professional confidence and are getting opportunities to engage in activities that were previously denied them' and that the work of the PSLN is proving to be a powerful force for change.

SUMMARY

This chapter has considered a range of issues related to the leadership and management of professional development and the growth of learning communities, networked or otherwise. The importance of the organisation's people resource cannot be under-estimated. Educational policy makers and practitioners worldwide are facing major challenges as education systems develop from predominantly bureaucratic, hierarchical models to those which give greater emphasis to school site management and where institutional level leaders take decision-making responsibilities with colleagues. Devolution to site-based management also means increased responsibility on the part of school leaders for the quality of staff, especially teaching staff and the education delivered to students; ongoing training and development is therefore crucial and whereas it was once seen as an activity that was predominantly 'done to' teachers, it has been shown that adult learners must now fulfil a more active role as they learn to create and use the opportunities available. The role of educational leaders in all this is crucial as they encourage teachers and other staff to participate in institutional-based development. Principals and other leaders themselves need to be up to date and demonstrate a commitment to CPD, to be 'lead learners' promoting a learning climate or culture and monitoring and evaluating the progress of teachers' and other staff's professional development.

It is important to create a culture where learning is seen as central to everything that is done, where there is a *community of learners* or a *professional learning community*. To summarise:

- CPD should be fully integrated into the life of the school, not seen as something brought in from the outside by 'experts';
- clear and consistent means of identifying the need for CPD and assessing its effectiveness should exist;
- a balance of the CPD needs of the individual and the institution is important;
- a positive and participative attitude to CPD from school leaders and managers is required;

- there is an acceptance of the need for continuous individual improvement and learning;
- opportunities should exist to learn from colleagues on an ongoing basis (e.g. mutual observations, mentoring, coaching and other reflective practices);
- knowledge can occur through informal interactions (e.g. in the staffroom);
- teachers and other staff should learn from each other and with each other;
- inter-school networking is a valuable form of professional development.

RECOMMENDED FURTHER READING

Earley, P. and Bubb, S. (2004) *Leading and Managing Continuing Professional Development: Developing people—developing schools*, London: PCP/Sage.

Foskett, N. and Lumby, J. (2003) *Leading and Managing Education: International Dimensions*, London: Paul Chapman Publishing.

Both of the above books are useful for exploring further many of the themes in this chapter. The first is very practical and gives lots of advice and guidance for those in educational establishments, like heads and professional development coordinators, who are responsible for leading and managing the process and ensuring people (and thereby pupils) come first. The second reference takes a much broader perspective and is international in focus. Sections 2 and 3 are especially useful.

USEFUL WEBSITES

www.ncsl.org.uk
www.dfes.gov.uk
www.teachernet.gov.uk/professional_development

Endnote—Leading for Learning and Improvement

Peter Earley and Marianne Coleman

Key themes of this book have been leadership and the importance of learning—learning for all: students, teachers, and educational leaders and managers, often in a context of increasing institutional autonomy. The contributors to the book have considered the variety of ways in which leadership and management can contribute towards the development and enhancement of students' learning, the development of staff—all staff—and the growth of institutions. What is clear is that the move away from centralised control of resources towards more institutional autonomy is likely to continue as more and more educational systems throughout the world decentralise and give greater emphasis to institutional improvement, as discussed by Anderson in Chapter 4. Such developments give great emphasis to the role of educational leaders; it is assumed not only that they can cope with any new responsibilities thrust upon them but also that they will welcome them as providing new opportunities. However, the stress on targets for schools and colleges and the increasing accountability of leaders can also be seen as threatening their professionality.

The last decade or so has therefore seen a huge growth in interest in educational leaders and leadership development and we have seen the dominant discourse, shift in the USA, UK and elsewhere, from management to leadership. Some English examples make this clear. In England in 1990 the government set up the 'School Management Task Force', whilst exactly ten years later came the establishment of the 'National College for School Leadership'. Schools in England have been encouraged to think in terms of 'leadership teams' rather than the more traditional 'senior management teams' (DfEE, 2000) and middle managers are now increasingly referred to as middle leaders (Earley and Weindling, 2004). A similar stress on leadership was evident in a review of courses preparing aspiring school principals in Australia, Canada, the USA, Hong Kong, New Zealand, Singapore and Sweden (Bush and Jackson, 2002), and the same report commented on the Commonwealth Secretariat's concern in 1996 to train for leadership (and management) in schools throughout Africa. In most cases, the transition from 'manager' to 'leader' has taken place although reflected in the differing emphasis that is given to each over time and from culture to culture. This transition from teacher to school leader is a challenging one (Hobson et al, 2003) and has been reflected in the growing interest in leadership preparation and development, and building leadership capacity. But what kinds of leaders are being developed and what models of leadership are being promulgated? To what extent are they predicated on Western thinking? (See Chapter 2.)

The emerging model(s) of leadership that underpins current discourse is one of transformational and instructional leadership (Hallinger, 2003) and 'learning-centred leadership' (Southworth, 2003), these styles of leadership were discussed by Coleman in Chapter 1 where they are related to both Western and non-Western examples. These forms of leadership focus less on the leader—leadership is not perceived as simply a trait of an individual—and more on the sharing of leadership throughout the organisation. It is an inclusive leadership and one that is *distributed* throughout the school. Learning-centred leadership also has close connections to learning and pedagogy and andragogy. It is unashamedly about learning—pupil learning, adult learning (teachers, staff and governors), organisational learning and leadership networks—and teaching. The notion of learning-centred leadership has developed from both transformational and instructional leadership. (see Chapters 12 and 13.)

Hallinger (2003) sees headteachers who share leadership responsibilities with others as less subject to burnout than principal 'heroes' who attempt the challenges and complexities of leadership alone. Therefore the modern conception of educational leadership focuses strongly on 'learning' and does not reside within any one individual. It is part of leaders' role to develop leadership capacity—and learning—within the organisation (Harris and Lambert, 2003). In this model, leadership must become dispersed and it is not the leader but leadership that is the key factor. Today's leadership is therefore seen to be decentralised and distributed in every part of the organisation so those on the periphery who are first to spot challenges can act on them instantly (Pedlar et al, 2003).

Part of that style of leadership is to distribute or disperse responsibility and to empower others to give of their best and to keep learning at the centre of their activities. As Egan (1993, p.80) writing in a business context notes: 'if your organisation has only one leader then it is almost certainly short of leadership'. Leaders are people who, as Senge comments, 'lead through developing new skills, capabilities and understandings. And they come from many places within the organisation' (Senge, 1990, p.15). It could also be argued that leadership can be 'remote' and come from outside the organisation as discussed by Brighouse in Chapter 5.

Educational leaders are working in complex and uncertain ever-changing environments and as such need to possess qualities that will equip them to cope and thrive in such situations. Crucially, they need to be skilled in developing leadership capabilities in others. Leaders are seen as change agents whose focus must increasingly be on institutional development and the improvement of learning. As we have argued in this book, educational organisations that give high priority to learning and which maintain a culture to support it at all levels, are the ones able to react most imaginatively to and meet the challenges of an uncertain world. Educational leaders increasingly have to be improvement driven and 'learning-centred'. Some examples of this are given by Riley and Khamis in Chapter 7.

Educational leaders and managers are now vested with greater control and responsibility and they must ensure that they create a positive climate or culture in which staff can work and learn together. Leadership and management need to be embedded throughout the organisation by increasingly providing training for staff at all levels. It is through such arrangements that the learning of all will be enhanced and organisational outcomes achieved. However it would be naïve to see effective leadership and management as solving all our problems—neither leadership nor education can, in Basil Bernstein's famous phrase, 'compensate for society'. Thrupp and Wilmott (2003) have pointed out that if leadership now encompasses management it may be prone to managerialist assumptions, that even transformational leadership can be criticised for overlooking or disregarding the role of education in perpetuating social injustice. Nevertheless there is no shortage of evidence to show that schools and their leaders are very important in bringing about improvements, particularly where programmes are being implemented which address low achievement and social inclusion, including those facing challenging circumstances (Ofsted, 2003).

It is hoped that this book, based as it is on the contributions of leading writers in their fields, will provide you with insights into the nature of leadership and management in a variety of contexts and help ensure that 'learning' is at the heart of all your practice and a key consideration in all you do. It is our view that the practice of effective educational leadership and management will, ultimately, help enhance the life chances of future generations.

Glossary

Accountability—requirement for those with decision-making power to be open to scrutiny and sanction; responsibility for them to account for their decisions.

Adequacy and equity—criteria used for evaluating resource allocation.

Administration—in UK often refers to 'lower level' office work, whereas in other parts of the world it is equivalent with 'management' activities, such as planning, controlling and budgeting. May also include leadership.

Autonomy—decision-making rights over certain domains and/or resources.

Budgeting—the planning, implementation and evaluation of the use of given resources.

Bureaucracy—a form of organisation characterised by specialization of labour, a hierarchy of authority, a formal set of rules and rigid promotion and selection criteria.

Coaching—see the related term *mentoring*.

Co-constructivist model of learning—the co-constructivist model is an expanded version of the constructivist model. The essential features of this model are that it relies on dialogue and that the responsibility for learning shifts from individuals to emphasise collaboration in the construction of knowledge.

Collaboration (collaborative or participative leadership)—a process of working closely with colleagues, implying common ownership, some shared values, goals and/or a common vision of teaching; characterised by trust, care and mutual respect. Closely related to *collegiality*.

Collegiality—a culture of mutual support and shared decision-making, ideally by consensus between colleagues in professional organisations.

Constructivist model of learning—the learners' construction of meaning is at the heart of this model. They actively construct knowledge through such activities as discussion, discovery learning, open-ended questioning, usually related to their everyday experiences, often with the help of those around them.

Continuing professional development—training and development that is ongoing, commencing with initial training and continuing throughout the individual's career or work-life; related to life-long learning.

Culture—organisational: the norms and values underpinning work or, in broad terms, 'the way things are done around here'.

Culture—societal: the beliefs and values of a society or, in broad terms, a way of life.

Decentralisation—the process whereby decision-making authority for particular functions and, therefore, power over deployment and use of resources, is shifted from a certain location to one that is less central or 'lower'.

Distributive (or distributed) leadership—leadership which is distributed among the senior leadership team, the teachers and other staff of a school and (in some definitions) the students.

Effective learning—an activity of construction, handled with (or in the context of) others, driven by learners' agency and the monitoring and review of whether approaches and strategies are proving effective for the particular goals and context.

Effectiveness (in relation to finance)—refers just to the extent to which an organisation is judged to meet its objectives regardless of cost. It is a concept that endeavours to bring together both the measurable and the more subjective elements of education. It is the relationship between the school's objectives and its outputs.

Effectiveness (in relation to an individual school or college)—the relationship between the expected and actual academic and other outcomes.

Multi-level effectiveness—the extent to which each level (e.g. department and class) is effective.

Efficacy—the feeling of competence and confidence in self and colleagues that leads to effective performance.

Efficiency—relates to the relationship between an institution's inputs and its outputs. Efficiency entails securing minimum inputs for a given quality and quantity of education provided. This is achieved when a given quantity of output is achieved at minimum cost. A criterion used in evaluating resource use.

Emotional intelligence—emphasises the importance of a range of emotional qualities and skills that leaders need to be truly effective and stresses the affective rather than the rational aspect of relationships including leadership.

Empowerment—sharing decision-making and responsibility with those you manage in order to encourage commitment, efficacy and a high level of performance.

Equity—a system or procedure that is considered to be fair and socially just.

Evaluation—a process which involves looking back systematically at what has been accomplished and measuring the present position against the original aims.

Governance—the processes, procedures and rules relating to the governing and accountability of educational institutions.

Human resource management—the process of selecting, managing and developing people to ensure their effective performance and sense of efficacy. Often divided into 'hard' and 'soft' variants.

Improvement (school)—a systematic effort to improve some aspect of the organisation with the ultimate intention of improving learning outcomes.

Induction—a process by which an individual taking up a new post or position is introduced or socialised into the workings of the organisation.

Inspection—involves checking through quality procedures by external authorities with a stress on accountability and measurable performance.

Instructional (or educational, or educative) leadership—assumes that the key focus for leaders in education is the learning of their students, so the influence of leaders would tend to be based in their expert knowledge and intended to improve the effectiveness of teachers in the classroom.

Leadership—an over-arching concept that is difficult to define. Many definitions are available, one might be: a process of influencing the activities of a group in its efforts towards achieving its goals.

Learning communities—an organisation where the learning of all its members is given a high priority. Networked learning communities include groups of learners, especially those connected electronically or 'virtually'.

Loosely coupled systems—staff relate to a subsystem or department which is one of a loose collection of other subsystems within the organisation as a whole.

Management—activities undertaken to assist organisations to achieve their goals and may include planning, organising, resourcing, controlling and leading.

Managerialism—a term that is generally used pejoratively to describe management for its own sake, often linked to the achievement of targets and strict accountability. An associated term is new public management.

Mentoring—defined in many different ways but usually involves a process by which an individual is linked to another, usually a more senior staff member, for professional guidance, support and advice; to act as a critical friend or buddy. A related term is *coaching*, which is more related to skill development but both are tools for developing people.

Micro-politics—a perspective which sees organisations composed of groups with separate interests, goals and values, each vying with each other to reach their preferred outcomes. Conflict and power struggles are endemic.

Monitoring—checking on an activity whilst it is going on.

Moral leadership—stresses the importance of values in leadership and aims for morally justified actions and democratic schools.

Motivation—the complex individual drive to perform in order to achieve desired goals and to satisfy perceived needs. This depends on individual mentality, in particular self-image, self-esteem, goal-orientation and expectations, as well as on the work and broader environment.

NCSL—the National College for School Leadership, established in November 2000 and funded by UK government, to develop school leaders through providing training programmes and other activities.

New public management—the introduction of business management practices such as market competition, performance management and accountability into the public services. An associated term is 'managerialism'.

Normative—decision based on opinion rather than backed by evidence.

NPQH—the National Professional Qualification for Headteachers is a training programme for aspiring heads in England. Since April 2004 all applicants for headships have needed to possess this qualification or to be studying for it.

Open organisation or system—one which interacts with its environment, for example an environment which has regional, national and international levels.

Opportunity cost—the value of resources measured in terms of the next best alternative use of the resources that are given up in order to spend them in a particular way.

Outliers—those cases (schools) which lie well outside what might be expected as 'normal'. They may be schools which are particularly effective, or particularly ineffective.

Performance management—agreeing goals, objectives or targets for individuals, teams, organisation and even countries, using monitoring and review processes, incentives and development activities to achieve and measure progress towards these targets.

Performance-related pay (PRP)—the payment of bonuses or salary increases based on formal appraisal.

Policy—an external directive or general plan of action often stipulated by central government and underpinned by statute or circular/directive. Organisations may also devise their own (internal) policies.

Power—the capacity of individuals to overcome resistance on the part of others, to exert their will and to produce results consistent with their interests and objectives.

Reception model of learning—in this model the learner is a passive recipient of knowledge which is transmitted by the teacher.

Remote leadership—leadership exercised at a distance from a number of institutions, e.g. by a regional director.

Resources—the human and physical resources used in the educational process—these include:

- admissions—decisions over which pupils are to be admitted to the schools;
- assessment—the methods of assessment employed;
- finance—the allocation of money;
- funding—the setting of fees for the admission of pupils;
- information—the selection of data to be published about the school's performance;
- knowledge—including the curriculum and the goals or purposes of education;
- materials—the use of facilities;
- people—the management of human resources;
- power—the authority to make decisions;
- time;
- school governance—decisions over the power and composition of the governing body;
- technology—the means of teaching and learning.

Review—the action following an evaluation which usually involves making a decision about whether to continue with an activity, reject it, or modify it in the light of it being evaluated.

Self-evaluation—an activity conducted for development and improvement not for the production of a report for external accountability.

Situational or contingent or contextual leadership—the ability of a leader to vary their response in different leadership situations to maximise their leadership.

Structure—the manner in which something is constructed or made up, often associated with organisations, e.g. a hierarchical structure.

Transactional leadership—a formal exchange relationship between leader and follower, where the follower does what is expected in return for salary and other rewards.

Transformational leadership—(often contrasted with transactional leadership) which relates strongly to building the capacity of members of the organisation. Leadership of this type might be exercised by people other than the formal leader, and the outcomes would be greater capacity and continuing improvement.

Value-added—the process by which an effective school 'adds value' to its students' achievements in comparison with schools serving similar intakes.

Value for money. If an organisation is both efficient *and* effective it is said to be providing value for money. This concept attempts to bring the measurable and the immeasurable, the objective and the subjective together.

References

CHAPTER 1

Bass, B. M. and Avolio, B. J. (1994) *Improving Organizational Effectiveness Through Transformational Leadership*, Thousand Oaks: Sage.

Bhindi, M. N. and Duignan, P. (1997) 'Leadership for a New Century: authenticity, intentionality, spirituality and sensibility', *Educational Management and Administration*, 25(2), 117–132.

Blake, R. R. and Mouton, J. S. (1964) *The Managerial Grid*, Houston: Gulf Publishing Co.

Burns, J. M. (1978) *Leadership*, New York: Harper and Row.

Bush, T. (1999) 'Crisis or Crossroads? The discipline of educational management in the late 1990s', *Educational Management and Administration*, 27(3), 239–252.

Bush, T. and Jackson, D. (2002) 'A preparation for school leadership: International perspectives', *Educational Management and Administration*, 30(4), 417–430.

Cohen, O. (2003) *Headteachers Leading Change*, unpublished PhD thesis, University of Leicester.

Coleman, M. (2002) *Women as Headteachers: Striking the balance*, Stoke on Trent: Trentham Books.

DfES (2000) *National Standards for Headteachers*, London: Department for Education and Skills.

Day, C., Harris, A., Hadfield, M., Tolley, H. and Beresford, J. (2000) *Leading Schools in Times of Change*, Buckingham: Open University Press.

Dimmock, C. and Walker, A. (2000) Globalization and societal culture: Redefining schooling and school leadership in the 21st Century, *Compare* 30(3), 303–312.

Earley, P., Evans, J., Collarbone, P., Gold, A. and Halpin, D. (2002) *Establishing the Current State of School Leadership in England*, Research Brief, London: DfES.

Fiedler, F. E. (1967) *A Theory of Leadership Effectiveness*, New York: McGraw-Hill.

Foskett, N. and Lumby, J. (2003) *Leading and Managing Education: International Dimensions*, London: Paul Chapman Publishing.

Fullan, M. (2002) Leadership and sustainability, *Principal Leadership*, 3(4)

Gerwirtz, S. (2002) *The Managerial School*, London: RoutledgeFalmer.

Gibton, D., Sabar, N. and Goldring, E. B. (2000) 'How principals of autonomous schools in Israel view implementation of decentralization and restructuring policy: Risks, rights, and wrongs', *Educational Evaluation and Policy Analysis*, 22(2), 193–210.

Glatter, R., Preedy, M., Riches, C. and Masterton, M. (eds.) (1988) *Understanding School Management*, Milton Keynes: Open University Press.

Gold, A., Evans, J., Earley, P., Halpin D. and Collarbone, P. (2003) 'Principled principals? Values-driven leadership: Evidence from ten case studies of "outstanding" school leaders', *Educational Management and Administration*, 31(2), 125–136.

Goleman, D. (1996) *Emotional Intelligence: Why it Matters More than IQ*, London: Bloomsbury Paperbacks.

Gronn, P. (1999) *The Making of Educational Leaders*, London: Cassell.

—— (2003) *The New Work of Educational Leaders*, London: Paul Chapman Publishing.

Hallinger, P. and Kantamara, P. (2000) 'Educational Change in Thailand: Opening a window onto leadership as a cultural process', *School Leadership and Management*, 20(2), 189–205.

Harber, C. and Davies, L. (1997) *School Management and Effectiveness in Developing Countries: The Post-Bureaucratic School*, London: Cassell.

Harris, A. (2002) 'Effective leadership in schools facing challenging contexts', *School Leadership and Management*, 22(1), 15–26.

HayGroup (2000) *The Lessons of Leadership*, London: Hay Group.

Hersey, P. and Blanchard, K. H. (1988) *Management of Organisational Resources: Utilising Human Resources*, Englewood Cliffs N. J.: Prentice-Hall.

Hofstede, G. (1991) *Culture and Organizations: Software of the Mind*, New York: McGraw-Hill.

Huen, Y., Leithwood, K. and Jantzi, D. (2002) 'The effects of transformational leadership on teachers' commitment to change in Hong Kong', *Journal of Educational Administration*, 40(4), 368–389.

James, C. and Vince, R. (2001) 'Developing the leadership capability of headteachers', *Educational Management and Administration*, 29(3), 307–317.

Lahui-Ako, B. (2001) 'The instructional leadership behaviour of Papua New Guinea high school principals: a provincial case study', *Journal of Educational Administration*, 39(3), 233–265.

Law, S. and Glover, D. (2000) *Educational Leadership and Learning: Practice, Policy and Research*, Buckingham: Open University Press.

Lee, J. C. K. and Walker, A. (2000) 'Pre-service primary teachers' perceptions about principals in Hong Kong: implications for teacher and principal education', *Asia-Pacific Journal of Teacher Education*, 28(1), 53–67.

Leithwood, K., Jantzi, D. and Steinback, R. (1999) *Changing Leadership for Changing Times*, Buckingham: Open University Press.

Riley, K. and MacBeath, J. (2003) *Effective Leaders and Effective Schools*, in Bennett, N., Crawford, M. and Cartwright, M., London: Paul Chapman Publishing.

Schein, V. E. (1994) Managerial sex typing: A persistent and pervasive barrier to women's opportunities, in Davidson, M. J. and Burke, R. J. (eds.) *Women in Management: Current Research Issues*, London: Paul Chapman.

Stogdill, P. (1969) 'Personal factors associated with leadership: a survey of the literature', in Gibb, C.A. (ed.), *Leadership*, Harmondsworth: Penguin.

Tannenbaum, R. and Schmidt, W. H. (1973) 'How to choose a leadership pattern', *Harvard Business Review*, May-June, 162–180.

Taylor, F. (1911) *Principles of Scientific Management*, New York: Norton.

Thrupp, M. and Wilmott, R. (2003) *Education Management in Managerialist Times: Beyond the Textual Apologists*, Maidenhead: Open University Press.

Wright, N. (2001) 'Leadership, "bastard leadership" and managerialism: Confronting twin paradoxes in the Blair education project', *Educational Management and Administration*, 29(3), 275–290.

CHAPTER 2

Arthur, L. and Preston, R. (1995) *The Changing Nature of International Consultancy in Human Development: Report to the British Council*, International Centre for Education in Human Development, University of Warwick.

Ball, S. (1987) *The Micro-Politics of the School*, London: Routledge.

—— (1993) *Understanding Culture's Influences on Behaviour*, New York: Harcourt Brace Jovanovich College Publishers.

Brislin, R., Cushner, K., Cherrie, C. and Yong, M. (1986) *Intercultural Interactions: A Practical Guide*, Newbury Park: Sage.

Bullock, A. and Thomas, H. (1997) *Schools at the Centre? A study of decentralisation*, London: Routledge

Cray, D. and Mallory, G. (1998) *Making Sense of Managing Culture*, London: International Thompson Business Press.

Fadil, P. (1995) 'The effect of cultural stereotypes on leader attributions of minority subordinates', *Journal of Managerial Issues*, 7(2), 193–208.

Goffee, R. and Jones, G. (1995)' Developing managers for Europe: a re-examination of cross-cultural differences', *European Management Journal*, 13(3), 245–250.

Harber, C. (1995) 'Democratic education and the international agenda', in Harber, C. (ed.) *Developing Democratic Education*, Derby: Education Now Publishing Group.

—— (1998) *Voices for Democracy*, Nottingham: Education Now, in association with British Council.

—— and Davies, L. (1997) *School Management and Effectiveness in Developing Countries: the post-bureaucratic school*, London: Cassell.

Harris, A. (2001) 'Contemporary perspectives on school effectiveness and school improvement', in Harris, A. and Bennett, N. (eds.) *School Effectiveness and School Improvement: alternative perspectives,* London: Continuum.

Heller, R. (1997) *In Search of European Excellence*, HarperCollins Business.

Helson, H. (1964) *Adaptation Level Theory*, New York: Harper and Row.

Hersey, P. (1985) *Situational Selling*, Escondido, CA: Centre for Leadership Studies.

—— and Blanchard, K. (1988) *Management of Organizational Behavior: Utilizing Human Resources* (5th edn), Englewood Cliffs: Prentice-Hall International.

Hofstede, G. (1991) *Cultures and Organizations*, London: Harper Collins.

Jameson, D. (1994) 'Strategies for overcoming barriers inherent in cross-cultural research', *Bulletin for the Association for Business Communication*, 57(3), 39–40.

Kanter, R. M. and Corn, R. (1994) 'Do cultural differences make a business difference? Contextual factors affecting cross-cultural relationships', *Journal of Management Development*, 13(2), 5–23.

Kraiger, K. and Ford, J. (1985) 'A meta-analysis of ratee race effects in performance ratings', *Journal of Applied Psychology*, 70, 56–65.

Little, A. (1996) 'Globalisation and international research: whose context counts?' *International Journal of Educational Development*, 16(4), 427–438.

MacBeath, J. and Mortimore, P. (eds.) (2001) *Improving School Effectiveness*, Buckingham: Open University Press.

McMahon, A. (2001) 'A cultural perspective on school effectiveness, school improvement and teacher professional development', in Harris, A. and Bennett, N. (eds.) *School Effectiveness and School Improvement: alternative perspectives*, London: Continuum.

Mbiti, J. (1990) *African Religions and Philosophy*, London: Heinemann.

Riordan, C. and Vandenburg, R. (1994) 'A central question in cross-cultural research: do employees of different cultures interpret work-related measures in an equivalent manner?', *Journal of Management*, 20(3), 643–671.

Rodwell, S. (1998) 'Internationalisation or indigenisation of educational management development? Some issues of cross-cultural transfer', *Comparative Education*, 34(1), 41–54.

Ross, I. (1977) 'The intuitive psychologist and his shortcomings: distortion in the attribution process', *Advances in Experimental Social Psychology*, 10, 173–220.

Schein, E. (1985) *Organizational Culture and Leadership*, Oxford: Jossey-Bass.

Schwartz, S. (1992) 'The universal content and structure of values: theoretical advances and empirical tests in 20 countries', in M. Zanna (ed.) *Advances in Experimental Social Psychology*, 25, 1–65, New York: Academic Press.

Shaw, M. (2001a) 'Managing mixed-culture teams in international schools', in Blandford, S. and Shaw, M., *Managing International Schools*, London: Routledge.

—— (2001b) 'The application of Western educational management praxis in different cultural contexts: a case study in Namibia', Unpublished PhD thesis, University of Birmingham.

—— and Ormston, M. (2001) 'Values and vodka: Cross-cultural anatomy of an Anglo-Russian educational project', *International Journal of Educational Development*, 21, 119–133.

Smith, P. and Bond, M. (1993) *Social Psychology Across Cultures*, Hemel Hempstead: Harvester Wheatsheaf.

Tayeb, M. (1994) 'Organizations and national culture: Methodology considered', *Organization Studies*, 15(3), 429–446.

Trompenaars, F. (1993) *Riding the Waves of Culture*, London: Nicholas Brearley.

CHAPTER 3

Ball, S. (1987) *The Micropolitics of the School: Towards a Theory of School Organization*, London: Methuen.

Bishop, P. and Mulford, B. (1999) 'When will they ever learn?: another failure of centrally-imposed change', *School Leadership and Management*, 19(2), 179–187.

Blackmore, J. (1999) *Troubling Women*, Buckingham: Open University Press.

Bolman L. G. and Deal, T. E. (1997) *Reframing Organizations: Artistry, Choice and Leadership*, San Francisco: Jossey-Bass.

Brown, M., Boyle, B. and Boyle, T. (1999) 'Commonalities, between perception and practice in models of school decision-making in secondary schools', *School Leadership and Management*, 19(3), 319–330.

Bush, T. (2003) *Theories of Educational Management and Leadership*, London: Paul Chapman Publishing.

—— Coleman, M. and Si, X. (1998) 'Managing secondary schools in China', *Compare*, 28(2), 183–196.

Busher, H. (2001) 'The micro-politics of change, improvement and effectiveness in schools', in Harris, A. and Bennett, N. (eds.) *School Effectiveness and School Improvement: Alternative perspectives*, London: Continuum.

Coleman, M. (2003) 'Gender and the orthodoxies of leadership, in *School Leadership Management*' 23(3), 325–341.

—— (2002a) *Women as Headteachers: Striking the balance*, Stoke on Trent: Trentham Books.

—— (2002b) 'Managing for equal opportunities', in Bush, T. and Bell, L. (eds.) *The Principles and Practice of Educational Management*, London: Paul Chapman Publishing, pp. 135–150.

—— Qiang, H. and Li, Y. (1998) 'Women in educational management in China: Experience in Shaanxi Province, *Compare*', 28(2), 141–154.

Connell, R. W. (1991) *Gender and Power*, Cambridge: Polity Press.

Deal, T. and Kennedy, A. (1982) *Corporate Rituals: the Rites and Rituals of Corporate Life*, Reading, M.A.: Addison Wesley.

Detert, J. R., Seashore Louis, K. and Schroeder, R. G. (2001) 'A culture framework for education: Defining quality values and their impact in U.S. high schools', *School Effectiveness and School Improvement*, 12(2), 183–212.

Fidler, B. (1997) 'Organisational structure and organizational effectiveness', in Harris, A., Bennett, N. and Preedy, M. (eds.) *Organizational Effectiveness and Improvement in Education*, Buckingham: Open University Press.

Gerth, H. and Wright Mills, C. (1947) *From Max Weber; Essays in Sociology*, London: Routledge and Kegan Paul.

Hales, C. (1997) 'Power, authority and influence', in Harris, A., Bennett, N. and Preedy, M. (eds.) *Organizational Effectiveness and Improvement in Education*, Buckingham: Open University Press.

Hanna, D. (1997) 'The organization as an open system', in Harris A., Bennett, N. and Preedy, M. (eds.) *Organizational Effectiveness and Improvement in education*, Buckingham: Open University Press.

Hannay, L. M. and Ross, J. A. (1999) 'Department heads as middle managers? Questioning the black box', *School Leadership and Management*, 19(3), 345–358.

Hargreaves, A. (1991) 'Contrived collegiality: the micropolitics of teacher collaboration', in Blase, J. (ed.) *The Politics of Life in Schools*, London: Sage.

Hargreaves, D. (1997) 'School culture, school effectiveness and school improvement', in Harris, A. Bennett, N. and Preedy, M. (eds.) *Organizational Effectiveness and Improvement in Education*, Buckingham: Open University Press.

Harling, P. (1989) 'The organizational framework for educational leadership', in Bush, T. (ed.) *Managing Education: Theory and Practice*, Milton Keynes: Open University Press.

Hoyle, E. (1986) *The Politics of School Management*, London: Hodder and Stoughton.

Kang, S. (2002) 'Democracy and human rights education in South Korea', *Comparative Education*, 38(3), 315–325.

Lewin, K., Xu, H., Little, A. and Zheng, J. (1994) *Educational Innovation in China: Tracing the impact of the 1985 reforms*, Harlow: Longman.

Morgan, G. (1998) *Images of Organization*, The Executive Edition, San Francisco: Berrett-Kochler Publications Inc. and Thousand Oaks: Sage Publications Inc.

Mulford, B., Kendall, L., Kendall, D., Hogan, D. and Lamb, S. (2001) 'Decision-making in Australian high schools', *International Studies in Educational Administration*, 29(2), 1–20.

Nsaliwa, C. and Ratsoy, E. (1998) 'Educational decisions in Malawi', *International Studies in Educational Administration*, 26(2), 63–72.

O'Neill, J. (1994) 'Organizational structure and culture, in Bush, T. and West-Burnham, J. (eds.) *The Principles of Educational Management*, Harlow: Longman.

Senge, P. M. (1990) *The Fifth Discipline: The Art and Practice of the Learning Organisation,* London: Century Business.

Singapore Ministry of Education (1997–98) *Learning to Think: Thinking to Learn*, Singapore: Ministry of Education.

Stoll, L. and Fink, D. (1996) *Changing our Schools: Linking school effectiveness and school improvement*, Buckingham: Open University Press.

Timperley, H. and Robinson, M. J. (2000) 'Workload and the professional culture of teachers', *Educational Management and Administration*, 28(1), 47–62.

Torrington, D. and Weightman, J. (1989) *The Reality of School Organisation*, Oxford: Blackwell Education.

Tuohy, D. and Coghlan, D. (1997) 'Development in schools: A systems approach based on organizational levels', *Educational Management and Administration*, 25(1), 65–78.

Vogt, F. (2002) 'Teacher teamwork—supportive cultures and coercive policies?', paper presented at the Annual Conference of BERA, University of Exeter, England, September, on *Education Line*, www/leeds.ac.uk/edcol/documents.

Walker, M. (1998) 'Academic Identities: women on a South African landscape', *British Journal of Sociology of Education*, 19(3), 335–355.

Weick, K. E. (1976) 'Educational organisations as loosely coupled systems', *Administrative Science Quarterly*, 21(1), 1–19.

West, M. (1999) 'Micropolitics, leadership and all that . . . The need to increase the micropolitical awareness and skills of school leaders', *School Leadership and Management*, 19(2), 189–195.

Wildy, H. and Louden, W. (2000) 'School restructuring and the dilemmas of principals' work', *Educational Management and Administration*, 28(2), 173–184.

Yariv, E. (unpublished doctoral course work, 2000) *An application of educational management theories to the solving of discipline problems by headteachers*.

CHAPTER 4

Ainley, P. and Bailey, J. (1997) *The Business of Learning: Staff and Student Experiences of Further Education in the 1990s*, London: Cassell.

Angus, L. (1993) 'Democratic participation or efficient site management: the social and political location of the self-managing school' in J. Smyth (ed.) *A Socially Critical View of the Self-managing School*, London: The Falmer Press.

Archer, M. (1979) *Social Origins of Educational Systems*, London: Sage.

Atkinson, R. (1997) *Towards Self-governing Schools*, London: The Institute of Economic Affairs, Education and Training Unit.

Babyegeya, E. B. N. K. (2000) 'Education reforms in Tanzania: from nationalisation to decentralization of schools', *International Studies in Educational Administration*, 28(1), 2–10.

Bell, L. (1998) 'Back to the future: the development of site-based management in England with messages, challenges and a vision for Australia', Keynote address to the 25th Australian Council for Educational Administration International Conference, Gold Coast, 27–30 September.

Blackmore, J., Bigum, C., Hodgens, J. and Laskey, L. (1996) 'Managed change and self-management in schools of the future', paper presented at the joint Conference of the Educational Research Association, Singapore and the Australian Association for Research in Education, 25–29 November, www.swin.edu.au/aare/conf96/BLACJ96.133.

Brooke, J. Z. (1984) *Centralization and Autonomy: A Study in Organisational Behaviour*, New York: Holt, Rinehart and Winston.

Brown, D. (1990) *Decentralization and School-based Management*, Lewes: The Falmer Press.

Bullock, A. and Thomas, H. (1997) *Schools at the Centre?*, London: Routledge.

Bush, T. (1995) *Theories of Educational Management*, London: Paul Chapman.

—— Coleman, M. and Glover, D. (1993) *Managing Autonomous Schools: The Grant Maintained Experience*, London: Paul Chapman.

Caldwell, B. (2000) 'Local management and learning outcomes: Mapping the links in three generations of international research' in Coleman, M. and Anderson, L. (eds.) *Managing Finance and Resources in Education*, London: Paul Chapman.

Caldwell, B. (2001) *A Theory of Learning in the Self-Managing School*, Context paper for Technology Colleges Trust, Vision 2020, First International On-Line Conference 4 June-1 July, www.cybertext.net.au

—— (2002) 'Autonomy and self-management: Concepts and evidence', in T. Bush and L. Bell (eds.) *The Principles and Practice of Educational Management*, London: Paul Chapman.

—— (1993) 'Paradox and Uncertainty in the Governance of Education', in H. Beare and W. L. Boyd (eds.) *Restructuring Schools*, London: The Falmer Press.

—— and Spinks, J. (1988) *The Self-managing School*, Lewes: The Falmer Press.

—— and Spinks, J. (1992) *Leading the Self-managing School*, Lewes: The Falmer Press.

—— and Spinks, J. (1998) *Beyond the Self-managing School*, Lewes: The Falmer Press.

Caillods, F. (1999) Preface, in N. McGinn and T. Welsh (eds.) *Decentralization of Education: Why, When, What and How?* Paris, UNESCO.

Carnoy, M. (1998) 'National voucher plans in Chile and Sweden: did privatization reforms make for better education?' *Comparative Educational Review*, 42(3), 309–337.

Chubb, J. and Moe, T. (1990) *Politics, Markets and America's Schools*, Washington DC: Brookings Institution.

Cortina, R. (1995) 'Education and political change in Mexico', paper presented at the CIES Conference, Boston, MA.

Cruz, R. de la (ed.) (1992) *Descentralización, Deocracia*: Caracas: Nueva Sociedad.

Davies, B. and Anderson, L. (1992) *Opting for Self-management*, London: Routledge.

Davies, L., Harber, C. and Dzimadzi, C. (2003) 'Educational Decentralisation in Malawi: a study of process', *Compare*, 33(2), 139–154.

De la Fuente, M. T., Luck, E. and Ramos, C. (1998) 'Monitoring and evaluation of educational reform initiatives in the state of Paraná, Brazil', in B. Alvarez and M. Ruis-Casares (eds.) *Evaluation and Educational reform: Policy Options*, Washington DC: Academy for Educational Development.

DEET (2001) 'An "actuals" school global budget: Steps towards enhanced self management', Melbourne: Department of Education, Employment and Training.

Dempster, N. (2000) 'Guilty or not: the impact and effects of site-based management on schools', *Journal of Educational Administration*, 38(1), 47–63.

Derouet, J.-L. (2000) 'School autonomy in a society with multi-faceted political references: the search for new ways of coordinating', *Journal of Education Policy,* 15(1), 61–69.

Elmore, R. F. (1993) 'School decentralization: Who gains? Who loses?', In. J. Hannaway and M. Carnoy (eds.) *Decentralization and school improvement*, San Francisco, CA: Jossey-Bass.

Feintuck, M. (1994) *Accountability and Choice in Schooling*, Buckingham: Open University Press.

Fernandez Lamarra, N. and Vitar, A. (1991) *Planificación, Federalismo, y Descentralización en la Argentina*, Buenos Aires: Ministerio de Educación y Justicia.

Fidler, B., Russell, S. and Simkins, T. (1997) *Choices for Self-managing Schools: Autonomy and Accountability*, London: Paul Chapman.

Fitz, J., Halpin, D. and Power, S. (1993) *Grant Maintained Schools: Education in the Market Place*, London: Kogan Page.

Fullan, M. (1993) *Changing Forces: probing the depths of educational reform*, London: Falmer Press.

—— and Watson, N. (2000) 'School-based management: Reconceptualizing to improve learning outcomes', *School Effectiveness and School Improvement*, 11(4), 453–473.

Gammage, D. T., Sipple, P. and Partridge, P. (1996) 'Research on school-based management in Victoria', *Journal of Educational Administration*, 34(1), 24–40.

Gewirtz, S., Ball, S. J. and Bowe, R. (1995) *Markets, Choice and Equity in Education*, Buckingham: Open University Press.

Gibton, D., Sabar, N. and Goldring, E. (2000) 'How principals of autonomous schools in Israel view implementation of decentralization and restructuring policy: risks, rights and wrongs', *Educational Evaluation and Policy Analysis*, 22(2), 193–210.

Giddens, A. (1998) *The Third Way*, Cambridge: Polity Press.

Glatter, R. (2002) 'Governance, Autonomy and Accountability in Education', in T. Bush and L. Bell (eds.) *The Principles and Practice of Educational Management*, London: Paul Chapman.

Glatter, R., Woods, P. and Bagley, C. (1997) *Choice and Diversity in Schooling*, London: Routledge.

Gorostiaga Derqui, J. M. (2001) 'Educational decentralization policies in Argentina and Brazil: exploring the new trends', *Journal of Education Policy*, 16(6), 561–583.

Green, A. (1999) 'Education and globalisation in Europe and East Asia: convergent and divergent trends', *Journal of Educational Policy*, 14(1), 55–72.

Hales, C. (1997) 'Power, authority and influence,' in Harris, A., Bennett, N. and Preedy, M. (eds.) *Organizational Effectiveness and Improvement in Education*, Buckingham: Open University Press.

Hallak, J. (1991) *Managing schools for educational quality and equity: Finding the proper mix to make it work*, paper presented at the 3rd SEAMEO INNOTECH International Conference, Manila, The Philippines.

Halpin, D., Fitz, J. and Power, S. (1993) 'The early impact and long term implications of the grant maintained schools policy', in *Warwick Papers on Education Policy No. 4*, Stoke-on-Trent: Trentham Books.

Hanson, E. M. (1976) 'Decentralization and regionalization in the ministry of education: the case of Venezuela', *International Review of Education*, 22(2), 155–176.

—— (1986) *Educational Reform and Administrative Development: The Cases of Columbia and Venezuela*, Stanford, CA: Hoover Institution Press.

—— (1998) 'Strategies of educational decentralization: key questions and core issues', *Journal of Educational Administration*, 36(2), 111–128.

Kang, S. (2002) 'Democracy and Human Rights Education in South Korea', *Comparative Education*, 38(3), 315–325.

Karlsen, G. E. (2000) 'Decentralized centralism: framework for a better understanding of governance in the filed of education', *Journal of Education Policy*, 15(5), 525–538.

Karstanje, P. (1999) 'Decentralization and deregulation in Europe: towards a conceptual framework', in T. Bush, L. Bell, R. Bolam, R. Glatter and P. Ribbins (eds.) *Educational Management: Redefining Theory, Policy and Practice*, London: Paul Chapman.

King, E. and Osler, B. (1998) *'What's decentralization got to do with learning?: the case of Nicaragua's school autonomy reform'*, paper presented to the Annual Conference of the American Educational Research Association, San Diego, CA, 13–17 April.

Kogan, M. (1986) Education Accountability: An Analytic Overview, London: Hutchinson.

Krawczyk, N. (1999) 'A gesto escolar: um campo minado . . . Análise das propostas de 11 municipios brasileiros', *Educçao & Sociedade*, ano XX(67), 112–149.

Le Grand, J. and Bartlett, W. (1993) 'Introduction', in J. Le Grand and W. Bartlett (eds.) *Quasi-Markets and Social Policy*, London: Macmillan Press.

Lauglo, J. (1996) 'Forms of decentralization and their implications for education', in J. D. Chapman, W. L. Boyd, R. Lander and D. Reynolds (eds.) *The Reconstruction of Education*, London: Cassell.

Levacic, R. (2002) 'Efficiency, Equity and Autonomy', in T. Bush and L. Bell (eds.) *The Principles and Practice of Educational Management*, London: Paul Chapman.

—— (1995) *Local Management of Schools*, Buckingham: Open University Press.

Levin, B. and Young, J. (1994) *Understanding Canadian Schools: An Introduction to Educational Administration*, Canada: Harcourt Brace and Company.

Lockheed, M. E. and Verspoor, A. M. (1991) *Improving Primary Education in Developing Countries*, Oxford: Oxford University Press.

Lundgren, U. P. and Mattsson, K. (1996) 'Decentralization by or for School Improvement', in J. D. Chapman, W. L. Boyd, R. Lander and D. Reynolds (eds.) *The Reconstruction of Education*, London: Cassell.

McGinn, N. and Street, S. (1986) 'Educational decentralization: weak state or strong state?', *Comparative Education Review*, 30, 471–490.

Mintzberg (1983) *Structure in Fives: Designing effective organizations*, N. J.: Prentice-Hall Inc.

Nir, A. E. (2002) 'School-based management and its effect on teacher commitment', *International Journal of leadership in Education*, 5(4), 323–341.

Nunez, I., Gonźalez, L. and Espinoza, O. (1993) *La Práctica de la Planificación Educativa en el Contexto del Proceso de Descentralización en Chile*, Paris: Instituto Internacional de Planeamiento de la Educación.

Office for Official Publications of the European Communities (2001) *Key Topics in Education, Volume 2: The Financing and Management of Resources in Compulsory Education in Europe—Trends in National Policies*, Brussels: OOFPEC.

Organisation for Economic Co-operation and Development (OECD) (2000) *Education at a Glance*, Paris: OECD.

Papagiannis, G. J., Easton, P. A. and Owens, J. T. (1998) *The school restructuring movement in the USA: An analysis of major issues and policy implications*, Paris: IIEP-UNESCO.

Plank, D. N., Sobrinho, J. A. and Xavier, A. C. (1996) 'Why Brazil lags behind in educational development', in N. Birdsall and R. H. Sabot (eds.) *Opportunity Foregone: Education in Brazil*, Washington DC: International American Development Bank.

Ranson (1996) 'Markets or Democracy for Ecucation', in J. Ahier, B. Cosin and M. Hales (eds.) *Diversity and Choice*, London: Routledge.

Rhoten, D. (2000) 'Education decentralization in Argentina: a "global-local conditions of possibility" approach to state, market and socity change', *Journal of Education Policy*, 15(6), 593–619.

Rondinelli, D. A., Nellis, J. R. and Cheema, G. S. (1983) *Decentralization in Developing Countries: A Review of Recent Experience*, World Bank Staff Working Papers, No. 581, Washington DC: Management and Development Series, No. 8.

Sabar, N. (1988) 'School-based curriculum development', in T. Hussen and N. Postlewaite (eds.) *The International Encyclopedia of Education* (Supp. Vol. 1): *Research and Studies* (201–203) Oxford: Pergamon Press.

Sackney, L. E. and Dibski, D. J. (1994) 'School-based management: a critical perspective', *Educational Management and Administration*, 22(2), 104–12.

Sharpe, F. (1994) 'Devolution: towards a research framework', *Educational Management and Administration*, 22(2), 85–95.

Sherratt, B. (1994) *Grant Maintained Schools: Considering the Options*, Harlow: Longman.

Silberstein, M. (1990) 'The autonomous school: A combination of planning approaches', in I. Friedman (ed.) *Autonomy in Education* (2nd edn., pp. 100–129) Jerusalem: Szold Institute.

Simkins, T. (1997) 'Autonomy and Accountability', in B. Fidler, S. Russell and T. Simkins (1997) *Choices for Self-managing Schools: Autonomy and Accountability*, London: Paul Chapman.

Smith, B. C. (1985) *Decentralization*, London: George Allen and Unwin.

Simon, H. A.(1957) *Administrative Behaviour* (2nd edn.), New York: Free Press.

Smyth, J. (ed.) (1993) *A Socially Critical View of the self-managing School*, London: The Falmer Press.

Sosale, S. (2000) 'Trends in private sector development in World Bank education projects', *World Bank Policy Research Working Paper* 2452, 49.

Souza, M. Z. (1997) 'Avaliaçao do rendimen to escolar como instrumento de gestao educaciaonal', in D. A. Oliveira (ed.) *Gestao Democratica da Educaçao,* Petropolis: Vozes.

Stinnette, L. (1992) *Decentralization: why, how and towards what ends?* Policy Briefs, Washington, DC: USDE.

Thélot, C. (1993) *L'evaluation du systéme éducatif*, Paris: Natham.

Thomas, H. and Martin, J. (1996) *Managing Resources for School Improvement*, London: Routledge.

Tooley, J. (1998) 'Scepticism about school effectiveness research: Lessons from school improvement. Paper presented at the International Congress on School Effectiveness and Improvement, Manchester, January.

Van Langen, A. and Dekkers, H. (2001) 'Decentralization and Combating Educational Exclusion', *Comparative Education*, 37(3), 367–384.

Van Zanten, A. (2002) 'Educational change and new cleavages between headteachers, teachers and parents: global and local perspectives on the French case', *Journal of Education Policy*, 17(3), 289–304.

—— and Robert, A. (2000) ' "Plus ca change . . . " Changes and continuities in education policy in France', *Journal of Education Policy*, 15(1), 1–4.

Weiler, H. (1993) 'Control versus legitimization: The politics of ambivalence', in J. Hannaway and M. Carnoy (eds.) *Decentralization and School Improvement*, San Francisco, CA: Jossey-Bass.

—— (1990) 'Decentralization in educational governance: an exercise in contradiction', in M. Granheim, M. Kogan, and U. Lundgren (eds.), *Evaluation as Policymaking: Introducing Evaluation into a National Decentralised Educational System*, London: Jessics Kingsley Publishers.

Whitty, G. (1990) 'The New Right and the National Curriculum: State control or market forces?', in M. Flude and M. Hammer (eds.) *The Education Reform Act 1988*, London: The Falmer Press.

——, Power, S. and Halpin, D. (1998) *Devolution and Choice in Education: The School, the State and the Market*, Buckingham: Open University Press.

Wildy, H. (1991) 'School-based management and its linkage with school effectiveness: research issues arising from a preliminary study of three government secondary schools in Western Australia', in McKay, I. and Caldwell, B. J. (eds.) *Researching Educational Administration Theory and Practice*, ACEA Pathways Series 2, Australian Council for Educational Administration, Victoria: Hawthorne.

Winkler, D. (1993) 'Fiscal decentralization and accountability in education: experiences in four countries', in J. Hannaway and M. Carnoy (eds.) *Decentralization and School Improvement*, San Francisco, CA: Jossey-Bass.

World Bank (1995) *Priorities and Strategies for Education: A review*, Washington, DC: World Bank.

Wylie, C. (1996) 'Finessing site-based management with balancing acts', *Educational Leadership*, 53(4), 54–59.

CHAPTER 5

Abrahamsson, B. (1977) *Bureaucracy or Participation?*, London: Sage.

Advisory Group on Citizenship (1998) *Education for Citizenship and the Teaching of Democracy in Schools*, London: Qualifications and Curriculum Authority.

Bacon, W. (1978) *Public Accountability and the School System*, London: Harper Row.

Ball, S. J. (2003) *Class Strategies and the Education Market*, London: RoutledgeFalmer.

Bastiani, J. (1993) 'Parents as partners: genuine progress or empty rhetoric?', in Munn, P. (ed.) *Parents and Schools: Customers, Managers or Partners?*, London: Routledge.

—— (2002) *Parental Involvement in Children's Learning: A practical framework for the review and development of home-school work*, London: Tower Hamlets Education.

Benavot, A. and Resh, N. (2003) 'Educational governance, school autonomy, and curriculum implementation: a comparative study of Arab and Jewish schools in Israel', *Journal of Curriculum Studies*, 35(2), 171–196.

Brehony, K. (1992) "Active citizens": the case of school governors', *International Studies in the Sociology of Education*, 2(2).

Bush, T. and Heystek, J. (2003) 'School governance in the new South Africa', *Compare*, 33(2), 127–138.

Deem, R., Brehony, K. and Heath, S. (1995) *Active Citizenship and the Governing of Schools*, Buckingham: Open University Press.

Demerath, P. (1999) 'The cultural production of educational utility in Pere Village, Papua New Guinea', *Comparative Education Review*, 43(2), 162–192.

Field, L. (1993) 'School governing bodies: the lay-professional relationship', *School Organisation*, 13(2), 165–174.

Frances, J., Levačić, R., Mitchell, J. and Thompson, G. (1991) 'Introduction', in G. Thompson, J. Frances, R. Levačić and J. Mitchell (eds.) *Markets, Hierarchies & Networks: The Co-ordination of Social Life*, London: Sage.

Furman, G. (2002) '*School as Community*, Albany: State University of New York Press.

Gelsthorpe, T. (2003) 'Engaging communities and schools', in Gelsthorpe, T. and West-Burnham, J. (eds.) *Educational Leadership and the Community: Strategies for School Improvement through Community Engagement*, Harlow: Pearson Education.

Gewirtz, S. (2000) 'Bringing the politics back in: A critical analysis of quality discourses in education', *British Journal of Educational Studies*, 48(4), 352–370.

Glatter, R. (2003) 'Governance, autonomy and accountability in education', in M. Preedy, R.Glatter and C. Wise (eds.) *Strategic Leadership and Educational Improvement*, London: Paul Chapman.

Kogan, M. (1986) *Education Accountability: An Analytic Overview*, London: Hutchinson.

Lawton, D. and Cowen, R. (2001) 'Values, culture and education: an overview', in J. Cairns, D. Lawton and R. Gardner (eds.) *Values, Culture and Education*, London: Kogan Page.

Lucey, H. and Reay, D. (2002) 'A market in waste: psychic and structural dimensions of school-choice policy in the UK and children's narratives on "demonized" schools', *Discourse: studies in the cultural politics of education*, 23(3), December.

Macbeth, A. (1989) *Involving Parents: Effective parent-teacher relations*, Oxford: Heinemann.

Martin, J. (1999) 'Social justice, education policy and the role of parents: A question of choice or voice?', *Education and Social Justice*, 1(2), 48–61.

—— Tett, L. with Kay, H. (1999) 'Developing collaborative partnerships: limits and possibilities for schools, parents and community education', *International Studies in Sociology of Education*, 9(1), 59–75.

McClelland, V. A. (1996) 'Weakness, faith and the distinctiveness of the Catholic school', in McLaughlin, T., O'Keefe, J. and O'Keeffe, B. (eds.) *The Contemporary Catholic School*, London: Falmer.

Mirza, H. S. and Reay, D. (2000) 'Redefining citizenship: Black women educators and "the third space"', in M. Arnot and J.-A. Dillabough (eds.) *Challenging Democracy*, London: Routledge Falmer.

Muskin, J. A. (1999) 'Including local priorities to assess school quality: The case of Save the Children Community Schools in Mali', *Comparative Education Review*, 43(1), 36–65.

Neill, A. S. (1991) *Summerhill*, London: Penguin.

Newman, J. (2001) *Modernising Governance*, London: Sage.

Osborne, D. and Gaebler, T. (1993) *Reinventing Government*, New York: Penguin.

Power, S., Edwards, T., Whitty, G. and Wigfall, V. (2003) *Education and the Middle Class*, Buckingham: Open University Press.

Ranson, S. (1990) 'From 1944 to 1988: Education, citizenship and democracy,' in M. Flude and M. Hammer (eds.) *The Education Reform Act 1988: Its origins and implications*, Basingstoke: Falmer.

Reay, D. (2002) 'Shaun's story: troubling discourses of white working class masculinities', *Gender and Education* 14(3), 221–234.

—— and Lucy, H. (2003) 'The limits of "choice": Children and inner city schooling', *Sociology*, 37(1), 121–142.

Rhodes, S. A. W. (1999) Foreword, in G. Stoker (ed.) *The New Management of British Local Governance*, Basingstoke: Macmillan.

Rose, P. (2003) 'Community participation in school policy and practice in Malawi: balancing local knowledge, national policies and international agency priorities', *Compare*, 33(1), 47–64.

Sayed, Y. (1999) 'Discourses of the policy of educational decentralization in South Africa since 1994: an examination of the South Africa Schools Act', *Compare*, 29, pp. 141–152.

Sergiovanni, T. J. (2000) *The Lifeworld of Leadership*, San Francisco: Jossey-Bass.

Suzuki, I. (2002) 'Parental participation and accountability in primary schools in Uganda', *Compare*, 32(2), 243–259.

Ungoed-Thomas, J. (1997) *Vision of a School*, London: Cassell.

Vincent, C. and Martin, J. (2002) 'Parents as citizens: Making the case', paper presented to the ESRC funded seminar series *Parents and Schools: Diversity, Participation and Democracy*, March.

West-Burnham, J. (2003) 'Education, leadership and the community', in Gelsthorpe, T. and West-Burnham, J. (eds.) *Educational Leadership and the Community: Strategies for School Improvement through Community Engagement*, Harlow: Pearson Education.

Whitty, G. (2002) *Making Sense of Education Policy*, London: Paul Chapman.

Wolfendale, S. and Bastiani, J. (eds.) (2000) *The Contribution of Parents to School Effectiveness*, London: David Fulton.

Woods, P. A. (1993) 'Parents as consumer-citizens', in R. Merttens, D. Mayers, A. Brown and J. Vass (eds.) *Ruling the Margins: Problematising parental involvement*, London: University of North London Press.

—— (1995) *Parents as Consumer-Citizens: An investigation into parent governors*, unpublished PhD thesis, Open University.

—— (2002) 'Space for idealism? Politics and education in the United Kingdom', *Journal of Educational Policy*, 16(1), 118–138.

—— (2003) 'Building on Weber to understand governance: Exploring the links between identity, democracy and "inner distance" ', *Sociology*, 37(1), 143–163.

CHAPTER 6

Anderson, L. and Bennett, N. (eds.) (2003) *Developing Educational Leadership: Using Evidence for Policy and Practice*, London: Sage Publications.

Belbin, M. (1993) *Team Roles at Work*, London: Butterworth Heinemann.

Brighouse, T. and Woods, D. (1999) *How to Improve your School*, London: Routledge Falmer.

Bush, T., Coleman, M. and Glover, D. (1993) *Managing Autonomous Schools: The Grant-Maintained Experience*, London: Paul Chapman Publishing.

Fullan, M. (1992) *The New Meaning of Educational Change* (3rd edn., 2001), London: Routledge Falmer.

—— (2001) *Leading in a Culture of Change*, London: John Wiley.

—— (2003) *The Moral Imperative of Leadership*, London: PCP/Sage.

Hargreaves, D. (2003) *Education Epidemic*, London: Demos.

Rosenholtz, S. (1989) *Teachers' Workplace: the social organisation of schools*, New York: Teachers College Press.

Stoll, L. and Fink, D. (1996) *Changing our Schools*, Buckingham: Open University Press.

CHAPTER 7

Bacchus, M. K. (1996) 'The role of teacher education in contributing to qualitative improvements in basic education in developing countries', in Brock-Utne, B. and Nagel, T. (eds.) *The Role of Aid in the Development of Education for All*, NASEDEC Conference, Norway, pp. 134–160.

Curle, A. (1966) *Planning for Education in Pakistan: A Personal Case Study*, Boston: Harvard University Press.

Darling-Hammond, L. (1997) *The Right to Learn*, San Francisco: Jossey-Bass Publishers.

Elmore, R. F. (1995) 'Getting to scale with good educational practice', *Harvard Educational Review*, 66(1), 1–26.

Gray, J. and Wilcox, B. (1995) *Good School, Bad School*, Buckingham: Open University Press.

Greenland, J. (2002) 'Evolution of School Improvement with the Aga Khan Foundation, from 1984–2000',. in Anderson, S. E. (ed.) *Improving Schools Through Teacher Development: Case Studies of the Aga Khan Foundation Projects in East Africa*, Tokyo: Swets and Zeitlinger.

Khamis, A. (1997), *The AKU-IED Documentation and Evaluation Study—Report 3*, The International Development and Research Centre, Ottawa, Canada.

—— (2000) *The Various Impacts of the Institute for Educational Development in its Co-operating Schools in Pakistan*, unpublished thesis, London: University of London.

Louis, K. S., Toole, J. and Hargreaves, A. (1999) 'Rethinking school improvement'. in J. Murphy and K. S. Louis (eds.), *Handbook of Research on Educational Administration* (2nd edn., pp. 251–275), San Francisco: Jossey Bass.

Mortimore, P. (1998) *The Road to Improvement*, Lisse: Swets and Zeitlinger.

——, Gopinathan, S., Leo, S., Myers, K., Sharpe, L., Stoll, L. and Mortimore, J. (2000) *The Culture of Change: Case Studies of Improving Schools in Singapore and London*, London: Institute of Education, Bedford Papers.

Murphy, J. and Adams, J. E. (1998) 'Reforming America's Schools, 1980–2000', web-site discussion paper, USA: Vanderbilt University.

OECD (2001) *Thematic Review of National Policies for Education in Macedonia—FYRoM*, OECD 5 Sept. CCNM/DEELSA/ED.

Riley, K. A. (2000) 'Leadership, learning and systemic reform', *Journal of Educational Change*, 1(1), 29–55.

—— (2001) 'Re-ignite the flame',. *Times Educational Supplement*, p.11, 17 August.

—— (2005) 'Schooling the Citizens of Tomorrow: The challenges for teaching and learning across the global North/South divide', *Journal of Education Change*, 5(4).

——, Docking, J. with Jackson, P. (2002) *Evaluation of Woolwich Reach and Plumstead Pathfinder, Excellence in Cities, Action Zones* (WRaPP), London: London Borough of Greenwich.

——, ——, Giffen, J. and Tilley-Riley, J. (2003) *Evaluation of the Interactive Learning Project*, Macedonia: Unicef/Ministry of Education and Science.

—— and Jordan, J. (2002) *'Reforming Classrooms from the Bottom-up'*, paper to the British Educational Research Association, Exeter, September.

Sammons, P. (1999) *School Effectiveness: Coming of Age in the Twenty-First Century*, Lisse: Swets and Zeitlinger.

Sarason, S. (1990) *The Predictable Failure of Educational Reform*, San Francisco and Oxford: Jossey-Bass Publishers.

Saunders, L. (2001) 'School Effectiveness and Improvement', in Riley, K. (ed.), *Promoting Good Teaching and Learning: An Education Source Book*, Washington DC: World Bank Human Development Network.

Sen, A. (1999) *Development as Freedom*, Oxford: Oxford University Press.

Slee, R., Weiner, G. and Tomlinson, S. (eds.) (1998) *School Effectiveness for Whom? Challenges to the School Effectiveness and School Improvement Movements*, London: Falmer Press.

Teddlie, C. and Reynolds. D. (2000) *The International Handbook of School Effectiveness Research*, London: Falmer Press.

Tyack, D. and Cuban, L. (1995), *Tinkering toward utopia: A century of public school reform*, Cambridge, MA: Harvard University Press.

Warwick, D. P. and Reimer, F. (1995) *Hope or Despair? Learning in Pakistan's Primary Schools*, Westport, Conn.: Praeger Publishers.

CHAPTER 8

Allsop, T. (1991) 'A proposal to the AKU Board of Trustees', Karachi: Aga Khan University.

Blair, M. (2002) Effective school leadership: the multi-ethnic context, *British Journal of Sociology of Education*, 23(2), 179–191.

Coleman, J. S., Campbell, E., Hobson, C., McPartland, J., Mood, A., Weinfeild, F. and York, R. (1966) *Equality of Educational Opportunity*, Washington: US Government Printing Office.

Davies, L. (1997) The rise of the school effectiveness movement, in White, J. and Barber, M. (eds.) *Perspectives on School Effectiveness and School Improvement*, University of London, Institute of Education.

—— and Iqbal, Z. (1997) 'Tensions in teacher training for school effectiveness: the case of Pakistan', *School Effectiveness and School Improvement*, vol. 8, pp. 254–266.

Fuller, B. (1991) *Growing Up Modern: The Western State Build Third World Schools*, London: Routledge.

Gray, J. (1995) 'The quality of schooling: frameworks for judgment', in Gray, J. and Wilcox, B. (1995) *Good School, Bad School: Evaluating Performance and Encouraging Improvement*, Buckingham: Open University Press.

—— (1998) *The Contribution of Educational Research to the Cause of School Improvement: A Professorial Lecture*, London University, Institute of Education.

Hallinger, P. and Heck, R. (1999) 'Can leadership enhance school effectiveness?' in Bush, T., Bell, L., Bolam, R., Glatter, R. and Ribbins, P. (eds.) *Redefining Educational Management: Policy, Practice and Research*, London: Paul Chapman.

Harber, C. and Davies, L. (1997) *School Management and Effectiveness in Developing Countries: The Post-Bureaucratic School*, London: Cassell.

—— and Muthukrishna, N. (2000) 'School effectiveness and school improvement in context: The case of South Africa', *School Effectiveness and School Improvement*, 11(4), 421–434.

Harbison, R. and Hanushek, E. (1992) *Educational Performance of the Poor: Lessons from North-East Brazil*. Washington DC: World Bank.

Harris, A., Jamieson, I. and Russ, J. (1995) 'A study of "effective" departments in secondary schools', *School Organisation*, 15(3), 283–299.

Heyneman, S. P. (1984) 'Research and education in developing countries', *International Journal of Educational Development*, 4(4), 293–304.

Hofman, R. J., Hofman, W. H. A. and Guldemond, H. (2001) 'The effectiveness of cohesive schools, *The International Journal of Leadership in Education*, 4(2), 115–135.

Jencks, C. S., Smith, M., Ackland, H., Bane, J. Cohen, D., Gintis, H. J., Heyns, B. and Micholson, S. (1972) *Inequality: Assessment of the Effect of Family and Schooling in America*, New York: Basic Books.

Khamis, A. (1997) *The International Documentation and Research Study: Report 3*, Ottawa: International Documentation and Research Centre.

—— (2000) 'The various impacts of the Institute for Educational Development in its co-operating schools in Pakistan', University of London, Ph.D. thesis.

Macbeath J. and Mortimore, P. (eds.) (2001) *Improving School Effectiveness* Buckingham: Open University Press.

Morley, L. and Rassool, N. (2000) 'School effectiveness: new managerialism, quality and the Japanization of education', *Journal of Education Policy*, 15(2), 169–183.

Mortimore, P. (1995) 'The positive effects of schooling' in M. Rutter (ed.) *Psycho-Social Disturbances in Young People: Challenges for Prevention*, Cambridge: Cambridge University Press.

——, Sammons, P., Stoll, L., Lewis, D. and Ecob, R. (1988) *School Matters: The Junior Years*, Wells: Open Books, republished, London: Paul Chapman.

Ouston, J. (1999) 'School effectiveness and school improvement: Critique of a movement', in Bush, T., Bell, L., Bolam, R., Glatter, R. and Ribbins, P. (eds.) *Educational Management: redefining theory, policy and practice*, London: Paul Chapman.

Pfau, R. (1980) 'The comparative study of classroom behaviours', *Comparative Education Review, 24(3)*, 400–414.

Qaisrani, M. N. (1990) *Effect of Teacher Level and Quality of Formal Schooling and Professional Training on Students' Achievement in Primary Schools in Pakistan*, Bridges, Harvard.

Reynolds, D. (1996) 'The problem of the ineffective school: some evidence and some speculations', in Gray, J., Reynolds, D., Fitz-Gibbon, C. and Jesson, D. (eds.), Merging Traditions: *The Future of Research on School Effectiveness and School Improvement*, London: Cassell.

—— and Creemers, B. (1990) 'School effectiveness and school improvement: a mission statement', *School Effectiveness and School Improvement*, 1(1), 1–3.

——, ——, Stringfield, S. and Schaffer, G. (2002) 'Creating world class schools: What have we learned?', in *World Class Schools: International perspectives on school effectiveness*, London: Routledge Falmer.

Rosenholtz, S. (1989) *Teachers' Workplace: The Social Organisation of Schools*, New York: Teachers College Press.

Rutter, M., Maughan, B., Mortimore, P. and Ouston, J. (1979) *Fifteen Thousand Hours—Secondary Schools and their Effects on Children*, London: Open Books.

Sammons, P. (1994) 'Findings from school effectiveness research: some implications for improving the quality of schools', in Ribbens, P. and Burridge, E. (eds.), *Improving Education*: The Issue is Quality, London: Cassell.

—— (1999) *School Effectiveness*: Coming of Age in the Twenty-first Century, Lisse: Swets and Zeitlinger.

——, Thomas, S. and Mortimore, P. (1997) *Forging Links: Effective Schools and Effective Departments*, London: Paul Chapman.

Scheerens, J. (2001) 'Monitoring school effectiveness in developing countries', *School Effectiveness and School Improvement*, 12(4), 359–384.

—— and Bosker, R. (1997) *The Foundations of Educational Effectiveness*, Oxford: Pergamon.

Slee, R. and Weiner, G. with Tomlinson, S. (eds.) (1998) *School Effectiveness for Whom? Challenges to the School Effectiveness and School Improvement Movements*, London: Falmer Press.

Stoll, L. and Fink, D. (1996) *Changing our Schools: Linking school effectiveness and school improvement*, Buckingham: Open University Press.

Teddlie, C. and Reynolds, D. (2000) *The International Handbook of School Effectiveness Research*, London: RoutledgeFalmer.

—— and Stringfield, S. (1993) *Schools Make a Difference: Lessons Learned from a 10 Year Study of School Effects*, New York: Teachers College Press.

Thrupp, M. (1999) *Schools Making a Difference: Let's Be Realistic!*, Buckingham: Open University Press.

Verspoor, A. (1990) *Implementing Educational Change: The World Bank Experience*, Washington DC, World Bank.

Warwick, D. P., Reimers, F. M., and McGinn, N. F. (1991) 'The implementation of educational innovations: Lessons from Pakistan', *International Journal of Educational Development*, 12(4), 297–307.

 CHAPTER 9

Anderson, S. (ed.) (2002) *Improving Schools Through Teacher Development: Case studies of the Aga Khan Foundation Projects in East Africa*, Lisse: Swets and Zeitlinger.

CERI (1995) *Schools Under Scrutiny: Strategies for the Evaluation of School Performance*, Paris: OECD.

Coleman, M. and Briggs A. (2002) *Research Methods for Educational Leadership and Management*, London: Paul Chapman Publishing.

Earley, P. (ed.) (1998) *School Improvement after Inspection? School and LEA Responses*, London: Paul Chapman Publishing.

Ferguson, N., Earley, P., Fidler, B. and Ouston, J. (2000) *Improving Schools and Inspection: The self-inspecting school*, London: Sage/PCP.

Geall, V. (2000) 'The expectations and experience of first-year students at City University of Hong Kong', *Quality in Higher Education*, 6(1), 77–89.

Goldstein, H. (2001) 'Using pupil performance data for judging schools and teachers', *British Educational Research Journal*, Vol. 27, pp. 433–442.

Kolitch, E. and Dean, A. V. (1999) 'Student ratings of instruction in the USA: hidden assumptions and missing conceptions about 'good' teaching', *Studies in Higher Education*, 24(1), 27–42.

Lonsdale, P. and Parsons, C. (1998) 'Inspection and the school improvement hoax' in Earley, P. (ed.) *School Improvement after Inspection? School and LEA responses*, London: Paul Chapman Publishing.

MacBeath, J. (1999) *Schools Must Speak for Themselves: The case for school self-evaluation*, London: Routledge.

—— with Schratz, M., Meuret, D. and Jakobsen, L. (2000) 'Methods of self-evaluation', in *Self-Evaluation in European Schools: A story of change*, London: Routledge.

Maychell, K. and Pathak, S. (1997) *Planning for Action, part 1: A survey of Schools' Post-Inspection Action Planning*, Slough: NFER.

McMahon, A., Bolam, R., Abbott, R. and Holly, P. (1984) *Guidelines for review and internal development in schools: Secondary school handbook*, Harlow: Longman.

Meuret, D. and Morlaix, S. (2003) 'Conditions of success of a school's self-evaluation: Some lessons of an European experience', *School Effectiveness and School Improvement*, 14(1), 53–71.

Ouston, J., Fidler, B. and Earley, P. (1996) 'Secondary schools' responses to Ofsted: Improvement through Inspection?' in Ouston, J., Earley, P. and Fidler, B. (eds.) *Ofsted Inspections: The Early Experience*, London: David Fulton Publishers.

Patton, M. Q. (1981) *Creative Evaluation*, Newbury Park and London: Sage.

—— (1987) *How to Use Qualitative Methods in Evaluation*, Newbury Park: Sage Publications.

Robson, C. (1993) *Real World Research*, Oxford: Blackwell.

Scheerens, J., van Amelsvoort, H. W. C. G. and Donoghue, C. (1999) 'Aspects of the organizational and political context of school evaluation in four European Countries', *Studies in Educational Evaluation*, Vol. 25, pp. 79–108.

Suchman, E. A. (1967) *Evaluative Research: Principles in public service and action programs*, New York: Russell Sage.

CHAPTER 10

Caldwell , B. J. and Spinks, J. M. (1992) *Leading the Self-managing School*, Lewes: Falmer Press.

Glover, D. (2000) 'Financial management and strategic planning', in Coleman, M. and Anderson, L. (eds.) *Managing Finance and Resources in Education,* London: Paul Chapman.

Gunter, H. (1997) *Re-thinking Education: the consequences of Jurassic management*, London: Cassell.

Kremer, M., Moulin, S., Myatt, D. and Namunyu, R. (1997) *The quality-quantity trade-off in education: evidence from a prospective evaluation in Kenya*, World Bank and Harvard University.

Levačić, R. (1995) *Local Management of Schools: Analysis and Practice*, Buckingham: Open University Press.

—— and Vignoles, A. (2002) 'Researching the links between school resources and student outcomes in the UK: a review of issues and evidence', *Education Economics*, 10(3), 312–331.

Mintzberg, H. and Quinn, J. B. (1996) *The Strategy Process: Concepts, contexts, cases*, (3 edn.), London: Prentice Hall.

Ross, K. N. and Levačić, R. (eds.) (1999) *Needs-based Resource Allocation in Education*, Paris: UNESCO.

Scheerens, J. (1997) 'Conceptual models and theory-embedded principles on effective schooling', *School Effectiveness and School Improvement*, 8(3), 269–310.

Simkins, T. (2000) 'Cost analysis in education', in Coleman, M. and Anderson, L. (eds.) *Managing Finance in Education*, London: Paul Chapman.

Weindling, D. (1997) 'Strategic planning in schools: some practical techniques', in Preedy, M., Glatter, R. and Levačić, R. (eds.) *Educational Management: Strategy, Quality and Resources*, Buckingham: Open University Press.

Whitaker, P. (1993) *Managing Change in Schools*, Buckingham: Open University Press.

CHAPTER 11

Belbin, M. (1993) *Team Roles at Work,* London: Butterworth-Heinemann.

Bhindi, M. and Duignan, P. (1997) 'Leadership for a new century: Authenticity, intentionality, spirituality and sensibility', *Educational Management and Administration*, 25(2), 117–132.

Blanchard, K. (1990) *The One-minute Manager Builds High-performing Teams*, London: Harper Collins.

Bottery, M. (1992) *The Ethics of Educational Management*, London: Cassell.

Bush, T. and West-Burnham, J. (eds.) (1994) *The Principles of Educational Management*, Harlow: Longman.

Evans, L. (1999) *Managing to Motivate: a guide for school leaders*, London: Cassell.

—— (2003) 'Managing morale, job satisfaction and motivation' in Davies, B. and West-Burnham, J. (eds.) *Handbook of Educational Leadership and Management*, London: Pearson Publishing.

Fidler, B. (1988) 'Theory, concepts and experience in other organisations', in Fidler, B. and Cooper, R. (eds.) *Staff Appraisal in Schools and Colleges,* Harlow: Longman.

Foskett, N. and Lumby, J. (2002) *Leading and Managing Education: International Dimensions*, London: Paul Chapman Publishing.

Gold, A., Evans, J., Earley, P., Halpin, D. and Collarbone, P. (2003) 'Principled principals? Values-driven leadership: Evidence from ten case studies of "outstanding" school leaders', *Educational Management and Administration*, 31(2), 125–136.

Goleman, D. (1998) *Working with Emotional Intelligence,* London: Bloomsbury.

Hargreaves, A. (1994) *Changing Teachers; Changing Times,* London: Cassell.

Hoyle. E. (1996) 'Professional collaboration in schools', *Curriculum Forum*, 5(2).

Little, J. W. (1990) 'Teachers as colleagues' in Lieberman A. (ed.) *Schools as Collaborative Cultures: creating the future now,* Basingstoke: Falmer Press.

Oldroyd, D. (2002) 'Educational leadership for results or for learning? Contrasting directions in times of transition', *Managing Global Transitions*, 1(1), 49–68.

——, Elsner, D. and Poster, C. (1996) *Educational Management Today: A Concise dictionary and guide*, London: Paul Chapman.

Owens, R. G. (2002) *Organisational Behaviour in Education* (6th edn.), New york: Prentice Hall.

Rayman, P. M. (2001) *Beyond the Bottom Line: the search for dignity at work*, New York: St Martins Press.

Storey, J. and Sissons, K. (1993) *Managing Human Resources and Industrial Relations,* Buckingham: Open University Press.

Tice, L. (1990) *Investment in Excellence,* Seattle: The Pacific Institute.

CHAPTER 12

Askew, S., (ed.) (2000) *Feedback for Learning*, London: Routledge Falmer.

Carnell, E. and Lodge, C. (2002) *Supporting Effective Learning*, London: Paul Chapman.

Clarke, P. (2000) *Learning Schools, Learning Systems*, London: Continuum.

Entwistle, N. and Ramsden, P. (1983) *Understanding Student Learning*, London: Croom Helm.

Hallinger, P. and Heck R. (2003) 'Understanding the contribution of leadership to school improvement', in Wallace, M. and Poulson, L. (eds.) *Learning to Read Critically in Educational Leadership and Management*, London: Sage.

Hammond, S. A. (1996) *The Thin Book of Appreciative Inquiry*, Plano, Texas: Kodiak Consulting.

Harris, D. (2002) 'Children's conceptions of learning: an investigation into what children think learning is in three contrasting schools, unpublished MA dissertation, Institute of Education, University of London.

Hay-McBer (nd), *Model of Excellence for School Leaders*, www.ncsl.org.uk/index.cfm?pageid? = hayhome2.

Marton, F., Dall'Allba, G. and Beaty, E. (1993) 'Conceptions of learning', *International Journal of Educational Research,* 19(3), 277–300.

Mitchell, C. and Sackney, L. (2001) 'Building capacity for a learning community', *Canadian Journal of Educational Administration and Policy*, February (19): online www.umanitoba.ca/publications/cjeap.

Mulford, B. and Silins, H. (2003) 'Leadership for organisational learning and improved student outcomes— What do we know?', *Cambridge Journal of Education*, 33(2), 175–196.

O'Connor, J. and McDermott, I. (1997) *The Art of Systems Thinking: essential skills for creativity and problem solving*, London: Thorsons.

Reed, J. and Stoll, L. (2000) 'Promoting organisational learning in schools—the role of feedback', in Askew, S. (ed.) *Feedback for Learning*, London: Routledge Falmer.

Resnick, L. (1987) 'Learning in school and out', *Educational Researcher*, 16(99), 13–40.

Silins, H. and Mulford, B. (2004) 'Leadership and school results', in Leithwood, K., Hallinger, P. and Lewis, K. (eds.) *Second International Handbook of Educational Leadership and Adminsitration*, Dordrecht: Kluwer.

Watkins, C., Carnell, E., Lodge, C., Wagner, P. and Whalley, C. (2002) 'Effective Learning', *Research Matters* (17), London: School Improvement Network, Institute of Education.

Williams, E. (2002) 'Enriched learning narratives' (unpublished), Institute of Education, University of London.

CHAPTER 13

Aspinwall, K. (1998) *Leading the Learning School*, London: Lemos and Crane.

Barthes, R. (1990) *Improving Schools from Within*, San Francisco: Jossey-Bass.

Bezzina, C. (2002) 'Rethinking teachers' professional development in Malta: agenda for the twenty first century', *Journal of In-service Education*, 28(1), 57–78.

Bolam, R. (1993) 'Recent developments and emerging issues', in *The Continuing Professional Development of Teachers*. General Teaching Council for England and Wales, London: GTC.

—— (2002) 'Professional development and professionalism', in Bush, T. and Bell, L. (eds.) *The Principles and Practice of Educational Management*, London: Sage/PCP.

Bubb, S., Heilbronn, R., Jones, C., Totterdell, M. and Bailey, M. (2002) *Improving Induction*, London: Routledge Falmer.

—— and Hoare, P. (2001) *Performance Management*, London: David Fulton.

Cibulka, J. and Nakayama, M. (2000) *Practitioners' Guide to Learning Communities*, National Partnership for Excellence and Accountability in Teaching, Deliverable No. 2530@www.ericsp.org/digests/guide.htm

Craft, A. (2000) *Continuing Professional Development: A Practical Guide for Teachers* (2nd edn.), London: Routledge Falmer.

Day, C. (1999) *Developing Teachers: The challenge of lifelong learning*, London: Falmer.

—— Hadfield M. and Kellow, M. (2003) *Schools as Learning Communities: Professional Development through Network Learning*, paper presented to AERA conference, Chicago, April.

Department for Education and Employment (2001) *Learning and Teaching: A Strategy for Professional Development*, London: DfEE.

Department for Education and Skills (2001) *Helping you develop: Guidance on producing a professional development record*, London: DfES.

Department of Education and Science (1972) *Teacher Education and Training (James Report)*, DES, London: HMSO.

Diggins, P. (1997) 'Reflections on leadership characteristics necessary to develop and sustain learning school communities', *School Leadership and Management*, 17(3), 413–425.

Durrant, J. (2003) 'Partnership, leadership and learning: building individual and organisational capacity through an accredited programme', *Professional Development Today*, 6(2), 6–12.

Earley, P., Evans, J., Gold, A., Collarbone, P. and Halpin, D. (2002) *Establishing the Current State of School Leadership in England*, London: DfES.

Frost, D. and Durrant, J. (2003) *Teacher-led Development Work*, London: David Fulton.

GTC (1993) *The Continuing Professional Development of Teachers*, General Teaching Council for England and Wales, London: GTC.

Guskey, T. (2002) 'Does it make a difference? Evaluating professional development', *Educational Leadership*, March, pp. 45–51.

—— (2000) *Evaluating Professional Development*, New York: Corwin Press.

Harris, A. and Anthony, P. (2001) 'Collegiality and its role in teacher evaluation: perspectives from veteran and novice teachers', *Teacher Development*, 5(3), 371–389.

Harris, B. (2000) 'A strategy for identifying the professional development needs of teachers: a report from New South Wales', *Journal of In-service Education*, 26(1), 25–47.

Harvey, S. (1999) 'The impact of coaching in South African primary science INSET', *International Journal of Educational Development*, 19(3), 191–205.

Jackson, D. (2003) 'Building schools' capacity as learning communities', *Professional Development Today*, 5(3), 17–24.

Jalongo, M. (1991) *Creating Learning Communities*, Indiana: National Education Service.

Jones, T. (2003) 'Continuing professional development in Wales: An entitlement for all', *Professional Development Today*, 6(1), 35–42.

Joyce, B. and Showers, B. (1995) *Student Achievement through Staff Development*, New York: Longman.

Kellow, M. (2003) 'Developing learning through networking learning communities', *Professional Development Today*, 6(2), 6–12.

Lee, B. (2002) 'What is effective CPD?', *Professional Development Today*, 5(3), 53–62.

Lieberman, A. (1999) 'Networks', *Journal of Staff Development*, 20(3).

Little, J. W. (1990) 'The persistence of privacy: autonomy and initiative in teachers' professional relations', *Teachers' College Record*, 91(4), 509–536.

Madden, C. and Mitchell, V. (1993) *Professions, Standards and Competence: A Survey of Continuing Education for the Professions*, Department for Continuing Education, University of Bristol.

Oldroyd, D. and Hall, V. (1991) *Managing Staff Development: A Handbook for Secondary Schools*, London: Paul Chapman Publishing.

O'Sullivan, M. (2000) 'Needs assessment for INSET for unqualified primary teachers in Namibia: An effective model', *Compare*, Vol. 30, pp. 211–234.

Sachs, J. (1997) 'Reclaiming the agenda of teachers' professionalism: the Australian experience', *Journal of Education for Teachers*, Vol. 23, pp. 263–275.

Senge, P. (1990) *The Fifth Discipline: the art and practice of the learning organisation*, New York: Century Business Books.

—— Cambron-McCabe, N., Lucas, T., Smith, B., Dutton, J. and Kleiner, A. (2000) *Schools that Learn*, London: Nicholas Brearley.

Shimahara, N. (1998) 'The Japanese model of professional development: Teaching as craft', *Teaching and Teacher Education*, Vol.14, pp. 451–462.

Thijs, A. and Van den Berg, E. (2002) 'Peer coaching as part of a professional development program for science teachers in Botswana', *International Journal of Educational Development*, Vol. 22, pp. 55–68.

Waters, M. (1998) 'Personal development for teachers', *Professional Development Today*, 1(2), 29–38.

Wenger, E. (1998) *Communities of Practice*, Cambridge: CUP.

END NOTES

Bush, T. and Jackson, D. (2002) 'A preparation for school leadership: International perspectives', *Educational Management and Administration*, 30(4), 417–430.

DfEE (2000) *The Leadership Group*, London: DfEE.

Egan, G. (1993) *Adding Value: a systematic guide to business-driven management and leadership*, San Francisco: Jossey Bass.

Earley, P. and Weindling, D. (2004) *Understanding School Leadership*, London: Paul Chapman/Sage.

Hallinger, P. (2003) 'Leading educational change: reflections on the practice of instructional and transformational leadership', *Cambridge Journal of Education*, 33(3), 329–51.

Harris, A. and Lambert, L. (2003) *Building Leadership Capacity for School Improvement*, Maidenhead: Open University Press.

Hobson, A., Brown, E., Ashby, P., Keys, W., Sharp, C. and Benefield, P. (2003) *Issues of Early Headship—problems and support strategies*. NCSL available from www.ncsl.org.uk.

Ofsted (2003) *Leadership and management—what inspection tells us*, London: Ofsted.

Pedlar, M., Burgoyne, J. and Boydell, T. (2003) *A Manager's Guide to Leadership*, Maidenhead: McGraw Hill.

Senge, P. (1990) *The Fifth Discipline: the art and practice of the learning organisation*, New York: Century Business Books.

Southworth, G. (2003) *Primary School Leadership in Context: Leading small, medium and large sized primary schools*, London: Routledge Falmer.

Thrupp, M. and Wilmott, R. (2003) *Education Management in Managerialist Times: Beyond the Textual Apologists*, Maidenhead: Open University Press.

Index